Guide to the Secure Configuration of Red Hat Enterprise Linux 5

Revision 4.1

February 28, 2011

Operating Systems Division Unix Team
of the
Systems and Network Analysis Center

National Security Agency
9800 Savage Rd. Suite 6704
Ft. Meade, MD 20755-6704

2

Warnings

- Do not attempt to implement any of the recommendations in this guide without first testing in a non-production environment.

- This document is only a guide containing recommended security settings. It is not meant to replace well-structured policy or sound judgment. Furthermore this guide does not address site-specific configuration concerns. Care must be taken when implementing this guide to address local operational and policy concerns.

- The security changes described in this document apply only to Red Hat Enterprise Linux 5. They may not translate gracefully to other operating systems.

- Internet addresses referenced were valid as of 1 Dec 2009.

Trademark Information

Red Hat is a registered trademark of Red Hat, Inc. Any other trademarks referenced herein are the property of their respective owners.

Change Log

Revision 4.1 is an update of Revision 4 dated September 14, 2010.

- Added section 2.2.2.6, Disable All GNOME Thumbnailers if Possible.

- Added Common Configuration Enumeration (CCE) identifiers to associated sections within the guide, and a note about CCE in section 1.2.4, Formatting Conventions.

- Updated section 2.3.3.2, Set Lockouts for Failed Password Attempts. There is no longer the need to add the `pam_tally2` module into each program's PAM configuration file, or to comment out some lines from `/etc/pam.d/system-auth`. The `pam_tally2` module can now be referenced directly from `/etc/pam.d/system-auth`.

- Corrected section 2.6.2.4.5 title from Ensure auditd Collects Logon and Logout Events to Record Attempts to Alter Logon and Logout Event Information.

- Corrected section 2.6.2.4.6 title from Ensure auditd Collects Process and Session Initiation Information to Record Attempts to Alter Process and Session Initiation Information

Note: The above changes did not affect any of the section numbering.

Table of Contents

1. Introduction

The purpose of this guide is to provide security configuration recommendations for the Red Hat Enterprise Linux (RHEL) 5 operating system. The guidance provided here should be applicable to all variants (Desktop, Server, Advanced Platform) of the product. Recommended settings for the basic operating system are provided, as well as for many commonly-used services that the system can host in a network environment.

The guide is intended for system administrators. Readers are assumed to possess basic system administration skills for Unix-like systems, as well as some familiarity with Red Hat's documentation and administration conventions. Some instructions within this guide are complex. All directions should be followed completely and with understanding of their effects in order to avoid serious adverse effects on the system and its security.

1.1 General Principles

The following general principles motivate much of the advice in this guide and should also influence any configuration decisions that are not explicitly covered.

1.1.1 Encrypt Transmitted Data Whenever Possible

Data transmitted over a network, whether wired or wireless, is susceptible to passive monitoring. Whenever practical solutions for encrypting such data exist, they should be applied. Even if data is expected to be transmitted only over a local network, it should still be encrypted. Encrypting authentication data, such as passwords, is particularly important. Networks of RHEL5 machines can and should be configured so that no unencrypted authentication data is ever transmitted between machines.

1.1.2 Minimize Software to Minimize Vulnerability

The simplest way to avoid vulnerabilities in software is to avoid installing that software. On RHEL, the RPM Package Manager (originally Red Hat Package Manager, abbreviated RPM) allows for careful management of the set of software packages installed on a system. Installed software contributes to system vulnerability in several ways. Packages that include setuid programs may provide local attackers a potential path to privilege escalation. Packages that include network services may give this opportunity to network-based attackers. Packages that include programs which are predictably executed by local users (e.g. after graphical login) may provide opportunities for trojan horses or other attack code to be run undetected. The number of software packages installed on a system can almost always be significantly pruned to include only the software for which there is an environmental or operational need.

1.1.3 Run Different Network Services on Separate Systems

Whenever possible, a server should be dedicated to serving exactly one network service. This limits the number of other services that can be compromised in the event that an attacker is able to successfully exploit a software flaw in one network service.

1.1.4 Configure Security Tools to Improve System Robustness

Several tools exist which can be effectively used to improve a system's resistance to and detection of unknown attacks. These tools can improve robustness against attack at the cost of relatively little configuration effort. In particular, this guide recommends and discusses the use of Iptables for host-based firewalling, SELinux for protection against vulnerable services, and a logging and auditing infrastructure for detection of problems.

1.1.5 Least Privilege

Grant the least privilege necessary for user accounts and software to perform tasks. For example, do not allow users except those that need administrator access to use `sudo`. Another example is to limit logins on server systems to only those administrators who need to log into them in order to perform administration tasks. Using SELinux also follows the principle of least privilege: SELinux policy can confine software to perform only actions on the system that are specifically allowed. This can be far more restrictive than the actions permissible by the traditional Unix permissions model.

1.2 How to Use This Guide

Readers should heed the following points when using the guide.

1.2.1 Read Sections Completely and in Order

Each section may build on information and recommendations discussed in prior sections. Each section should be read and understood completely; instructions should never be blindly applied. Relevant discussion will occur after instructions for an action. The system-level configuration guidance in Chapter 2 must be applied to all machines. The guidance for individual services in Chapter 3 must be considered for all machines as well: apply the guidance if the machine is *either* a server or a client for that service, and ensure that the service is disabled according to the instructions provided if the machine is neither a server nor a client.

1.2.2 Test in Non-Production Environment

This guidance should always be tested in a non-production environment before deployment. This test environment should simulate the setup in which the system will be deployed as closely as possible.

1.2.3 Root Shell Environment Assumed

Most of the actions listed in this document are written with the assumption that they will be executed by the root user running the `/bin/bash` shell. Commands preceded with a hash mark (#) assume that the administrator will execute the commands as root, i.e. apply the command via `sudo` whenever possible, or use `su` to gain root privileges if `sudo` cannot be used. Commands which can be executed as a non-root user are are preceded by a dollar sign ($) prompt.

1.2.4 Formatting Conventions

Commands intended for shell execution, as well as configuration file text, are featured in a `monospace font`. *Italics* are used to indicate instances where the system administrator must substitute the appropriate information into a command or configuration file.

Common Configuration Enumeration (CCE) identifiers are presented at the lower right corner of those sections for which an associated identifier exists. More information about CCE is available at `http://cce.mitre.org`.

1.2.5 Reboot Required

A system reboot is implicitly required after some actions in order to complete the reconfiguration of the system. In many cases, the changes will not take effect until a reboot is performed. In order to ensure that changes are applied properly and to test functionality, always reboot the system after applying a set of recommendations from this guide.

2. System-wide Configuration

2.1 Installing and Maintaining Software

The following sections contain information on security-relevant choices during the initial operating system installation process and the setup of software updates.

2.1.1 Initial Installation Recommendations

The recommendations here apply to a clean installation of the system, where any previous installations are wiped out. The sections presented here are in the same order that the installer presents, but only installation choices with security implications are covered. Many of the configuration choices presented here can also be applied after the system is installed. The choices can also be automatically applied via Kickstart files, as covered in [8].

2.1.1.1 Disk Partitioning

Some system directories should be placed on their own partitions (or logical volumes). This allows for better separation and protection of data.

The installer's default partitioning scheme creates separate partitions (or logical volumes) for /, /boot, and swap.

- If starting with any of the default layouts, check the box to "Review and modify partitioning." This allows for the easy creation of additional logical volumes inside the volume group already created, though it may require making /'s logical volume smaller to create space. In general, using logical volumes is preferable to using partitions because they can be more easily adjusted later.

- If creating a custom layout, create the partitions mentioned in the previous paragraph (which the installer will require anyway), as well as separate ones described in the following sections.

If a system has already been installed, and the default partitioning scheme was used, it is possible but nontrivial to modify it to create separate logical volumes for the directories listed above. The Logical Volume Manager (LVM) makes this possible. See the LVM HOWTO at `http://tldp.org/HOWTO/LVM-HOWTO/` for more detailed information on LVM.

2.1.1.1.1 Create Separate Partition or Logical Volume for /tmp

The /tmp directory is a world-writable directory used for temporary file storage. Ensure that it has its own partition or logical volume.

CCE 14161-4

Because software may need to use /tmp to temporarily store large files, ensure that it is of adequate size. For a modern, general-purpose system, 10GB should be adequate. Smaller or larger sizes could be used, depending on the availability of space on the drive and the system's operating requirements.

2.1.1.1.2 Create Separate Partition or Logical Volume for /var

> The /var directory is used by daemons and other system services to store frequently-changing data. It is not uncommon for the /var directory to contain world-writable directories, installed by other software packages. Ensure that /var has its own partition or logical volume.
>
> **CCE 14777-7**

Because the yum package manager and other software uses /var to temporarily store large files, ensure that it is of adequate size. For a modern, general-purpose system, 10GB should be adequate.

2.1.1.1.3 Create Separate Partition or Logical Volume for /var/log

> System logs are stored in the /var/log directory. Ensure that it has its own partition or logical volume. Make certain that it is large enough to store all the logs that will be written there.
>
> **CCE 14011-1**

See Section 2.6 for more information about logging and auditing.

2.1.1.1.4 Create Separate Partition or Logical Volume for /var/log/audit

> Audit logs are stored in the /var/log/audit directory. Ensure that it has its own partition or logical volume. Make absolutely certain that it is large enough to store all audit logs that will be created by the auditing daemon.
>
> **CCE 14171-3**

See 2.6.2.2 for discussion on deciding on an appropriate size for the volume.

2.1.1.1.5 Create Separate Partition or Logical Volume for /home if Using Local Home Directories

> If user home directories will be stored locally, create a separate partition for /home. If /home will be mounted from another system such as an NFS server, then creating a separate partition is not necessary at this time, and the mountpoint can instead be configured later.
>
> **CCE 14559-9**

2.1.1.2 Boot Loader Configuration

> Check the box to "Use a boot loader password" and create a password. Once this password is set, anyone who wishes to change the boot loader configuration will need to enter it. More information is available in Section 2.3.5.2.

Assigning a boot loader password prevents a local user with physical access from altering the boot loader configuration at system startup.

2.1.1.3 Network Devices

The default network device configuration uses DHCP, which is not recommended.

> Unless use of DHCP is *absolutely necessary*, click the "Edit" button and:
>
> - Uncheck "Use Dynamic IP configuration (DHCP)."
> - Uncheck "Enable IPv4 Support" if the system does not require IPv4. (This is uncommon.)
> - Uncheck "Enable IPv6 Support" if the system does not require IPv6.
> - Enter appropriate IPv4 and IPv6 addresses and prefixes as required.
>
> With the DHCP setting disabled, the hostname, gateway, and DNS servers should then be assigned on the main screen.

Sections 3.9.1 and 3.9.2 contain more information on network configuration and the use of DHCP.

2.1.1.4 Root Password

The security of the entire system depends on the strength of the root password. The password should be at least 12 characters long, and should include a mix of capitalized and lowercase letters, special characters, and numbers. It should also not be based on any dictionary word.

2.1.1.5 Software Packages

Uncheck all package groups, including the package groups "Software Development" and "Web Server," unless there is a specific requirement to install software using the system installer. If the machine will be used as a web server, it is preferable to manually install the necessary RPMs instead of installing the full "Web Server" package group. See Section 3.16 for installation and configuration details.

Use the "Customize now" radio box to prune package groups as much as possible. This brings up a two-column view of categories and package groups. If appropriate, uncheck "X Window System" in the "Base System" category to avoid installing X entirely. Any other package groups not necessary for system operation should also be unchecked.

Much finer-grained package selection is possible via Kickstart as described in [8].

2.1.1.6 First-boot Configuration

The system presents more configuration options during the first boot after installation. For the screens listed, implement the security-related recommendations:

Screen	Recommendation
Firewall	Leave set to "Enabled." Only check the "Trusted Services" that this system needs to serve. Uncheck the default selection of SSH if the system does not need to serve SSH.
SELinux	Leave SELinux set to "Enforcing" mode.
Kdump	Leave Kdump off unless the feature is required, such as for kernel development and testing.

Screen	Recommendation
Set Up Software Updates	If the system is connected to the Internet now, click "Yes, I'd like to register now." This will require a connection to either the Red Hat Network servers or their proxies or satellites. This can also be configured later as described in Section 2.1.2.1.
Create User	If the system will require a local user account, it can be created here. Even if the system will be using a network-wide authentication system as described in Section 2.3.6, do not click on the "Use Network Login..." button. Manually applying configuration later is preferable.

2.1.2   Updating Software

The `yum` command line tool is used to install and update software packages. Yum replaces the `up2date` utility used in previous system releases. The system also provides two graphical package managers, `pirut` and `pup`. The `pirut` tool is a graphical front-end for `yum` that allows users to install and update packages while `pup` is a simple update tool for packages that are already installed. In the **Applications** menu, `pirut` is labeled **Add/Remove Software** and `pup` is labeled **Software Updater**.

It is recommended that these tools be used to keep systems up to date with the latest security patches.

2.1.2.1   Configure Connection to the RHN RPM Repositories

The first step in configuring a system for updates is to register with the Red Hat Network (RHN). For most systems, this is done during the initial installation. Successfully registered systems will appear on the RHN web site. If the system is not listed, run the Red Hat Network Registration tool, which can be found in the **Applications** menu under **System Tools** or on the command line:

```
# rhn_register
```

Follow the prompts on the screen. If successful, the system will appear on the RHN web site and be subscribed to one or more software update channels. Additionally, a new daemon, `rhnsd`, will be enabled.

If the system will not have access to the Internet, it will not be able to directly subscribe to the RHN update repository. Updates will have to be downloaded from the RHN web site manually. The command line tool `yum` and the graphical front-ends `pirut` and `pup` can be configured to handle this situation.

2.1.2.1.1   Ensure Red Hat GPG Key is Installed

To ensure that the system can cryptographically verify update packages (and also connect to the Red Hat Network to receive them if desired), run the following command to ensure that the system has the Red Hat GPG key properly installed:

```
$ rpm -q --queryformat "%{SUMMARY}\n" gpg-pubkey
```

The command should return the string:

```
gpg(Red Hat, Inc. (release key <security@redhat.com>)
```

CCE 14440-2

To verify that the Red Hat GPG key itself has not been tampered with, its fingerprint can be compared to the one from Red Hat's web site at `http://www.redhat.com/security/team/key`. The following command can be used to print the installed release key's fingerprint, which is actually contained in the file referenced below:

```
$ gpg --quiet --with-fingerprint /etc/pki/rpm-gpg/RPM-GPG-KEY-redhat-release
```

More information on package signing is also available at `https://fedoraproject.org/keys`.

2.1.2.2 Disable the `rhnsd` Daemon

The `rhnsd` daemon polls the Red Hat Network web site for scheduled actions. Unless it is actually necessary to schedule updates remotely through the RHN website, it is recommended that the service be disabled.

```
# chkconfig rhnsd off
```

CCE 3416-5

The `rhnsd` daemon is enabled by default, but until the system has been registered with the Red Hat Network, it will not run. However, once the registration process is complete, the `rhnsd` daemon will run in the background and periodically call the `rhn_check` utility. It is the `rhn_check` utility that communicates with the Red Hat Network web site.

This utility is not required for the system to be able to access and install system updates. Once the system has been registered, either use the provided `yum-updatesd` service or create a cron job to automatically apply updates.

2.1.2.3 Obtain Software Package Updates with `yum`

The `yum` update utility can be run by hand from the command line, called through one of the provided front-end tools, or configured to run automatically at specified intervals.

2.1.2.3.1 Manually Check for Package Updates

The following command prints a list of packages that need to be updated:

```
# yum check-update
```

To actually install these updates, run:

```
# yum update
```

2.1.2.3.2 Configure Automatic Update Retrieval and Installation with Cron

The `yum-updatesd` service is not mature enough for an enterprise environment, and the service may introduce unnecessary overhead. When possible, replace this service with a cron job that calls `yum` directly.

Disable the `yum-updatesd` service:

```
# chkconfig yum-updatesd off
```

Create the file `yum.cron`, make it executable, and place it in `/etc/cron.daily`:

```
#!/bin/sh

/usr/bin/yum -R 120 -e 0 -d 0 -y update yum
/usr/bin/yum -R 10 -e 0 -d 0 -y update
```

CCE 4218-4

This particular script instructs `yum` to update any packages it finds. Placing the script in `/etc/cron.daily` ensures its daily execution. To only apply updates once a week, place the script in `/etc/cron.weekly` instead.

2.1.2.3.3   Ensure Package Signature Checking is Globally Activated

The `gpgcheck` option should be used to ensure that checking of an RPM package's signature always occurs prior to its installation.

To force yum to check package signatures before installing them, ensure that the following line appears in `/etc/yum.conf` in the [main] section:

```
gpgcheck=1
```

CCE 14914-6

2.1.2.3.4   Ensure Package Signature Checking is Not Disabled For Any Repos

---

To ensure that signature checking is not disabled for any repos, ensure that the following line *DOES NOT* appear in any repo configuration files in `/etc/yum.repos.d` or elsewhere:

```
gpgcheck=0
```

CCE 14813-0

2.1.3   Software Integrity Checking

The AIDE (Advanced Intrusion Detection Environment) software is included with the system to provide software integrity checking. It is designed to be a replacement for the well-known Tripwire integrity checker. The RPM software also includes the ability to compare the hashes of installed files with those in its own metadata database. Integrity checking cannot *prevent* intrusions into your system, but can detect that they have occurred. Such integrity checking software should be configured before the system is deployed and able to provides services to users. Ideally, the integrity checking database would be built before the system is connected to any network, though this may prove impractical due to registration and software updates.

2.1.3.1 Configure AIDE

Requirements for software integrity checking should be defined by policy, and this is highly dependent on the environment in which the system will be used. As such, a general strategy for implementing integrity checking is provided, but precise recommendations (such as to check a particular file) cannot be. Documentation for AIDE, including the quick-start on which this advice is based, is available in `/usr/share/doc/aide-0.12`.

The prelinking feature can interfere with the operation of AIDE, because it changes binaries in an attempt to decrease their startup time. Set `PRELINKING=no` *inside* `/etc/sysconfig/prelink` *and run* `/usr/sbin/prelink -ua` *to restore binaries to a non-prelinked state and prevent prelinking from causing false positive results from AIDE.*

2.1.3.1.1 Install AIDE

AIDE is not installed by default. Install it with the command:

```
# yum install aide
```

CCE 4209-3

2.1.3.1.2 Customize Configuration File

Customize `/etc/aide.conf` to meet your requirements. The default configuration is acceptable for many environments.

The man page `aide.conf(5)` provides detailed information about the configuration file format.

2.1.3.1.3 Build, Store, and Test Database

Generate a new database:

```
# /usr/sbin/aide --init
```

By default, the database will be written to the file `/var/lib/aide/aide.db.new.gz`.

The database, as well as the configuration file `/etc/aide.conf` and the binary `/usr/sbin/aide` (or hashes of these files) should be copied and stored in a secure location. Storing these copies or hashes on read-only media may provide further confidence that they will not be altered.

Install the newly-generated database:

```
# cp /var/lib/aide/aide.db.new.gz /var/lib/aide/aide.db.gz
```

Run a manual check:

```
# /usr/sbin/aide --check
```

If this check produces any unexpected output, investigate.

2.1.3.1.4   Implement Periodic Execution of Integrity Checking

By default, AIDE does not install itself for periodic execution.

Implement checking with whatever frequency is required by your security policy. A once-daily check may be suitable for many environments. For example, to implement a daily execution of AIDE at 4:05am, add the following line to `/etc/crontab`:

```
05 4 * * * root /usr/sbin/aide --check
```

AIDE output may be an indication of an attack against your system, or it may be the result of something innocuous such as an administrator's configuration change or a software update. The steps in Section 2.1.3.1.3 should be repeated when configuration changes or software updates necessitate. This will certainly be necessary after applying guidance later in this guide.

2.1.3.1.5   Manually Verify Integrity of AIDE

Because integrity checking is a means of intrusion detection and not intrusion prevention, it cannot be guaranteed that the AIDE binaries, configuration files, or database have not been tampered with. An attacker could disable or alter these files after a successful intrusion. Because of this, manual and frequent checks on these files is recommended. The safely stored copies (or hashes) of the database, binary, and configuration file were created earlier for this purpose.

Manually verify the integrity of the AIDE binaries, configuration file, and database. Possibilities for doing so include:

1. Use `sha1sum` or `md5sum` to generate checksums on the files and then visually compare them to those generated from the safely stored versions. This does not, of course, preclude the possibility that such output could also be faked.

2. Mount the stored versions on read-only media and run `/bin/diff` to verify that there are no differences between the files.

3. Copying the files to another system and performing the hash or file comparisons there may impart additional confidence that the manual verification process is not being interfered with.

2.1.3.2   Verify Package Integrity Using RPM

The RPM package management system includes the ability to verify the integrity of installed packages by comparing the installed files with information about the files taken from the package metadata stored in the RPM database. Although an attacker could corrupt the RPM database (analogous to attacking the AIDE database as described above), this check can still reveal modification of important files.

To determine which files on the system differ from what is expected by the RPM database:

```
# rpm -qVa
```

A "c" in the second column indicates that a file is a configuration file (and may be expected to change). In order to exclude configuration files from this list, run:

```
# rpm -qVa | awk '$2!="c" {print $0}'
```

The man page `rpm(8)` describes the format of the output. Any files that do not match the expected output demand further investigation if the system is being seriously examined. This check could also be run as a cron job.

2.2 File Permissions and Masks

Traditional Unix security relies heavily on file and directory permissions to prevent unauthorized users from reading or modifying files to which they should not have access. Adhere to the principle of least privilege — configure each file, directory, and filesystem to allow only the access needed in order for that file to serve its purpose.

However, Linux systems contain a large number of files, so it is often prohibitively time-consuming to ensure that every file on a machine has exactly the permissions needed. This section introduces several permission restrictions which are almost always appropriate for system security, and which are easy to test and correct.

Note: Several of the commands in this section search filesystems for files or directories with certain characteristics, and are intended to be run on every local `ext2` or `ext3` partition on a given machine. When the variable *PART* appears in one of the commands below, it means that the command is intended to be run repeatedly, with the name of each local partition substituted for *PART* in turn.

The following command prints a list of `ext2` and `ext3` partitions on a given machine:

```
$ mount -t ext2,ext3 | awk '{print $3}'
```

If your site uses a local filesystem type other than `ext2` or `ext3`, you will need to modify this command.

2.2.1 Restrict Partition Mount Options

System partitions can be mounted with certain options which limit what files on those partitions can do. These options are set in the file `/etc/fstab`, and can be used to make certain types of malicious behavior more difficult.

2.2.1.1 Add `nodev` Option to Non-Root Local Partitions

Edit the file `/etc/fstab`. The important columns for purposes of this section are column 2 (mount point), column 3 (filesystem type), and column 4 (mount options). For any line which satisfies all of the conditions:

- The filesystem type is `ext2` or `ext3`

- The mount point is *not* `/`

add the text ",`nodev`" to the list of mount options in column 4.

CCE 4249-9

The `nodev` option prevents users from mounting unauthorized devices on any partition which is known not to contain any authorized devices. The root partition typically contains the `/dev` directory, which is the primary location for authorized devices, so this option should not be set on `/`.

However, if system programs are being run in `chroot` jails, this advice may need to be modified further, since it is often necessary to create device files inside the `chroot` directory for use by the restricted program.

2.2.1.2 Add `nodev`, `nosuid`, and `noexec` Options to Removable Storage Partitions

> Edit the file `/etc/fstab`. Filesystems which represent removable media can be located by finding lines whose mount points contain strings like `floppy` or `cdrom`.
>
> For each line representing a removable media mountpoint, add the text `noexec,nodev,nosuid` to the list of mount options in column 4.
>
> **CCE 3522-0, 4275-4, 4042-8**

Filesystems mounted on removable media also provide a way for malicious executables to potentially enter the system, and should be mounted with options which grant least privilege. Users should not be allowed to introduce arbitrary devices or setuid programs to a system. In addition, while users are usually allowed to add executable programs to a system, the `noexec` option prevents code from being executed directly from the media itself, and may therefore provide a line of defense against certain types of worms or malicious code.

Mount points in `/etc/fstab` may not exist on a modern system with typical hardware. The dynamic mounting mechanism may be controlled through other means (which may or may not allow control of the mount options). Adding `noexec` will cause problems if it is necessary in your environment to execute code from removable media, though that behavior carries risks as well.

2.2.1.3 Add `nodev`, `nosuid`, and `noexec` Options to Temporary Storage Partitions

Temporary storage directories such as `/tmp` and `/dev/shm` potentially provide storage space for malicious executables. Although mount options options cannot prevent interpreted code stored there from getting executed by a program in another partition, using certain mount options can be disruptive to malicious code.

2.2.1.3.1 Add `nodev`, `nosuid`, and `noexec` Options to `/tmp`

> Edit the file `/etc/fstab`. Add the text `,nodev,nosuid,noexec` to the list of mount options in column 4.
>
> **CCE 14412-1, 14940-1, 14927-8**

2.2.1.3.2 Add `nodev`, `nosuid`, and `noexec` Options to `/dev/shm`

> Edit the file `/etc/fstab`. Add the text `,nodev,nosuid,noexec` to the list of mount options in column 4.
>
> **CCE 15007-8, 14306-5, 14703-3**

2.2.1.4 Bind-mount `/var/tmp` to `/tmp`

> Edit the file `/etc/fstab`. Add the following line:
>
> ```
> /tmp          /var/tmp          none          rw,noexec,nosuid,nodev,bind  0 0
> ```
>
> **CCE 14584-7**

This line will bind-mount the world-writeable `/var/tmp` directory onto `/tmp`, using the restrictive mount options specified. See the `mount(8)` man page for further explanation of bind mounting.

2.2.2   Restrict Dynamic Mounting and Unmounting of Filesystems

Linux includes a number of facilities for the automated addition and removal of filesystems on a running system. These facilities may increase convenience, but they all bring some risk, whether direct risk from allowing unprivileged users to introduce arbitrary filesystems to a machine, or risk that software flaws in the automated mount facility itself will allow an attacker to compromise the system.

Use caution when enabling any such facility, and find out whether better configuration management or user education might solve the same problem with less risk.

2.2.2.1   Restrict Console Device Access

The default system configuration grants the console user enhanced privileges normally reserved for the root user, including temporary ownership of most system devices. If not necessary, these privileges should be removed and restricted to root only.

Restrict device ownership to root only.

Edit `/etc/security/console.perms.d/50-default.perms` and locate the section prefaced by the following comment:

```
# permission definitions
```

Prepend a `#` symbol to comment out each line in that section which starts with `<console>` or `<xconsole>`:

```
#<console>  0660 <floppy>      0660 root.floppy
#<console>  0600 <sound>       0600 root
...
#<xconsole> 0600 /dev/console 0600 root.root
#<console>  0600 <dri>         0600 root
```

Edit `/etc/security/console.perms` and make the following changes:

```
<console>=tty[0-9][0-9]* vc/[0-9][0-9]* :0\.[0-9] :0
<xconsole>=:0\.[0-9] :0
```

CCE 3685-5

2.2.2.2   Disable USB Device Support

USB flash or hard drives allow an attacker with physical access to a system to quickly copy an enormous amount of data from it.

2.2.2.2.1   Disable Modprobe Loading of USB Storage Driver

If USB storage devices should not be used, the `modprobe` program used for automatic kernel module loading should be configured to not load the USB storage driver upon demand.

Add the following line to `/etc/modprobe.conf` to prevent loading of the `usb-storage` kernel module:

```
install usb-storage /bin/true
```

CCE 4187-1

This will prevent the `modprobe` program from loading the `usb-storage` module, but will not prevent an administrator (or another program) from using the `insmod` program to load the module manually.

2.2.2.2.2   Remove USB Storage Driver

If your system never requires the use of USB storage devices, then the supporting driver can be removed. Though more effective (as USB storage certainly cannot be used if the driver is not available at all), this is less elegant than the method described in Section 2.2.2.2.1.

To remove the USB storage driver from the system:

> `rm /lib/modules/`*`kernelversion(s)`*`/kernel/drivers/usb/storage/usb-storage.ko`

This command will need to be repeated every time the kernel is updated. This command will also cause the command `rpm -q --verify kernel` to fail, which may be an undesirable side effect.

CCE 4006-3

Note that this guidance will not prevent USB storage devices from being mounted if a custom kernel (i.e., not the one supplied with the system) with built-in USB support is used.

2.2.2.2.3   Disable Kernel Support for USB via Bootloader Configuration

Another means of disabling USB storage is to disable all USB support provided by the operating system. This can be accomplished by adding the "nousb" argument to the kernel's boot loader configuration.

Disabling all kernel support for USB will cause problems for systems with USB-based keyboards, mice, or printers. This guidance is inappropriate for systems which require USB connectivity.

To disable kernel support for USB, append "nousb" to the kernel line in `/etc/grub.conf` as follows:

> `kernel /vmlinuz-`*`version`* `ro vga=ext root=/dev/VolGroup00/LogVol00 rhgb quiet nousb`

CCE 4173-1

2.2.2.2.4   Disable Booting from USB Devices

An attacker with physical access could try to boot the system from a USB flash drive and then access any data on the system's hard drive, circumventing the normal operating system's access controls. To prevent this, configure the BIOS to disallow booting from USB drives. Also configure the BIOS or firmware password as described in Section 2.3.5.1 to prevent unauthorized configuration changes.

CCE 3944-6

2.2.2.3   Disable the Automounter if Possible

If the `autofs` service is not needed to dynamically mount NFS filesystems or removable media, disable the service:

```
# chkconfig autofs off
```
CCE 4072-5

The `autofs` daemon mounts and unmounts filesystems, such as user home directories shared via NFS, on demand. In addition, `autofs` can be used to handle removable media, and the default configuration provides the cdrom device as `/misc/cd`. However, this method of providing access to removable media is *not* common, so `autofs` can almost always be disabled if NFS is not in use.

Even if NFS is required, it is almost always possible to configure filesystem mounts statically by editing `/etc/fstab` rather than relying on the automounter.

2.2.2.4 Disable GNOME Automounting if Possible

The system's default desktop environment, GNOME, runs the program `gnome-volume-manager` to mount devices and removable media (such as DVDs, CDs and USB flash drives) whenever they are inserted into the system.

Execute the following commands to prevent `gnome-volume-manager` from automatically mounting devices and media:

```
# gconftool-2 --direct \
            --config-source xml:readwrite:/etc/gconf/gconf.xml.mandatory \
            --type bool \
            --set /desktop/gnome/volume_manager/automount_media false
# gconftool-2 --direct \
            --config-source xml:readwrite:/etc/gconf/gconf.xml.mandatory \
            --type bool \
            --set /desktop/gnome/volume_manager/automount_drives false
```

Verify the changes by executing the following command, which should return a list of settings:

```
# gconftool-2 -R /desktop/gnome/volume_manager
```

The `automount_drives` and `automount_media` settings should be set to `false`. Survey the list for any other options that should be adjusted.

CCE 4231-7

The system's capabilities for automatic mounting should be configured to match whatever is defined by security policy. Disabling USB storage as described in Section 2.2.2.2.1 will prevent the use of USB storage devices, but this step can also be taken as an additional layer of prevention and to prevent automatic mounting of CDs and DVDs if required.

Particularly for kiosk-style systems, where users should have extremely limited access to the system, more detailed information can be found in Red Hat Desktop: Deployment Guide [5]. The `gconf-editor` program, available in an RPM of the same name, can be used to explore other settings available in the GNOME environment.

2.2.2.5 Disable Mounting of Uncommon Filesystem Types

Append the following lines to `/etc/modprobe.conf` in order to prevent the usage of uncommon filesystem types:

```
install cramfs /bin/true
install freevxfs /bin/true
install jffs2 /bin/true
install hfs /bin/true
install hfsplus /bin/true
install squashfs /bin/true
install udf /bin/true
```

CCE 14089-7, 14457-6, 15087-0, 14093-9, 14853-6, 14118-4, 14871-8

Using the `install` command inside `/etc/modprobe.conf` instructs the kernel module loading system to run the command specified (here, `/bin/true`) instead of inserting the module in the kernel as normal. This effectively prevents usage of these uncommon filesystems.

2.2.2.6   Disable All GNOME Thumbnailers if Possible

The system's default desktop environment, GNOME, uses a number of different thumbnailer programs to generate thumbnails for any new or modified content in an opened folder.

Execute the following command to prevent the thumbnailers from automatically creating thumbnails for new or modified folder contents:

```
# gconftool-2 --direct \
              --config-source xml:readwrite:/etc/gconf/gconf.xml.mandatory \
              --type bool \
              --set /desktop/gnome/thumbnailers/disable_all true
```

This effectively prevents an attacker from gaining access to a system through a flaw in GNOME's Nautilus thumbnail creators.

2.2.3   Verify Permissions on Important Files and Directories

Permissions for many files on a system should be set to conform to system policy. This section discusses important permission restrictions gshadow which should be checked on a regular basis to ensure that no harmful discrepancies have arisen.

2.2.3.1   Verify Permissions on `passwd`, `shadow`, `group` and `gshadow` Files

```
# cd /etc
# chown root:root passwd shadow group gshadow
# chmod 644 passwd group
# chmod 400 shadow gshadow
```

CCE 3988-3, 3883-6, 3276-3, 3932-1, 4064-2, 4210-1, 3918-0, 3566-7, 3958-6, 3967-7, 3495-9, 4130-1

These are the default permissions for these files. Many utilities need read access to the `passwd` file in order to function properly, but read access to the `shadow` file allows malicious attacks against system passwords, and should never be enabled.

2.2.3.2   Verify that All World-Writable Directories Have Sticky Bits Set

Locate any directories in local partitions which are world-writable and do not have their sticky bits set. The following command will discover and print these. Run it once for each local partition *PART*:

```
# find PART -xdev -type d \( -perm -0002 -a ! -perm -1000 \) -print
```

If this command produces any output, fix each reported directory */dir* using the command:

```
# chmod +t /dir
```

CCE 3399-3

When the so-called "sticky bit" is set on a directory, only the owner of a given file may remove that file from the directory. Without the sticky bit, any user with write access to a directory may remove any file in the directory. Setting the sticky bit prevents users from removing each other's files. In cases where there is no reason for a directory to be world-writable, a better solution is to remove that permission rather than to set the sticky bit. However, if a directory is used by a particular application, consult that application's documentation instead of blindly changing modes.

2.2.3.3   Find Unauthorized World-Writable Files

The following command discovers and prints any world-writable files in local partitions. Run it once for each local partition *PART*:

```
# find PART -xdev -type f -perm -0002 -print
```

If this command produces any output, fix each reported file *file* using the command:

```
# chmod o-w file
```

CCE 3795-2

Data in world-writable files can be modified by any user on the system. In almost all circumstances, files can be configured using a combination of user and group permissions to support whatever legitimate access is needed without the risk caused by world-writable files.

It is generally a good idea to remove global (other) write access to a file when it is discovered. However, check with documentation for specific applications before making changes. Also, monitor for recurring world-writable files, as these may be symptoms of a misconfigured application or user account.

2.2.3.4   Find Unauthorized SUID/SGID System Executables

The following command discovers and prints any setuid or setgid files on local partitions. Run it once for each local partition *PART*:

```
# find PART -xdev \( -perm -4000 -o -perm -2000 \) -type f -print
```

If the file does not require a setuid or setgid bit as discussed below, then these bits can be removed with the command:

```
# chmod -s file
```

CCE 14340-4, 14970-8

The following table contains all setuid and setgid files which are expected to be on a stock system. The setuid or setgid bit on these files may be disabled to reduce system risk if only an administrator requires their functionality. The table indicates those files which may not be needed.

Note: Several of these files are used for applications which are unlikely to be relevant to most production environments, such as ISDN networking, SSH hostbased authentication, or modification of network interfaces by unprivileged users. It is extremely likely that your site can disable a subset of these files with no loss of functionality.

Any files found by the above command which are not in the table should be examined. If the files are not authorized, they should have permissions removed, and further investigation may be warranted.

File	Set-ID	Subsystem/Ref	Disable?
/bin/mount	uid root	filesystems	no
/bin/ping	uid root	net (3.3.9)	no
/bin/ping6	uid root	net (3.3.9),IPv6 (2.5.3)	unless IPv6 is used
/bin/su	uid root	auth (2.3.1.2)	no
/bin/umount	uid root	filesystems	no
/sbin/mount.nfs	uid root	NFS (3.13)	unless NFS is used
/sbin/mount.nfs4	uid root	NFS (3.13)	unless NFSv4 is used
/sbin/netreport	gid root	net (3.3.9)	unless users must modify interfaces
/sbin/pam_timestamp_check	uid root	PAM auth (2.3.3)	no
/sbin/umount.nfs	uid root	NFS (3.13)	unless NFS is used
/sbin/umount.nfs4	uid root	NFS (3.13)	unless NFSv4 is used
/sbin/unix_chkpwd	uid root	PAM auth (2.3.3)	no
/usr/bin/at	uid root	cron/at (3.4)	no
/usr/bin/chage	uid root	passwd expiry (2.3.1.7)	unless users must view expiry info
/usr/bin/chfn	uid root	user info	unless users must change finger info
/usr/bin/chsh	uid root	user info	unless users must change shells
/usr/bin/crontab	uid/gid root	cron/at (3.4)	unless users must use cron
/usr/bin/gpasswd	uid root	group auth	no
/usr/bin/locate	gid slocate	locate database	no
/usr/bin/lockfile	gid mail	procmail	unless procmail is used
/usr/bin/newgrp	uid root	group auth	no
/usr/bin/passwd	uid root	passwd auth	no
/usr/bin/rcp	uid root	rsh (3.2.3)	yes (rsh is obsolete)
/usr/bin/rlogin	uid root	rsh (3.2.3)	yes (rsh is obsolete)
/usr/bin/rsh	uid root	rsh (3.2.3)	yes (rsh is obsolete)
/usr/bin/ssh-agent	gid nobody	SSH (3.5)	no
/usr/bin/sudo	uid root	sudo (2.3.1.3)	no
/usr/bin/sudoedit	uid root	sudo (2.3.1.3)	no
/usr/bin/wall	gid tty	console messaging	unless console messaging is used
/usr/bin/write	gid tty	console messaging	unless console messaging is used
/usr/bin/Xorg	uid root	X11 (3.6)	unless X11 is used
/usr/kerberos/bin/ksu	uid root	Kerberos auth (2.3.6)	unless Kerberos is used
/usr/libexec/openssh/ssh-keysign	uid root	SSH (3.5)	unless sshd uses hostbased auth
/usr/libexec/utempter/utempter	gid utmp	terminal support	no
/usr/lib/squid/pam_auth	uid root	squid (3.19)	unless squid is used
/usr/lib/squid/ncsa_auth	uid root	squid (3.19)	unless squid is used
/usr/lib/vte/gnome-pty-helper	gid utmp	X11, Gnome (3.6)	unless X11 is used
/usr/sbin/ccreds_validate	uid root	PAM auth (2.3.3)	unless PAM auth caching is used
/usr/sbin/lockdev	gid lock	filesystems	no
/usr/sbin/sendmail.sendmail	gid smmsp	sendmail client (3.11.2)	no
/usr/sbin/suexec	uid root	apache (3.16)	unless apache is used
/usr/sbin/userhelper	uid root	PAM auth (2.3.3.4)	restrict (see section 2.3.3.4)
/usr/sbin/userisdnctl	uid root	ISDN	unless ISDN is used

File	Set-ID	Subsystem/Ref	Disable?
/usr/sbin/usernetctl	uid root	user network control	unless users must modify interfaces

2.2.3.5 Find and Repair Unowned Files

> The following command will discover and print any files on local partitions which do not belong to a valid user and a valid group. Run it once for each local partition *PART*:
>
>   # find *PART* -xdev \(-nouser -o -nogroup \) -print
>
> If this command prints any results, investigate each reported file and either assign it to an appropriate user and group or remove it.
>
> **CCE 4223-4, 3573-3**

Unowned files are not directly exploitable, but they are generally a sign that something is wrong with some system process. They may be caused by an intruder, by incorrect software installation or incomplete software removal, or by failure to remove all files belonging to a deleted account. The files should be repaired so that they will not cause problems when accounts are created in the future, and the problem which led to unowned files should be discovered and addressed.

2.2.3.6 Verify that All World-Writable Directories Have Proper Ownership

> Locate any directories in local partitions which are world-writable and ensure that they are owned by root or another system account. The following command will discover and print these (assuming only system accounts have a uid lower than 500). Run it once for each local partition *PART*:
>
>   # find *PART* -xdev -type d -perm -0002 -uid +500 -print
>
> If this command produces any output, investigate why the current owner is not root or another system account.

CCE 14794-2

Allowing a user account to own a world-writable directory is undesirable because it allows the owner of that directory to remove or replace any files that may be placed in the directory by other users.

2.2.4 Restrict Programs from Dangerous Execution Patterns

The recommendations in this section provide broad protection against information disclosure or other misbehavior. These protections are applied at the system initialization or kernel level, and defend against certain types of badly-configured or compromised programs.

2.2.4.1 Set Daemon `umask`

> Edit the file /etc/sysconfig/init, and add or correct the following line:
>
>   umask 027
>
> **CCE 4220-0**

The settings file /etc/sysconfig/init contains settings which apply to all processes started at boot time. The system umask must be set to at least 022, or daemon processes may create world-writable files. The more restrictive setting 027 protects files, including temporary files and log files, from unauthorized reading by unprivileged users on the system.

If a particular daemon needs a less restrictive umask, consider editing the startup script or sysconfig file of that daemon to make a specific exception.

2.2.4.2 Disable Core Dumps

> To disable core dumps for all users, add or correct the following line in /etc/security/limits.conf:
>
> ```
> *     hard core 0
> ```
>
> In addition, to ensure that core dumps can never be made by setuid programs, edit /etc/sysctl.conf and add or correct the line:
>
> ```
> fs.suid_dumpable = 0
> ```
>
> **CCE 4225-9, 4247-3**

A core dump file is the memory image of an executable program when it was terminated by the operating system due to errant behavior. In most cases, only software developers would legitimately need to access these files. The core dump files may also contain sensitive information, or unnecessarily occupy large amounts of disk space.

By default, the system sets a *soft limit* to stop the creation of core dump files for all users. This is accomplished in /etc/profile with the line:

```
ulimit -S -c 0 > /dev/null 2>&1
```

However, compliance with this limit is voluntary; it is a default intended only to protect users from the annoyance of generating unwanted core files. Users can increase the allowed core file size up to the hard limit, which is unlimited by default.

Once a hard limit is set in /etc/security/limits.conf, the user cannot increase that limit within his own session. If access to core dumps is required, consider restricting them to only certain users or groups. See the limits.conf(5) man page for more information.

The core dumps of setuid programs are further protected. The sysctl variable fs.suid_dumpable controls whether the kernel allows core dumps from these programs at all. The default value of 0 is recommended.

2.2.4.2.1 Ensure SUID Core Dumps are Disabled

> The sysctl variable fs.suid_dumpable should be checked to ensure that it has not been enabled at any time during system operation. To check this, issue the command:
>
> ```
> # sysctl fs.suid_dumpable
> ```
>
> The output should indicate that the setting is 0. (Use of the -n option causes output to consist of only the value, which may make automated checking easier.)

2.2.4.3   Enable ExecShield

ExecShield comprises a number of kernel features to provide protection against buffer overflows. These features include random placement of the stack and other memory regions, prevention of execution in memory that should only hold data, and special handling of text buffers.

To ensure ExecShield (including random placement of virtual memory regions) is activated at boot, add or correct the following settings in `/etc/sysctl.conf`:

```
kernel.exec-shield = 1
kernel.randomize_va_space = 1
```

CCE 4146-7, 4168-1

ExecShield uses the segmentation feature on all x86 systems to prevent execution in memory higher than a certain address. It writes an address as a limit in the code segment descriptor, to control where code can be executed, on a per-process basis. When the kernel places a process's memory regions such as the stack and heap higher than this address, the hardware prevents execution there. However, this cannot always be done for all memory regions in which execution should not occur, so follow guidance in Section 2.2.4.4 to further protect the system.

2.2.4.3.1   Ensure ExecShield is Enabled

Exec-shield protection is enabled by default, but the `sysctl` variables `kernel.exec-shield` and `kernel.randomize_va_space` should be checked to ensure that it has not been disabled at any time during system operation. To check that ExecShield (including random placement of virtual memory regions) is currently running, issue the following commands:

```
# sysctl kernel.exec-shield
# sysctl kernel.randomize_va_space
```

The output of both commands should be indicate that the setting is 1. (Use of the `-n` option causes output to consist of only the value, which may make automated checking easier.)

2.2.4.4   Enable `Execute Disable` (XD) or `No Execute` (NX) Support on 32-bit x86 Systems

Later 32-bit processors in the x86 family support the ability to prevent code execution on a per memory page basis. Generically and on AMD processors, this ability is called No Execute (NX), while on Intel processors it is called Execute Disable (XD). This ability can help prevent exploitation of buffer overflow vulnerabilities and should be activated whenever possible. Extra steps must be taken to ensure that this protection is enabled on 32-bit x86 systems. Other processors, such as Itanium, POWER, and 64-bit x86 (both AMD64 or Intel 64), have included such support since inception and the standard kernel for those platforms supports the feature.

2.2.4.4.1   Check for Processor Support on x86 Systems

Check to see if the processor supports the PAE and NX features:

```
$ cat /proc/cpuinfo
```

> If supported, the `flags` field will contain `pae` and `nx`.

2.2.4.4.2   Install New Kernel on Supported x86 Systems

> Systems that are using the 64-bit x86 kernel package do not need to install the `kernel-PAE` package because the 64-bit x86 kernel already includes this support. However, if the system is running 32-bit kernel package supports PAE and NX features as determined in the previous section, the `kernel-PAE` package should be installed to enable XD or NX support:
>
> ```
> # yum install kernel-PAE
> ```
>
> The installation process should also have configured the bootloader to load the new kernel at boot. Verify this at reboot and modify `/etc/grub.conf` if necessary.
>
> **CCE 4172-3**

The `kernel-PAE` package should not be installed on older systems that do not support the XD or NX bit, as this may prevent them from booting.

2.2.4.4.3   Enable NX or XD Support in the BIOS

Computers with the ability to prevent this type of code execution frequently put an option in the BIOS that will allow users to turn the feature on or off at will.

> Reboot the system and enter the BIOS or "Setup" configuration menu.
>
> Navigate the BIOS configuration menu and make sure that the option is enabled. The setting may be located under a "Security" section. Look for `Execute Disable` (XD) on Intel-based systems and `No Execute` (NX) on AMD-based systems.
>
> See Section 2.3.5.1 for information on protecting this and other BIOS settings.
>
> **CCE 4177-2**

2.2.4.5   Configure Prelink

Prelinking is designed to decrease process startup time by loading each shared library into an address for which the linking of needed symbols has already been performed. The `/etc/sysconfig/prelink` file describes what files the `/usr/sbin/prelink` program will modify and how often it should modify those files.

A cron job is run daily that determines if the `prelink` program should be run. There are two types of prelinking: quick and full. Full prelinking occurs by default every fourteen days and relinks all shared libraries and the binaries that use them. Quick mode is run every day, but it only runs on modified binaries and libraries.

After a binary has been prelinked, the address at which shared libraries will be loaded will no longer be random on a per-process basis, even if the `kernel.randomize_va_space` sysctl is set to 1. This is undesirable because it provides a stable address for an attacker to use during an exploitation attempt.

2.2.4.5.1 Disable Prelink

Prelink can be safely disabled by setting the following setting in `/etc/sysconfig/prelink`:

```
PRELINKING=no
```

2.2.4.5.2 Undo Existing Prelinking

Execute the following command to revert binaries and libraries to their original content before they were prelinked:

```
# /usr/sbin/prelink -ua
```

2.3   Account and Access Control

In traditional Unix security, if an attacker gains shell access to a certain login account, he can perform any action or access any file to which that account has access. Therefore, making it more difficult for unauthorized people to gain shell access to accounts, particularly to privileged accounts, is a necessary part of securing a system. This section introduces mechanisms for restricting access to accounts under RHEL5.

2.3.1   Protect Accounts by Restricting Password-Based Login

Conventionally, Unix shell accounts are accessed by providing a username and password to a login program, which tests these values for correctness using the `/etc/passwd` and `/etc/shadow` files. Password-based login is vulnerable to guessing of weak passwords, and to sniffing and man-in-the-middle attacks against passwords entered over a network or at an insecure console. Therefore, mechanisms for accessing accounts by entering usernames and passwords should be restricted to those which are operationally necessary.

2.3.1.1 Restrict Root Logins to System Console

Edit the file `/etc/securetty`. Ensure that the file contains only the following lines:

- The primary system console device:

```
console
```

- The virtual console devices:

```
tty1
tty2
tty3
tty4
tty5
tty6
...
```

- If required by your organization, the deprecated virtual console interface may be retained for backwards compatibility:

  ```
  vc/1
  vc/2
  vc/3
  vc/4
  vc/5
  vc/6
  ...
  ```

- If required by your organization, the serial consoles may be added:

  ```
  ttyS0
  ttyS1
  ```

  CCE 3820-8, 3485-0, 4111-1, 4256-4

Direct root logins should be allowed only for emergency use. In normal situations, the administrator should access the system via a unique unprivileged account, and use `su` or `sudo` to execute privileged commands. Discouraging administrators from accessing the root account directly ensures an audit trail in organizations with multiple administrators. Locking down the channels through which root can connect directly reduces opportunities for password-guessing against the root account.

The `login` program uses the file `/etc/securetty` to determine which interfaces should allow root logins. The virtual devices `/dev/console` and `/dev/tty*` represent the system consoles (accessible via the Ctrl-Alt-F1 through Ctrl-Alt-F6 keyboard sequences on a default installation). The default `securetty` file also contains `/dev/vc/*`. These are likely to be deprecated in most environments, but may be retained for compatibility.

Root should also be prohibited from connecting via network protocols. See Section 3.5 for instructions on preventing root from logging in via SSH.

2.3.1.2   Limit `su` Access to the Root Account

---

1. Ensure that the group `wheel` exists, and that the usernames of all administrators who should be allowed to execute commands as root are members of that group.

   ```
   # grep ^wheel /etc/group
   ```

2. Edit the file `/etc/pam.d/su`. Add, uncomment, or correct the line:

   ```
   auth          required          pam_wheel.so          use_uid
   ```

   CCE 14088-9, 15047-4

The `su` command allows a user to gain the privileges of another user by entering the password for that user's account. It is desirable to restrict the root user so that only known administrators are ever allowed to access the root account. This restricts password-guessing against the root account by unauthorized users or by accounts which have been compromised.

By convention, the group `wheel` contains all users who are allowed to run privileged commands. The PAM module `pam_wheel.so` is used to restrict root access to this set of users.

2.3.1.3   Configure `sudo` to Improve Auditing of Root Access

> 1. Ensure that the group `wheel` exists, and that the usernames of all administrators who should be allowed to execute commands as root are members of that group.
>
>    ```
>    # grep ^wheel /etc/group
>    ```
>
> 2. Edit the file `/etc/sudoers`. Add, uncomment, or correct the line:
>
>    ```
>    %wheel          ALL=(ALL)          ALL
>    ```
>
> **CCE 4044-4**

The `sudo` command allows fine-grained control over which users can execute commands using other accounts. The primary benefit of `sudo` when configured as above is that it provides an audit trail of every command run by a privileged user. It is possible for a malicious administrator to circumvent this restriction, but, if there is an established procedure that all root commands are run using `sudo`, then it is easy for an auditor to detect unusual behavior when this procedure is not followed.

Editing `/etc/sudoers` by hand can be dangerous, since a configuration error may make it impossible to access the root account remotely. The recommended means of editing this file is using the `visudo` command, which checks the file's syntax for correctness before allowing it to be saved.

Note that `sudo` allows any attacker who gains access to the password of an administrator account to run commands as root. This is a downside which must be weighed against the benefits of increased audit capability and of being able to heavily restrict the use of the high-value root password (which can be logistically difficult to change often). As a basic precaution, *never* use the `NOPASSWD` directive, which would allow anyone with access to an administrator account to execute commands as root without knowing the administrator's password.

The `sudo` command has many options which can be used to further customize its behavior. See the `sudoers(5)` man page for details.

2.3.1.4   Block Shell and Login Access for Non-Root System Accounts

Do not perform the steps in this section on the root account. Doing so might cause the system to become inaccessible.

> Using `/etc/passwd`, obtain a listing of all users, their UIDs, and their shells, for instance by running:
>
> ```
> # awk -F: '{print $1 ":" $3 ":" $7}' /etc/passwd
> ```
>
> Identify the system accounts from this listing. These will primarily be the accounts with UID numbers less than 500, other than root.
>
> For each identified system account *SYSACCT*, lock the account:
>
> ```
> # usermod -L SYSACCT
> ```
>
> and disable its shell:
>
> ```
> # usermod -s /sbin/nologin SYSACCT
> ```
>
> **CCE 3987-5**

These are the accounts which are not associated with a human user of the system, but which exist to perform some administrative function. Make it more difficult for an attacker to use these accounts by locking their passwords and by setting their shells to some non-valid shell. The RHEL5 default non-valid shell is `/sbin/nologin`, but any command which will exit with a failure status and disallow execution of any further commands, such as `/bin/false` or `/dev/null`, will work.

2.3.1.5 Verify Proper Storage and Existence of Password Hashes

CCE 4238-2

2.3.1.5.1 Verify that No Accounts Have Empty Password Fields

> To ensure that no accounts have an empty password field, the following command should have no output:
>
> ```
> # awk -F: '($2 == "") {print}' /etc/shadow
> ```
>
> If this produces any output, fix the problem by locking each account (see Section 2.3.1.4 above) or by setting a password.

If an account has an empty password, anybody may log in and run commands with the privileges of that account. Accounts with empty passwords should never be used in operational environments.

2.3.1.5.2 Verify that All Account Password Hashes are Shadowed

> To ensure that no password hashes are stored in `/etc/passwd`, the following command should have no output:
>
> ```
> # awk -F: '($2 != "x") {print}' /etc/passwd
> ```
>
> CCE 14300-8

The hashes for all user account passwords should be stored in the file `/etc/shadow` and never in `/etc/passwd`, which is readable by all users.

2.3.1.6 Verify that No Non-Root Accounts Have UID 0

> This command will print all password file entries for accounts with UID 0:
>
> ```
> # awk -F: '($3 == "0") {print}' /etc/passwd
> ```
>
> This should print only one line, for the user `root`. If any other lines appear, ensure that these additional UID-0 accounts are authorized, and that there is a good reason for them to exist.
>
> CCE 4009-7

In general, the best practice solution for auditing use of the root account is to restrict the set of cases in which root must be accessed anonymously by requiring use of `su` or `sudo` in almost all cases. Some sites choose to have more than one account with UID 0 in order to differentiate between administrators, but this practice may have unexpected side effects, and is therefore not recommended.

2.3.1.7 Set Password Expiration Parameters

> Edit the file `/etc/login.defs` to specify password expiration settings for new accounts. Add or correct the following lines:
>
> ```
> PASS_MAX_DAYS   60
> PASS_MIN_DAYS   7
> PASS_MIN_LEN    14
> PASS_WARN_AGE   7
> ```
>
> For each existing human user *USER*, modify the current expiration settings to match these:
>
> ```
> # chage -M 60 -m 7 -W 7 USER
> ```
>
> **CCE 4180-6, 4092-3, 4097-2**

Users should be forced to change their passwords, in order to decrease the utility of compromised passwords. However, the need to change passwords often should be balanced against the risk that users will reuse or write down passwords if forced to change them too often. Forcing password changes every 90-360 days, depending on the environment, is recommended. Set the appropriate value as `PASS_MAX_DAYS` and apply it to existing accounts with the `-M` flag.

The `PASS_MIN_DAYS` (`-m`) setting prevents password changes for 7 days after the first change, to discourage password cycling. If you use this setting, train users to contact an administrator for an emergency password change in case a new password becomes compromised. The `PASS_WARN_AGE` (`-W`) setting gives users 7 days of warnings at login time that their passwords are about to expire.

The `PASS_MIN_LEN` setting, which controls minimum password length, should be set to whatever is required by your site or organization security policy. The example value of 8 provided here may be inadequate for many environments. See Section 2.3.3 for information on how to enforce more sophisticated requirements on password length and quality.

2.3.1.7.1 Remove Password Parameters from libuser.conf

> Ensure the following line exists within the file `/etc/libuser.conf` under the `[import]` section.
>
> ```
> login_defs = /etc/login.defs
> ```
>
> Also ensure that no lines beginning with the following appear in the `[userdefaults]` section of the file, as these override settings from `/etc/login.defs`:
>
> ```
> LU_SHADOWMAX
> LU_SHADOWMIN
> LU_SHADOWWARNING
> ```

The `/etc/libuser.conf` file contains configuration options for the libuser library, which is intended to implement a standardized interface for manipulating and administering user and group accouts. By default, it sources password settings from `/etc/login.defs`, but it can override these parameters. The man page `libuser.conf(5)` contains more information.

2.3.1.8   Remove Legacy '+' Entries from Password Files

> The command:
>
> ```
> # grep "^+:" /etc/passwd /etc/shadow /etc/group
> ```
>
> should produce no output.
>
> **CCE 4114-5, 14675-3, 14071-5**

The + symbol was used by systems to include data from NIS maps into existing files. However, a certain configuration error in which a NIS inclusion line appears in `/etc/passwd`, but NIS is not running, could lead to anyone being able to access the system with the username + and no password. Therefore, it is important to verify that no such line appears in any of the relevant system files.

The correct way to tell the local system to consult network databases such as LDAP or NIS for user information is to make appropriate modifications to `/etc/nsswitch.conf`.

2.3.2   Use Unix Groups to Enhance Security

The access control policies which can be enforced by standard Unix permissions are limited, and configuring SELinux (Section 2.4) is frequently a better choice. However, this guide recommends that security be enhanced to the extent possible by enforcing the Unix group policies outlined in this section.

2.3.2.1   Create a Unique Default Group for Each User

> When running `useradd`, do *not* use the `-g` flag or otherwise override the default group.

The Red Hat default is that each new user account should have a unique primary group whose name is the same as that of the account. This default is recommended, in order to provide additional protection against files which are created with group write permission enabled.

2.3.2.2   Create and Maintain a Group Containing All Human Users

> Identify all user accounts on the system which correspond to human users. Depending on your system configuration, this may be all entries in `/etc/passwd` with UID values of at least 500. Once, you have identified such a set of users, create a group named *usergroup* (substitute some name appropriate to your environment) and populate it with each human user:
>
> ```
> # groupadd usergroup
> # usermod -G usergroup human1
> # usermod -G usergroup human2
> ...
> # usermod -G usergroup humanN
> ```
>
> Then modify your procedure for creating new user accounts by adding `-G usergroup` to the set of flags with which `useradd` is invoked, so that new human users will be placed in the correct group by default.

Creating a group of human users does not, by itself, enhance system security. However, as you work on securing your system, you will often find commands which never need to be run by system accounts, or which are only ever needed by users logged into the graphical console (which should only ever be available to human users, even on workstations). Once a group of users has been created, it is easy to restrict access to a given command, for instance */path/to/graphical/command*, to authorized users:

```
# chgrp usergroup /path/to/graphical/command
# chmod 750 /path/graphical/command
```

Without a group of human users, it is necessary to restrict access by somehow preventing each system account from running the command, which is an error-prone process even when it is possible at all.

2.3.3 Protect Accounts by Configuring PAM

PAM, or Pluggable Authentication Modules, is a system which implements modular authentication for Linux programs. PAM is the framework which provides the system's authentication architecture and can be configured to minimize your system's exposure to unnecessary risk. This section contains guidance on how to accomplish that, and how to ensure that the modules used by your PAM configuration do what they are supposed to do.

PAM is implemented as a set of shared objects which are loaded and invoked whenever an application wishes to authenticate a user. Typically, the application must be running as `root` in order to take advantage of PAM. Traditional privileged network listeners (e.g. `sshd`) or SUID programs (e.g. `sudo`) already meet this requirement. An SUID `root` application, `userhelper`, is provided so that programs which are not SUID or privileged themselves can still take advantage of PAM.

PAM looks in the directory `/etc/pam.d` for application-specific configuration information. For instance, if the program `login` attempts to authenticate a user, then PAM's libraries follow the instructions in the file `/etc/pam.d/login` to determine what actions should be taken.

One very important file in `/etc/pam.d` is `/etc/pam.d/system-auth`. This file, which is included by many other PAM configuration files, defines "default" system authentication measures. Modifying this file is a good way to make far-reaching authentication changes, for instance when implementing a centralized authentication service.

Be careful when making changes to PAM's configuration files. The syntax for these files is complex, and modifications can have unexpected consequences.[1] The default configurations shipped with applications should be sufficient for most users.

Running `authconfig` or `system-config-authentication` will re-write the PAM configuration files, destroying any manually made changes and replacing them with a series of system defaults.

2.3.3.1 Set Password Quality Requirements

The default `pam_cracklib` PAM module provides strength checking for passwords. It performs a number of checks, such as making sure passwords are not similar to dictionary words, are of at least a certain length, are not the previous password reversed, and are not simply a change of case from the previous password. It can also require passwords to be in certain character classes.

The `pam_passwdqc` PAM module provides the ability to enforce even more stringent password strength requirements. It is provided in an RPM of the same name.

The man pages `pam_cracklib(8)` and `pam_passwdqc(8)` provide information on the capabilities and configuration of each.

---

[1]One reference to the configuration file syntax can be found at `http://www.kernel.org/pub/linux/libs/pam/Linux-PAM-html/sag-configuration-file.html`.

CCE 3762-2

2.3.3.1.1 Set Password Quality Requirements, if using pam_cracklib

The pam_cracklib PAM module can be configured to meet recommendations for DoD systems as stated in [12].

To configure pam_cracklib to require at least one uppercase character, lowercase character, digit, and other (special) character, locate the following line in /etc/pam.d/system-auth:

```
password        requisite       pam_cracklib.so try_first_pass retry=3
```

and then alter it to read (placing the text on one line, which is not possible here):

```
password        required        pam_cracklib.so try_first_pass retry=3 minlen=14 \
                                     dcredit=-1 ucredit=-1 ocredit=-1 lcredit=-1
```

If necessary, modify the arguments to ensure compliance with your organization's security policy. Note that the password quality requirements are not enforced for the root account for some reason.

CCE 14113-5, 14672-0, 14712-4, 14122-6, 14701-7, 15054-0

2.3.3.1.2 Set Password Quality Requirements, if using pam_passwdqc

If password strength stronger than that guaranteed by pam_cracklib is required, configure PAM to use pam_passwdqc.

To activate pam_passwdqc, locate the following line in /etc/pam.d/system-auth:

```
password        requisite       pam_cracklib.so try_first_pass retry=3
```

and then replace it with the line:

```
password        requisite       pam_passwdqc.so min=disabled,disabled,16,12,8
```

If necessary, modify the arguments (min=disabled,disabled,16,12,8) to ensure compliance with your organization's security policy. Configuration options are described in the man page pam_passwdqc(8) and also in /usr/share/doc/pam_passwdqc-*version*. The minimum lengths provided here supercede that specified by the argument PASS_MIN_LEN as described in Section 2.3.1.7.

The options given in the example above set a minimum length for each of the password "classes" that pam_passwdqc recognizes. Setting a particular minimum value to disabled will stop users from choosing a password that falls into that category alone.

2.3.3.2 Set Lockouts for Failed Password Attempts

The pam_tally2 PAM module provides the capability to lock out user accounts after a number of failed login attempts. Its documentation is available in /usr/share/doc/pam-*version*/txts/README.pam_tally2.

The behavior of pam_tally2 has changed during the lifetime of RHEL 5. Earlier guidance is different from what is listed here, and this guidance may not properly function on RHEL systems that are not up to date.

> If locking out accounts after a number of incorrect login attempts is required by your security policy, implement use of `pam_tally2.so`.
>
> To enforce password lockout, add the following to `/etc/pam.d/system-auth`. First, add to the top of the `auth` lines:
>
> ```
> auth        required        pam_tally2.so deny=5 onerr=fail unlock_time=900
> ```
>
> Second, add to the top of the `account` lines:
>
> ```
> account required        pam_tally2.so
> ```
>
> Adjust the `deny` argument (which controls how many attempts are permitted before the account is locked) and the `unlock_time` argument (which controls how many seconds elapse before the account is automatically unlocked) to conform to your system security policy. The `pam_tally2` utility can also be used to unlock user accounts as follows:
>
> ```
> # /sbin/pam_tally2 --user username --reset
> ```
>
> **CCE 3410-8**

Locking out user accounts presents the risk of a denial-of-service attack. The security policy regarding system lockout must weigh the risk of a denial-of-service attack against an account against the benefits of thwarting password guessing attacks. The `unlock_time` argument can be used to adjust this risk.

2.3.3.3 Use `pam_deny.so` to Quickly Deny Access to a Service

> In order to deny access to a service *SVCNAME* via PAM, edit the file `/etc/pam.d/`*SVCNAME*. Prepend this line to the beginning of the file:
>
> ```
> auth            requisite       pam_deny.so
> ```

Under most circumstances, there are better ways to disable a service than to deny access via PAM. However, this should suffice as a way to quickly make a service unavailable to future users (existing sessions which have already been authenticated, are not affected). The `requisite` tag tells PAM that, if the named module returns failure, authentication should fail, and PAM should immediately stop processing the configuration file. The `pam_deny.so` module always returns failure regardless of its input.

2.3.3.4 Restrict Execution of `userhelper` to Console Users

> If your environment has defined a group, *usergroup* containing all the human users of your system, restrict execution of the `userhelper` program to only that group:
>
> ```
> # chgrp usergroup /usr/sbin/userhelper
> # chmod 4710 /usr/sbin/userhelper
> ```
>
> **CCE 4185-5, 3952-9**

The `userhelper` program provides authentication for graphical services which must run with `root` privileges, such as the `system-config-` family of graphical configuration utilities. Only human users logged into the system console are likely to ever have a legitimate need to run these utilities. This step provides some protection against possible flaws in `userhelper`'s implementation, and against further privilege escalation when system accounts are compromised. See Section 2.3.2.2 for more information on creating a group of human users.

The `userhelper` program is configured by the files in `/etc/security/console.apps/`. Each file specifies, for some program, what user the program should run as, and what program should be executed after successful authentication.

Note: The configuration in `/etc/security/console.apps/` is applied in combination with the PAM configuration of the service defined in `/etc/pam.d/`. First, `userhelper` determines what user the service should run as. (Typically, this will be `root`.) Next, `userhelper` uses the PAM API to allow the user who ran the program to attempt to authenticate as the desired user. The PAM API exchange is wrapped in a GUI if the application's configuration requests one.

2.3.3.5 Upgrade Password Hashing Algorithm to SHA-512

In order to configure the system to use the SHA-512 algorithm, three files need to be edited.

First, edit the file `/etc/pam.d/system-auth` to ensure that `sha512` is used by the pam_unix.so module in the password section, replacing any other algorithms (such as `md5`, `bigcrypt`, `blowfish`, or `sha256`) with `sha512`, as shown:

```
password    sufficient    pam_unix.so sha512 shadow nullok try_first_pass use_authtok
```

Second, edit the file `/etc/login.defs` to add or correct the following lines:

```
MD5_CRYPT_ENAB no
ENCRYPT_METHOD SHA512
```

Third, edit the file `/etc/libuser.conf` to add or correct the following line:

```
crypt_style = sha512
```

When users changes their passwords, hashes for the new passwords will be generated using the SHA-512 algorithm.

CCE 14063-2

The default algorithm for storing hashes in earlier releases of Red Hat Enterprise Linux 5 was MD5. In release 5.2 (and for those systems fully updated since its release), the algorithms SHA-256 and SHA-512 are available. The release notes available at `http://www.redhat.com/docs/en-US/Red_Hat_Enterprise_Linux/5.2/html/Release_Notes/singles/relnotesU2-x86.html` document this change. As noted there, only kickstart-installed systems can be configured to begin operation with this algorithm. Other systems will need to have this command issued and then all accounts will need to perform a password change in order to upgrade the stored hashes to the stronger algorithm.

2.3.3.6 Limit Password Reuse

Do not allow users to reuse recent passwords. This can be accomplished by using the `remember` option for the pam_unix PAM module. In order to prevent a user from re-using any of his or her last 5 passwords, append `remember=5` to the `password` line which uses the pam_unix module in the file `/etc/pam.d/system-auth`, as shown:

```
password sufficient pam_unix.so existing_options remember=5
```

CCE 14939-3

Old (and thus no longer valid) passwords are stored in the file `/etc/security/opasswd`.

2.3.3.7 Remove the `pam_ccreds` Package if Possible

> Unless its credential caching functionality is required, remove the pam_ccreds package:
>
> ```
> # yum erase pam_ccreds
> ```

The `pam_ccreds` package contains the setuid program `/usr/sbin/ccreds_validate` and should be removed unless it provides essential functionality. Any credentials cached on a system would also be compromised if an attacker obtains control of the system.

2.3.4 Secure Session Configuration Files for Login Accounts

When a user logs into a Unix account, the system configures the user's session by reading a number of files. Many of these files are located in the user's home directory, and may have weak permissions as a result of user error or misconfiguration. If an attacker can modify or even read certain types of account configuration information, he can often gain full access to the affected user's account. Therefore, it is important to test and correct configuration file permissions for interactive accounts, particularly those of privileged users such as root or system administrators.

2.3.4.1 Ensure that No Dangerous Directories Exist in Root's Path

The active path of the root account can be obtained by starting a new root shell and running:

```
# echo $PATH
```

This will produce a colon-separated list of directories in the path.

It is important to prevent root from executing unknown or untrusted programs, since such programs could contain malicious code. Therefore, root should not run programs installed by unprivileged users. Since root may often be working inside untrusted directories, the . character, which represents the current directory, should never be in the root path, nor should any directory which can be written to by an unprivileged or semi-privileged (system) user. The following sections describe some entries which should not be seen in root's path.

It is a good practice for administrators to always execute privileged commands by typing the full path to the command.

CCE 3301-9

2.3.4.1.1 Ensure that Root's Path Does Not Include Relative Paths or Null Directories

> For each directory *DIR* in the path, ensure that *DIR* is not equal to a single . character, or that it contains any instances that lead to relative path traversal, such as .. or beginning a path without the slash (/) character. Also ensure that there are no "empty" elements in the path, such as in these examples:
>
> ```
> PATH=:/bin
> PATH=/bin:
> PATH=/bin::/sbin
> ```
>
> These empty elements have the same effect as a single . character.

2.3.4.1.2   Ensure that Root's Path Does Not Include World-Writable or Group-Writable Directories

For each element in the path, run:

```
# ls -ld DIR
```

and ensure that write permissions are disabled for group and other.

CCE 14957-5

2.3.4.2   Ensure that User Home Directories are not Group-Writable or World-Readable

Sections 2.3.4.2–2.3.4.5 recommend modifying user home directories. Notify your user community, and solicit input if appropriate, before making this type of change.

For each human user USER of the system, view the permissions of the user's home directory:

```
# ls -ld /home/USER
```

Ensure that the directory is not group-writable and that it is not world-readable. If necessary, repair the permissions:

```
# chmod g-w /home/USER
# chmod o-rwx /home/USER
```

CCE 4090-7

User home directories contain many configuration files which affect the behavior of a user's account. No user should ever have write permission to another user's home directory. Group shared directories can be configured in subdirectories or elsewhere in the filesystem if they are needed. Typically, user home directories should not be world-readable. If a subset of users need read access to one another's home directories, this can be provided using groups.

2.3.4.3   Ensure that User Dot-Files are not World-writable

For each human user USER of the system, view the permissions of all dot-files in the user's home directory:

```
# ls -ld /home/USER/.[A-Za-z0-9]*
```

Ensure that none of these files are group- or world-writable. Correct each misconfigured file FILE by executing:

```
# chmod go-w /home/USER/FILE
```

A user who can modify another user's configuration files can likely execute commands with the other user's privileges, including stealing data, destroying files, or launching further attacks on the system.

2.3.4.4   Ensure that Users Have Sensible Umask Values

1. Edit the global configuration files `/etc/profile`, `/etc/bashrc`, and `/etc/csh.cshrc`. Add or correct the line:

   ```
   umask 077
   ```

2. Edit the user definitions file `/etc/login.defs`. Add or correct the line:

   ```
   UMASK           077
   ```

3. View the additional configuration files `/etc/csh.login` and `/etc/profile.d/*`, and ensure that none of these files redefine the umask to a more permissive value unless there is a good reason for it.

4. Edit the root shell configuration files `/root/.bashrc`, `/root/.bash_profile`, `/root/.cshrc`, and `/root/.tcshrc`. Add or correct the line:

   ```
   umask 077
   ```

CCE 3844-8, 4227-5, 3870-3, 14107-7, 14847-8

With a default umask setting of 077, files and directories created by users will not be readable by any other user on the system. Users who wish to make specific files group- or world-readable can accomplish this using the `chmod` command. Additionally, users can make all their files readable to their group by default by setting a umask of 027 in their shell configuration files. If default per-user groups exist (that is, if every user has a default group whose name is the same as that user's username and whose only member is the user), then it may even be safe for users to select a umask of 007, making it very easy to intentionally share files with groups of which the user is a member.

In addition, it may be necessary to change root's umask temporarily in order to install software or files which must be readable by other users, or to change the default umasks of certain service accounts such as the FTP user. However, setting a restrictive default protects the files of users who have not taken steps to make their files more available, and preventing files from being inadvertently shared.

2.3.4.5   Ensure that Users do not Have `.netrc` Files

For each human user *USER* of the system, ensure that the user has no `.netrc` file. The command:

```
# ls -l /home/USER/.netrc
```

should return the error "No such file or directory". If any user has such a file, approach that user to discuss removing this file.

The `.netrc` file is a configuration file used to make unattended logins to other systems via FTP. When this file exists, it frequently contains unencrypted passwords which may be used to attack other systems.

2.3.5   Protect Physical Console Access

It is impossible to fully protect a system from an attacker with physical access, so securing the space in which the system is located should be considered a necessary step. However, there are some steps which, if taken, make it more difficult for an attacker to quickly or undetectably modify a system from its console.

2.3.5.1 Set BIOS Password

The BIOS (on x86 systems) is the first code to execute during system startup and controls many important system parameters, including which devices the system will try to boot from, and in which order.

> Assign a password to prevent any unauthorized changes to the BIOS configuration. The exact steps will vary depending on your machine, but are likely to include:
>
> 1. Reboot the machine.
>
> 2. Press the appropriate key during the initial boot screen (F2 is typical).
>
> 3. Navigate the BIOS configuration menu to add a password.

The exact process will be system-specific and the system's hardware manual may provide detailed instructions. This password should prevent attackers with physical access from attempting to change important parameters, such as those described in Sections 2.5.2.2.1 and 2.2.2.2.4. However, an attacker with physical access can usually clear the BIOS password. The password should be written down and stored in a physically-secure location, such as a safe, in the event that it is forgotten and must be retrieved.

2.3.5.2 Set Boot Loader Password

During the boot process, the boot loader is responsible for starting the execution of the kernel and passing options to it. The boot loader allows for the selection of different kernels – possibly on different partitions or media. Options it can pass to the kernel include "single-user mode," which provides root access without any authentication, and the ability to disable SELinux. To prevent local users from modifying the boot parameters and endangering security, the boot loader configuration should be protected with a password.

> The default RHEL boot loader for x86 systems is called GRUB. To protect its configuration:
>
> 1. Select a password and then generate a hash from it by running:
>
>    ```
>    # grub-md5-crypt
>    ```
>
> 2. Insert the following line into /etc/grub.conf immediately after the header comments. (Use the output from grub-md5-crypt as the value of *password-hash*):
>
>    ```
>    password --md5 password-hash
>    ```
>
> 3. Verify the permissions on /etc/grub.conf (which is a symlink to ../boot/grub/grub.conf):
>
>    ```
>    # chown root:root /etc/grub.conf
>    # chmod 600 /etc/grub.conf
>    ```
>
> **CCE 4144-2, 3923-0, 3818-2, 4197-0**

Boot loaders for other platforms should offer a similar password protection feature.

2.3.5.3 Require Authentication for Single-User Mode

Single-user mode is intended as a system recovery method, providing a single user root access to the system by providing a boot option at startup. By default, no authentication is performed if single-user mode is selected. This provides a trivial mechanism of bypassing security on the machine and gaining root access.

> To require entry of the root password even if the system is started in single-user mode, add the following
> line to the `/etc/inittab` file:
>
> ```
> ~:S:wait:/sbin/sulogin
> ```
>
> **CCE 4241-6**

2.3.5.4   Disable Interactive Boot

> Edit the file `/etc/sysconfig/init`. Add or correct the setting:
>
> ```
> PROMPT=no
> ```
>
> **CCE 4245-7**

The `PROMPT` option allows the console user to perform an interactive system startup, in which it is possible to select the set of services which are started on boot. Using interactive boot, the console user could disable auditing, firewalls, or other services, weakening system security.

2.3.5.5   Implement Inactivity Time-out for Login Shells

If the system does not run X Windows, then the login shells can be configured to automatically log users out after a period of inactivity. The following instructions are not practical for systems which run X Windows, as they will close terminal windows in the X environment. For information on how to automatically lock those systems, see Section 2.3.5.6.

> To implement a 15-minute idle time-out for the default `/bin/bash` shell, create a new file `tmout.sh` in the
> directory `/etc/profile.d` with the following lines:
>
> ```
> TMOUT=900
> readonly TMOUT
> export TMOUT
> ```
>
> To implement a 15-minute idle time-out for the `tcsh` shell, create a new file `autologout.csh` in the directory
> `/etc/profile.d` with the following line:
>
> ```
> set -r autologout 15
> ```
>
> Similar actions should be taken for any other login shells used.
>
> **CCE 3689-7, 3707-7**

The example time-out here of 15 minutes should be adjusted to whatever your security policy requires. The `readonly` line for bash and the `-r` option for `tcsh` can be omitted if policy allows users to override the value.

The automatic shell logout only occurs when the shell is the foreground process. If, for example, a `vi` session is left idle, then automatic logout would not occur.

When logging in through a remote connection, as with SSH, it may be more effective to set the timeout value directly through that service. To learn how to set automatic timeout intervals for SSH, see Section 3.5.2.3.

2.3.5.6 Configure Screen Locking

When a user must temporarily leave an account logged-in, screen locking should be employed to prevent passersby from abusing the account. User education and training is particularly important for screen locking to be effective.

A policy should be implemented that trains all users to lock the screen when they plan to temporarily step away from a logged-in account. Automatic screen locking is only meant as a safeguard for those cases where a user forgot to lock the screen.

2.3.5.6.1 Configure GUI Screen Locking

In the default GNOME desktop, the screen can be locked by choosing **Lock Screen** from the **System** menu.

The `gconftool-2` program can be used to enforce mandatory screen locking settings for the default GNOME environment. Run the following commands to enforce idle activation of the screen saver, screen locking, a blank-screen screensaver, and 15-minute idle activation time:

```
# gconftool-2 --direct \
            --config-source xml:readwrite:/etc/gconf/gconf.xml.mandatory \
            --type bool \
            --set /apps/gnome-screensaver/idle_activation_enabled true
# gconftool-2 --direct \
            --config-source xml:readwrite:/etc/gconf/gconf.xml.mandatory \
            --type bool \
            --set /apps/gnome-screensaver/lock_enabled true
# gconftool-2 --direct \
            --config-source xml:readwrite:/etc/gconf/gconf.xml.mandatory \
            --type string \
            --set /apps/gnome-screensaver/mode blank-only
# gconftool-2 --direct \
            --config-source xml:readwrite:/etc/gconf/gconf.xml.mandatory \
            --type int \
            --set /apps/gnome-screensaver/idle_delay 15
```

CCE 3315-9, 3910-7, 14604-3, 14023-6, 14735-5

The setting of 15 minutes for idle activation is reasonable for many office environments, but the setting should conform to whatever policy is defined. The screensaver mode blank-only is selected to conceal the contents of the display from passersby.

Because users should be trained to lock the screen when they step away from the computer, the automatic locking feature is only meant as a backup. The **Lock Screen** icon from the **System** menu can also be dragged to the taskbar in order to facilitate even more convenient screen-locking.

The root account cannot be screen-locked, but this should have no practical effect as the root account should *never* be used to log into an X Windows environment, and should only be used to for direct login via console in emergency circumstances.

For more information about configuring GNOME screensaver, see `http://live.gnome.org/GnomeScreensaver`. For more information about enforcing preferences in the GNOME environment using the GConf configuration system, see `http://www.gnome.org/projects/gconf` and the man page `gconftool-2(1)`.

2.3.5.6.2 Configure Console Screen Locking

A console screen locking mechanism is provided in the `vlock` package, which is not installed by default.

> If the ability to lock console screens is necessary, install the `vlock` package:
>
>   # yum install vlock
>
> Instruct users to invoke the program when necessary, in order to prevent passersby from abusing their login:
>
> $ vlock

The -a option can be used to prevent switching to other virtual consoles.

2.3.5.7 Disable Unnecessary Ports

Though unusual, some systems may be managed only remotely and yet also exposed to risk from attackers with direct physical access to them. In these cases, reduce an attacker's access to the system by disabling unnecessary external ports (e.g. USB, FireWire, NIC) in the system's BIOS.

 *Disabling USB ports is particularly unusual and will cause problems for important input devices such as keyboards or mice attached to the system.*

> Disable ports on the system which are not necessary for normal system operation. The exact steps will vary depending on your machine, but are likely to include: 1. Reboot the machine. 2. Press the appropriate key during the initial boot screen (F2 is typical). 3. Navigate the BIOS conguration menu to disable ports, such as USB, FireWire, and NIC.

2.3.6 Use a Centralized Authentication Service

A centralized authentication service is any method of maintaining central control over account and authentication data and of keeping this data synchronized between machines. Such services can range in complexity from a script which pushes centrally-generated password files out to all machines, to a managed scheme such as LDAP or Kerberos.

If authentication information is not centrally managed, it quickly becomes inconsistent, leading to out-of-date credentials and forgotten accounts which should have been deleted. In addition, many older protocols (such as NFS) make use of the UID to identify users over a network. This is not a good practice, and these protocols should be avoided if possible. However, since most sites must still make use of some older protocols, having consistent UIDs and GIDs site-wide is a significant benefit.

Centralized authentication services do have the disadvantage that authentication information must be transmitted over a network, leading to a risk that credentials may be intercepted or manipulated. Therefore, these services must be deployed carefully. The following precautions should be taken when configuring any authentication service:

- Ensure that authentication information and any sensitive account information are never sent over the network unencrypted.

- Ensure that the `root` account has a local password, to allow recovery in case of network outage or authentication server failure.

This guide recommends the use of LDAP. Secure configuration of OpenLDAP for clients and servers is described in Section 3.12. Kerberos is also a good choice for a centralized authentication service, but a description of its configuration is beyond the scope of this guide. The NIS service is not recommended, and should be considered obsolete. (See Section 3.2.4.)

2.3.7   Warning Banners for System Accesses

Each system should expose as little information about itself as possible.

System banners, which are typically displayed just before a login prompt, give out information about the service or the host's operating system. This might include the distribution name and the system kernel version, and the particular version of a network service. This information can assist intruders in gaining access to the system as it can reveal whether the system is running vulnerable software. Most network services can be configured to limit what information is displayed.

Many organizations implement security policies that require a system banner provide notice of the system's ownership, provide warning to unauthorized users, and remind authorized users of their consent to monitoring.

2.3.7.1   Modify the System Login Banner

The contents of the file `/etc/issue` are displayed on the screen just above the login prompt for users logging directly into a terminal. Remote login programs such as SSH or FTP can be configured to display `/etc/issue` as well. Instructions for configuring each server daemon to show this file can be found in the relevant sections of Chapter 3.

By default, the system will display the version of the OS, the kernel version, and the host name.

Edit `/etc/issue`. Replace the default text with a message compliant with the local site policy or a legal disclaimer.

CCE 4060-0

2.3.7.2   Implement a GUI Warning Banner

In the default graphical environment, users logging directly into the system are greeted with a login screen provided by the GNOME display manager. The warning banner should be displayed in this graphical environment for these users.

The files for the default RHEL theme can be found in `/usr/share/gdm/themes/RHEL`. Add the following sample block of XML to `/usr/share/gdm/themes/RHEL/RHEL.xml` after the first two "pixmap" entries:

```
<item type="rect" id="custom-dod-banner">
  <pos anchor="nw" x="20%" y="10" width="80%" height="100%"/>
  <box>
    <item type="label">
      <normal font="Sans Bold 9" color="#ffffff"/>
      <text>
        Insert the text of your warning banner here.
      </text>
    </item>
```

```
    </box>
  </item>
```

CCE 4188-9

The full syntax that GDM theme files expect is documented elsewhere, but the above XML will create a text box at the top right of the screen. The font, text color, and exact positioning can all be easily modified by editing the appropriate values. The latest current GDM theme manual can be found at `http://library.gnome.org/admin/gdm/2.16/thememanual.html.en`.

2.4   SELinux

SELinux is a feature of the Linux kernel which can be used to guard against misconfigured or compromised programs. SELinux enforces the idea that programs should be limited in what files they can access and what actions they can take.

The default SELinux policy, as configured on RHEL5, has been sufficiently developed and debugged that it should be usable on almost any Red Hat machine with minimal configuration and a small amount of system administrator training. This policy prevents system services — including most of the common network-visible services such as mail servers, ftp servers, and DNS servers — from accessing files which those services have no valid reason to access. This action alone prevents a huge amount of possible damage from network attacks against services, from trojaned software, and so forth.

This guide recommends that SELinux be enabled using the default (`targeted`) policy on every Red Hat system, unless that system has requirements which make a stronger policy appropriate.

2.4.1   How SELinux Works

In the traditional Linux/Unix security model, known as Discretionary Access Control (DAC), processes run under a user and group identity, and enjoy that user and group's access rights to all files and other objects on the system. This system brings with it a number of security problems, most notably: that processes frequently do not need and should not have the full rights of the user who ran them; that user and group access rights are not very granular, and may require administrators to allow too much access in order to allow the access that is needed; that the Unix filesystem contains many resources (such as temporary directories and world-readable files) which are accessible to users who have no legitimate reason to access them; and that legitimate users can easily provide open access to their own resources through confusion or carelessness.

SELinux provides a Mandatory Access Control (MAC) system that greatly augments the DAC model. Under SELinux, every process and every object (e.g. file, socket, pipe) on the system is given a *security context*, a label which include detailed type information about the object. The kernel allows processes to access objects only if that access is explicitly allowed by the policy in effect. The policy defines transitions, so that a user can be allowed to run software, but the software can run under a different context than the user's default. This automatically limits the damage that the software can do to files accessible by the calling user — the user does not need to take any action to gain this benefit.

For an action to occur, both the traditional DAC permissions must be satisifed as well as SELinux's MAC rules. If either do not permit the action, then it will not be allowed. In this way, SELinux rules can only make a system's permissions more restrictive and secure.

SELinux requires a complex policy in order to allow all the actions required of a system under normal operation. Three such policies have been designed for use with RHEL5, and are included with the system. In increasing order of power and complexity, they are: `targeted`, `strict`, and `mls`. The `targeted` SELinux policy consists mostly of Type Enforcement (TE) rules, and a small number of Role-Based Access Control (RBAC) rules. It restricts the actions of many types of programs, but leaves interactive users largely unaffected. The `strict` policy also uses TE and RBAC rules, but on more programs and more aggressively. The `mls` policy implements Multi-Level Security (MLS), which introduces even more kinds of labels — sensitivity and category — and rules that govern access based on these.

The remainder of this section provides guidance for the configuration of the `targeted` policy and the administration of systems under this policy. Some pointers will be provided for readers who are interested in further strengthening their systems by using one of the stricter policies provided with RHEL5 or in writing their own policy.

2.4.2   Enable SELinux

Edit the file `/etc/selinux/config`. Add or correct the following lines:

```
SELINUX=enforcing
SELINUXTYPE=targeted
```

Edit the file `/etc/grub.conf`. Ensure that the following arguments **DO NOT** appear on any kernel command line in the file:

```
selinux=0
enforcing=0
```

CCE 3977-6, 3999-0, 3624-4

The directive `SELINUX=enforcing` enables SELinux at boot time. If SELinux is causing a lot of problems or preventing the system from booting, it is possible to boot into the warning-only mode `SELINUX=permissive` for debugging purposes. Make certain to change the mode back to `enforcing` after debugging, set the filesystems to be relabelled for consistency using the command `touch /.autorelabel`, and reboot.

However, the RHEL5 default SELinux configuration should be sufficiently reasonable that most systems will boot without serious problems. Some applications that require deep or unusual system privileges, such as virtual machine software, may not be compatible with SELinux in its default configuration. However, this should be uncommon, and SELinux's application support continues to improve. In other cases, SELinux may reveal unusual or insecure program behavior by design.

The directive `SELINUXTYPE=targeted` configures SELinux to use the default `targeted` policy. See Section 2.4.7 if a stricter policy is appropriate for your site.

The SELinux boot mode specified in `/etc/selinux/config` can be overridden by command-line arguments passed to the kernel. It is necessary to check `grub.conf` to ensure that this has not been done and to protect the bootloader as described in Section 2.3.5.2.

2.4.2.1   Ensure SELinux is Properly Enabled

Run the command:

```
$ /usr/sbin/sestatus
```

If the system is properly configured, the output should indicate:

- SELinux status: enabled

- Current mode: enforcing
- Mode from config file: enforcing
- Policy from config file: targeted

2.4.3 Disable Unnecessary SELinux Daemons

Several daemons are installed by default as part of the RHEL5 SELinux support mechanism. These daemons may improve the system's ability to enforce SELinux policy in a useful fashion, but may also represent unnecessary code running on the machine, increasing system risk. If these daemons are not needed on your system, they should be disabled.

2.4.3.1 Disable and Remove SETroubleshoot if Possible

Is there a mission-critical reason to allow users to view SELinux denial information using the `sealert` GUI? If not, disable the service and remove the RPM:

```
# chkconfig setroubleshoot off
# yum erase setroubleshoot
```

CCE 4254-9, 4148-3

The setroubleshoot service is a facility for notifying the desktop user of SELinux denials in a user-friendly fashion. SELinux errors may provide important information about intrusion attempts in progress, or may give information about SELinux configuration problems which are preventing correct system operation. In order to maintain a secure and usable SELinux installation, error logging and notification is necessary.

However, setroubleshoot is a service which has complex functionality, which runs a daemon and uses IPC to distribute information which may be sensitive, or even to allow users to modify SELinux settings, and which does not yet implement real authentication mechanisms. This guide recommends disabling `setroubleshoot` and using the kernel audit functionality to monitor SELinux's behavior.

In addition, since `setroubleshoot` automatically runs client-side code whenever a denial occurs, regardless of whether the `setroubleshootd` daemon is running, it is recommended that the program be removed entirely unless it is needed.

2.4.3.2 Disable MCS Translation Service (`mcstrans`) if Possible

Unless there is some overriding need for the convenience of category label translation, disable the MCS translation service:

```
# chkconfig mcstrans off
```

CCE 3668-1, 4129-3

The `mcstransd` daemon provides the category label translation information defined in `/etc/selinux/targeted/setrans.conf` to client processes which request this information.

Category labelling is unlikely to be used except in sites with special requirements. Therefore, it should be disabled in order to reduce the amount of potentially vulnerable code running on the system. See Section 2.4.7 for more information about systems which use category labelling.

2.4.3.3 Restorecon Service (`restorecond`)

The `restorecond` daemon monitors a list of files which are frequently created or modified on running systems, and whose SELinux contexts are not set correctly. It looks for creation events related to files listed in `/etc/selinux/restorecond.conf`, and sets the contexts of those files when they are discovered.

The `restorecond` program is fairly simple, so it brings low risk, but, in its default configuration, does not add much value to a system. An automated program such as `restorecond` may be used to monitor problematic files for context problems, or system administrators may be trained to check file contexts of newly-created files using the command `ls -lZ`, and to repair contexts manually using the `restorecon` command.

This guide makes no recommendation either for or against the use of `restorecond`.

2.4.4 Check for Unconfined Daemons

Daemons that SELinux policy does not know about will inherit the context of the parent process. Because daemons are launched during startup and descend from the init process, they inherit the initrc_t context. This is a problem because it may cause AVC denials, or it could allow privileges that the daemon does not require.

To check for unconfined daemons, run the following command:

```
# ps -eZ | egrep "initrc" | egrep -vw "tr|ps|egrep|bash|awk" | tr ':' ' ' | awk '{ print $NF }'
```

It should produce no output in a well-configured system.

2.4.5 Check for Unlabeled Device Files

Device files are used for communication with important system resources. SELinux contexts should exist for these. If a device file is not labeled, then misconfiguration is likely.

To check for unlabeled device files, run the following command:

```
# ls -Z | grep unlabeled_t
```

It should produce no output in a well-configured system.

CCE 14991-4

2.4.6 Debugging SELinux Policy Errors

SELinux's default policies have improved significantly over time, and most systems should have few problems using the `targeted` SELinux policy. However, policy problems may still occasionally prevent accesses which should be allowed. This is especially true if your site runs any custom or heavily modified applications.

This section gives some brief guidance on discovering and repairing SELinux-related access problems. Guidance given here is necessarily incomplete, but should provide a starting point for debugging.

> If you suspect that a permission error or other failure may be caused by SELinux (and are certain that misconfiguration of the traditional Unix permissions are not the cause of the problem), search the audit logs for AVC events:
>
> ```
> # ausearch -m AVC,USER_AVC -sv no
> ```
>
> The output of this command will be a set of events. The timestamp, along with the `comm` and `pid` fields, should indicate which line describes the problem.
>
> Look up the context under which the process is running. Assuming the process ID is *PID*, find the context by running:
>
> ```
> # ps -p PID -Z
> ```
>
> The AVC denial message should identify the offending file or directory. The `name` field should contain the filename (not the full pathname by default), and the `ino` field can be used to search by inode, if necessary. Assuming the file is *FILE*, find its SELinux context:
>
> ```
> # ls -Z FILE
> ```

An administrator should suspect an SELinux misconfiguration whenever a program gets a "permission denied" error but the standard Unix permissions appear to be correct, or a program fails mysteriously on a task which seems to involve file access or network communication.

As described in Section 2.4.1, SELinux augments each process with a context providing detailed type information about that process. The contexts under which processes run may be referred to as subject contexts. Similarly, each filesystem object is given a context.

The `targeted` policy consists of a set of rules, each of which allows a subject type to perform some operation on a given object type. The kernel stores information about these access decisions in an structure known as an Access Vector Cache (AVC), so authorization decisions made by the system are audited with the type `AVC`. It is also possible for userspace modules to implement their own policies based on SELinux, and these decisions are audited with the type `USER_AVC`.

AVC denials are logged by the kernel `audit` facility (see Section 2.6.2 for configuration guidance on this subsystem) and may also be visible via `setroubleshoot`. This guide recommends the use of the `audit` userspace utilities to find AVC errors. It is possible to manually locate these errors by looking in the file `/var/log/audit/audit.log` or in `/var/log/messages` (depending on the syslog configuration in effect), but the `ausearch` tool allows fine-grained searching on audit event types, which may be necessary if system call auditing is enabled as well. The command line above tells `ausearch` to look for kernel or userspace AVC messages (`-m AVC,USER_AVC`) where the access attempt did not succeed (`-sv no`).

If an AVC denial occurs when it should not have, the problem is generally one of the following:

- The program is running with the wrong subject context. This could happen as a result of an incorrect context on the program's executable file, which could happen if 3rd party software is installed and not given appropriate SELinux file contexts.

- The file has the wrong object context because the current file's context does not match the specification. This can occur when files are created or modified in certain ways. It is not atypical for configuration files to get the wrong contexts after a system configuration change performed by an administrator. To repair the file, use the command:

  ```
  # restorecon -v FILE
  ```

  This should produce output indicating that the file's context has been changed. The `/usr/bin/chcon` program can be used to manually change a file's context, but this is problematic because the change will not persist if it does not agree with the policy-defined contexts applied by `restorecon`.

- The file has the wrong object context because the specification is either incorrect or does not match the way the file is being used on this system. In this case, it will be necessary to change the system file contexts.

  Run the `system-config-selinux` tool, and go to the "File Labeling" menu. This will give a list of files and wildcards corresponding to file labelling rules on the system. Add a rule which maps the file in question to the desired context. As an alternative, file contexts can be modified from the command line using the `semanage(8)` tool.

- The program and file have the correct contexts, but the policy should allow some operation between those two contexts which is currently not allowed. In this case, it will be necessary to modify the SELinux policy.

  Run the `system-config-selinux` tool, and go to the "Boolean" menu. If your configuration is supported, but is not the Red Hat default, then there will be a boolean allowing real-time modification of the SELinux policy to fix the problem. Browse through the items in this menu, looking for one which is related to the service which is not working. As an alternative, SELinux booleans can be modified from the command line using the `getsebool(8)` and `setsebool(8)` tools.

  If there is no boolean, it will be necessary to create and load a policy module. A simple way to build a policy module is to use the `audit2allow` tool. This tool can take input in the format of AVC denial messages, and generate syntactically correct Type Enforcement rules which would be sufficient to prevent those denials. For example, to generate and display rules which would allow all kernel denials seen in the past five minutes, run:

  ```
  # ausearch -m AVC -sv no -ts recent | audit2allow
  ```

  It is possible to use `audit2allow` to directly create a module package suitable for loading into the kernel policy. To do this, invoke `audit2allow` with the `-M` flag:

  ```
  # ausearch -m AVC -sv no -ts recent | audit2allow -M localmodule
  ```

  If this is successful, several lines of output should appear. Review the generated TE rules in the file `localmodule.te` and ensure that they express what you wish to allow.

  The file `localmodule.pp` should also have been created. This file is a policy module package that can be loaded into the kernel. To do so, use `system-config-selinux`, go to the "Policy Module" menu and use the "Add" button to enable your module package in SELinux, or load it from the command line using `semodule(8)`:

  ```
  # semodule -i localmodule.pp
  ```

  Section 45.2 of [9] covers this procedure in detail.

2.4.7   Further Strengthening

The recommendations up to this point have discussed how to configure and maintain a system under the default configuration of the `targeted` policy, which constrains only the actions of daemons and system software. This guide strongly recommends that any site which is not currently using SELinux at all transition to the `targeted` policy, to gain the substantial security benefits provided by that policy.

However, the default policy provides only a subset of the full security gains available from using SELinux. In particular, the SELinux policy is also capable of constraining the actions of interactive users, of providing compartmented access by sensitivity level (MLS) and/or category (MCS), and of restricting certain types of system actions using booleans beyond the RHEL5 defaults.

This section introduces other uses of SELinux which may be possible, and provides links to some outside resources about their use. Detailed description of how to implement these steps is beyond the scope of this guide.

2.4.7.1   Strengthen the Default SELinux Boolean Configuration

SELinux booleans are used to enable or disable segments of policy to comply with site policy. Booleans may apply to the entire system or to an individual daemon. For instance, the boolean `allow_execstack`, if enabled, allows programs to make part of their stack memory region executable. This would apply to all programs on the system. The boolean `ftp_home_dir` allows `ftpd` processes to access user home directories, and applies only to daemons which implement FTP.

The command

```
$ getsebool -a
```

lists the values of all SELinux booleans on the system. Section 2.4.6 discussed loosening boolean values in order to debug functionality problems which occur under more restrictive defaults. It is also useful to examine and strengthen the boolean settings, to disable functionality which is not required by legitimate programs on your system, but which might be symptomatic of an attack.

See the manpages `booleans(8)`, `getsebool(8)`, and `setsebool(8)` for general information about booleans. There are also manual pages for several subsystems which discuss the use of SELinux with those systems. Examples include `ftpd_selinux(8)`, `httpd_selinux(8)`, and `nfs_selinux(8)`. Another good reference is the html documentation distributed with the `selinux-policy` RPM. This documentation is stored under

```
/usr/share/doc/selinux-policy-version/html/
```

The pages `global_tunables.html` and `global_booleans.html` may be useful when examining booleans.

2.4.7.2   Use a Stronger Policy

Using a stronger policy can greatly enhance security, but will generally require customization to be compatible with the particular system's purpose, and this may be costly or time consuming. Under the `targeted` policy, interactive processes are given the type `unconfined_t`, so interactive users are not constrained by SELinux even if they attempt to take strange or malicious actions. The first alternative policy available with RHEL5's SELinux distribution, called `strict`, extends the protections offered by the default policy from daemons and system processes to all processes. To use the `strict` policy, first ensure that the policy module is installed:

```
# yum install selinux-policy-strict
```

Then edit `/etc/selinux/config` and correct the line:

```
SELINUXTYPE=strict
```

The `mls` policy type can be used to enforce sensitivity or category labelling, and requires site-specific configuration of these labels in order to be useful. To use this policy, install the appropriate policy module:

```
# yum install selinux-policy-mls
```

Then edit `/etc/selinux/config` and correct the line:

```
SELINUXTYPE=mls
```

Note: Switching between policies typically requires the entire disk to be relabelled, so that files get the appropriate SELinux contexts under the new policy. Boot with the additional grub command-line options

```
enforcing=0 single autorelabel
```

to relabel the disk in single-user mode, then reboot normally.

2.4.8   SELinux References

- NSA SELinux resources:
  - Web page: `http://www.nsa.gov/research/selinux`
  - Mailing list information at: `http://www.nsa.gov/research/selinux/list.shtml`
- Fedora SELinux resources:
  - FAQ: `http://docs.fedoraproject.org/selinux-faq`
  - User Guide: `http://docs.fedoraproject.org/selinux-user-guide`
  - Managing Services Guide: `http://docs.fedoraproject.org/selinux-managing-confined-services-g`
- SELinux Project web page and wiki: `http://www.selinuxproject.org`
- Chapters 43–45 of Red Hat Enterprise Linux 5: Deployment Guide [9]
- The book SELinux by Example: Using Security Enhanced Linux [14]

2.5   Network Configuration and Firewalls

Most machines must be connected to a network of some sort, and this brings with it the substantial risk of network attack. This section discusses the security impact of decisions about networking which must be made when configuring a system.

This section also discusses firewalls, network access controls, and other network security frameworks, which allow system-level rules to be written that can limit attackers' ability to connect to your system. These rules can specify that network traffic should be allowed or denied from certain IP addresses, hosts, and networks. The rules can also specify which of the system's network services are available to particular hosts or networks.

2.5.1   Kernel Parameters which Affect Networking

The `sysctl` utility is used to set a number of parameters which affect the operation of the Linux kernel. Several of these parameters are specific to networking, and the configuration options in this section are recommended. The ability to query the state of the system's network stack is also important, and such information is also available in `/proc/net`.

2.5.1.1   Network Parameters for Hosts Only

Is this system going to be used as a firewall or gateway to pass IP traffic between different networks?

If not, edit the file `/etc/sysctl.conf` and add or correct the following lines:

```
net.ipv4.ip_forward = 0
net.ipv4.conf.all.send_redirects = 0
net.ipv4.conf.default.send_redirects = 0
```

CCE 4151-7, 4155-8, 3561-8

These settings disable hosts from performing network functionality which is only appropriate for routers.

2.5.1.2 Network Parameters for Hosts and Routers

Edit the file `/etc/sysctl.conf` and add or correct the following lines:

```
net.ipv4.conf.all.accept_source_route = 0
net.ipv4.conf.all.accept_redirects = 0
net.ipv4.conf.all.secure_redirects = 0
net.ipv4.conf.all.log_martians = 1
net.ipv4.conf.default.accept_source_route = 0
net.ipv4.conf.default.accept_redirects = 0
net.ipv4.conf.default.secure_redirects = 0
net.ipv4.icmp_echo_ignore_broadcasts = 1
net.ipv4.icmp_ignore_bogus_error_messages = 1
net.ipv4.tcp_syncookies = 1
net.ipv4.conf.all.rp_filter = 1
net.ipv4.conf.default.rp_filter = 1
```

CCE 3472-8, 4217-6, 4133-5, 4265-5, 3644-2, 4186-3, 4080-8, 3339-9, 4320-8, 3840-6, 4091-5, 4236-6

These options improve Linux's ability to defend against certain types of IPv4 protocol attacks.

The `accept_source_route`, `accept_redirects`, and `secure_redirects` options are turned off to disable IPv4 protocol features which are considered to have few legitimate uses and to be easy to abuse.

The `net.ipv4.conf.all.log_martians` option logs several types of suspicious packets, such as spoofed packets, source-routed packets, and redirects.

The `icmp_echo_ignore_broadcasts icmp_ignore_bogus_error_messages` options protect against ICMP attacks.

The `tcp_syncookies` option uses a cryptographic feature called SYN cookies to allow machines to continue to accept legitimate connections when faced with a SYN flood attack. See [13] for further information on this option.

The `rp_filter` option enables RFC-recommended source validation. It should not be used on machines which are routers for very complicated networks, but is helpful for end hosts and routers serving small networks.

For more information on any of these, see the kernel source documentation file `/Documentation/networking/ip-sysctl.txt`.[2]

2.5.1.3 Ensure System is Not Acting as a Network Sniffer

The system should not be acting as a network sniffer, which can capture all traffic on the network to which it is connected. The output of **/proc/net/packet** should display exactly one header line, with entries similar to:

```
sk       RefCnt Type Proto  Iface R Rmem   User   Inode
```

If numbers appear in a row below this header, then a sniffing process (such as tcpdump or wireshark) is using the interface and this should be investigated.

CCE 15013-6

---

[2]A recent version of this file can be found online at http://lxr.linux.no/source/Documentation/networking/ip-sysctl.txt.

2.5.2 Wireless Networking

Wireless networking (sometimes referred to as 802.11 or Wi-Fi) presents a serious security risk to sensitive or classified systems and networks. Wireless networking hardware is much more likely to be included in laptop or portable systems than desktops or servers. See Section 3.3.14 for information on Bluetooth wireless support. Bluetooth serves a different purpose and possesses a much shorter range, but it still presents serious security risks.

Removal of hardware is the only way to absolutely ensure that the wireless capability remains disabled. If it is completely impractical to remove the wireless hardware, and site policy still allows the device to enter sensitive spaces, every effort to disable the capability via software should be made. In general, acquisition policy should include provisions to prevent the purchase of equipment that will be used in sensitive spaces and includes wireless capabilities.

2.5.2.1 Remove Wireless Hardware if Possible

Identifying the wireless hardware is the first step in removing it. The system's hardware manual should contain information on its wireless capabilities.

Wireless hardware included with a laptop typically takes the form of a mini-PCI card or PC card. Other forms include devices which plug into USB or Ethernet ports, but these should be readily apparent and easy to remove from the base system.

A PC Card (originally called a PCMCIA card) is designed to be easy to remove, though it may be hidden when inserted into the system. Frequently, there will be one or more buttons near the card slot that, when pressed, eject the card from the system. If no card is ejected, the slot is empty.

A mini-PCI card is approximately credit-card sized and typically accessible via a removable panel on the underside of the laptop. Removing the panel may require simple tools.

In addition to manually inspecting the hardware, it is also possible to query the system for its installed hardware devices. The commands `/sbin/lspci` and `/sbin/lsusb` will show a list of all recognized devices on their respective buses, and this may indicate the presence of a wireless device.

2.5.2.2 Disable Wireless Through Software Configuration

If it is impossible to remove the wireless hardware from the device in question, disable as much of it as possible through software. The following methods can disable software support for wireless networking, but note that these methods do not prevent malicious software or careless users from re-activating the devices.

2.5.2.2.1 Disable Wireless in BIOS

Some laptops that include built-in wireless support offer the ability to disable the device through the BIOS. This is system-specific; consult your hardware manual or explore the BIOS setup during boot.

CCE 3628-5

2.5.2.2.2 Deactivate Wireless Interfaces

Deactivating the wireless interfaces should prevent normal usage of the wireless capability.

> First, identify the interfaces available with the command:
>
> ```
> # ifconfig -a
> ```
>
> Additionally,the following command may also be used to determine whether wireless support ("extensions") is included for a particular interface, though this may not always be a clear indicator:
>
> ```
> # iwconfig
> ```
>
> After identifying any wireless interfaces (which may have names like `wlan0`, `ath0`, `wifi0`, or `eth0`), deactivate the interface with the command:
>
> ```
> # ifdown interface
> ```
>
> These changes will only last until the next reboot. To disable the interface for future boots, remove the appropriate interface file from `/etc/sysconfig/network-scripts`:
>
> ```
> # rm /etc/sysconfig/network-scripts/ifcfg-interface
> ```
>
> **CCE 4276-2**

2.5.2.2.3   Disable Wireless Drivers

Removing the kernel drivers that provide support for wireless Ethernet devices will prevent users from easily activating the devices.

> To remove the wireless drivers from the system:
>
> ```
> # rm -r /lib/modules/kernelversion(s)/kernel/drivers/net/wireless
> ```
>
> **CCE 4170-7**

This command must also be repeated every time the kernel is upgraded.

2.5.3   IPv6

The system includes support for Internet Protocol version 6. A major and often-mentioned improvement over IPv4 is its enormous increase in the number of available addresses. Another important feature is its support for automatic configuration of many network settings.

2.5.3.1   Disable Support for IPv6 unless Needed

As with any networking protocol, IPv6 should be disabled unless needed. Despite configuration that suggests support for IPv6 has been disabled, link-local IPv6 address autoconfiguration occurs even when only an IPv4 address is assigned. The only way to effectively prevent execution of the IPv6 networking stack is to prevent the kernel from loading the IPv6 kernel module.

2.5.3.1.1   Disable Automatic Loading of IPv6 Kernel Module

> To prevent the IPv6 kernel module (`ipv6`) from being automatically loaded, add the following line to `/etc/modprobe.conf`:

```
install ipv6 /bin/true
```

CCE 3562-6

When the kernel requests the `ipv6` module, this line will direct the system to run the program `/bin/true` instead.

2.5.3.1.2 Disable Interface Usage of IPv6

To prevent configuration of IPv6 for all interfaces, add or correct the following lines in `/etc/sysconfig/network`:

```
NETWORKING_IPV6=no
IPV6INIT=no
```

For each network interface *IFACE*, add or correct the following lines in `/etc/sysconfig/network-scripts/ifcfg-IFACE` as an additional prevention mechanism:

```
IPV6INIT=no
```

CCE 3377-9, 4296-0, 3381-1

If it becomes necessary later to configure IPv6, only the interfaces requiring it should be enabled.

2.5.3.2 Configure IPv6 Settings if Necessary

A major feature of IPv6 is the extent to which systems implementing it can automatically configure their networking devices using information from the network. From a security perspective, manually configuring important configuration information is always preferable to accepting it from the network in an unauthenticated fashion.

2.5.3.2.1 Disable Automatic Configuration

Disable the system's acceptance of router advertisements and ICMP redirects by adding or correcting the following line in `/etc/sysconfig/network` (note that this does not disable sending router solicitations):

```
IPV6_AUTOCONF=no
```

CCE 4269-7, 4291-1, 4313-3, 4198-8

This setting results in ensuring that the following kernel (`sysctl`) parameters are set as follows, if IPv6 is used on the system:

```
net.ipv6.conf.default.accept_ra=0
net.ipv6.conf.default.accept_redirect=0
```

2.5.3.2.2 Manually Assign Global IPv6 Address

To manually assign an IP address for an interface *IFACE*, edit the file `/etc/sysconfig/network-scripts/ifcfg-IFACE`. Add or correct the following line (substituting the correct IPv6 address):

```
IPV6ADDR=2001:0DB8::ABCD/64
```

Manually assigning an IP address is preferable to accepting one from routers or from the network otherwise. The example address here is an IPv6 address reserved for documentation purposes, as defined by RFC3849.

2.5.3.2.3 Use Privacy Extensions for Address if Necessary

To introduce randomness into the automatic generation of IPv6 addresses, add or correct the following line in /etc/sysconfig/network-scripts/ifcfg-*IFACE*:

```
IPV6_PRIVACY=rfc3041
```

CCE 3842-2

Automatically-generated IPv6 addresses are based on the underlying hardware (e.g. Ethernet) address, and so it becomes possible to track a piece of hardware over its lifetime using its traffic. If it is important for a system's IP address to not trivially reveal its hardware address, this setting should be applied.

2.5.3.2.4 Manually Assign IPv6 Router Address

Edit the file /etc/sysconfig/network-scripts/ifcfg-*IFACE*, and add or correct the following line (substituting your gateway IP as appropriate):

```
IPV6_DEFAULTGW=2001:0DB8::0001
```

Router addresses should be manually set and not accepted via any autoconfiguration or router advertisement.

2.5.3.2.5 Limit Network-Transmitted Configuration

Add the following lines to /etc/sysctl.conf to limit the configuration information requested from other systems, and accepted from the network:

```
net.ipv6.conf.default.router_solicitations = 0

net.ipv6.conf.default.accept_ra_rtr_pref = 0

net.ipv6.conf.default.accept_ra_pinfo = 0

net.ipv6.conf.default.accept_ra_defrtr = 0

net.ipv6.conf.default.autoconf = 0

net.ipv6.conf.default.dad_transmits = 0

net.ipv6.conf.default.max_addresses = 1
```

CCE 4221-8, 4137-6, 4159-0, 3895-0, 4287-9, 4058-4, 4128-5

The `router_solicitations` setting determines how many router solicitations are sent when bringing up the interface. If addresses are statically assigned, there is no need to send any solicitations.

The `accept_ra_pinfo` setting controls whether the system will accept prefix info from the router.

The `accept_ra_defrtr` setting controls whether the system will accept Hop Limit settings from a router advertisement. Setting it to 0 prevents a router from changing your default IPv6 Hop Limit for outgoing packets.

The `autoconf` setting controls whether router advertisements can cause the system to assign a global unicast address to an interface.

The `dad_transmits` setting determines how many neighbor solicitations to send out per address (global and link-local) when bringing up an interface to ensure the desired address is unique on the network.

The `max_addresses` setting determines how many global unicast IPv6 addresses can be assigned to each interface. The default is 16, but it should be set to exactly the number of statically configured global addresses required.

2.5.4   TCP Wrapper

TCP Wrapper is a library which provides simple access control and standardized logging for supported applications which accept connections over a network. Historically, TCP Wrapper was used to support `inetd` services. Now that `inetd` is deprecated (see Section 3.2.1), TCP Wrapper supports only services which were built to make use of the `libwrap` library. To determine whether a given executable daemon */path/to/daemon* supports TCP Wrapper, check the documentation, or run:

```
$ ldd /path/to/daemon | grep libwrap.so
```

If this command returns any output, then the daemon probably supports TCP Wrapper.

An alternative to TCP Wrapper support is packet filtering using `iptables`. Note that `iptables` works at the network level, while TCP Wrapper works at the application level. This means that `iptables` filtering is more efficient and more resistant to flaws in the software being protected, but TCP Wrapper provides support for logging, banners, and other application-level tricks which `iptables` cannot provide.

2.5.4.1   How TCP Wrapper Protects Services

TCP Wrapper provides access control for the system's network services using two configuration files. When a connection is attempted:

1. The file `/etc/hosts.allow` is searched for a rule matching the connection. If one is found, the connection is allowed.

2. Otherwise, the file `/etc/hosts.deny` is searched for a rule matching the connection. If one is found, the connection is rejected.

3. If no matching rules are found in either file, then the connection is allowed. By default, TCP Wrapper does not block access to any services.

In the simplest case, each rule in `/etc/hosts.allow` and `/etc/hosts.deny` takes the form:

```
daemon: client
```

where *daemon* is the name of the server process for which the connection is destined, and *client* is the partial or full hostname or IP address of the client. It is valid for *daemon* and *client* to contain one item, a comma-separated list of items, or a special keyword like `ALL`, which matches any service or client. (See the `hosts_access(5)` manpage for a list of other keywords.)

Note: Partial hostnames start at the root domain and are delimited by the . character. So the client machine `host03.dev.example.com`, with IP address `10.7.2.3`, could be matched by any of the specifications:

```
.example.com
.dev.example.com
10.7.2.
```

2.5.4.2   Reject All Connections From Other Hosts if Appropriate

Restrict all connections to non-public services to localhost only. Suppose *pubsrv1* and *pubsrv2* are the names of daemons which must be accessed remotely. Configure TCP Wrapper as follows.

Edit `/etc/hosts.allow`. Add the following lines:

```
pubsrv1,pubsrv2: ALL
ALL: localhost
```

Edit `/etc/hosts.deny`. Add the following line:

```
ALL: ALL
```

These rules deny connections to all TCP Wrapper enabled services from any host other than `localhost`, but allow connections from anywhere to the services which must be publicly accessible. (If no public services exist, the first line in `/etc/hosts.allow` may be omitted.)

2.5.4.3   Allow Connections Only From Hosts in This Domain if Appropriate

For each daemon, *domainsrv*, which only needs to be contacted from inside the local domain, *example.com*, configure TCP Wrapper to deny remote connections.

Edit `/etc/hosts.allow`. Add the following line:

```
domainsrv: .example.com
```

Edit `/etc/hosts.deny`. Add the following line:

```
domainsrv: ALL
```

There are many possible examples of services which need to communicate only within the local domain. If a machine is a local compute server, it may be necessary for users to connect via SSH from their desktop workstations, but not from outside the domain. In that case, you should protect the daemon `sshd` using this method. As another example, RPC-based services such as NFS might be enabled within the domain only, in which case the daemon `portmap` should be protected.

Note: This example protects only the service *domainsrv*. No filtering is done on other services unless a line is entered into `/etc/hosts.deny` which refers to those services by name, or which restricts the special service `ALL`.

2.5.4.4   Monitor Syslog for Relevant Connections and Failures

Ensure that the following line exists in `/etc/syslog.conf`. (This is the default, so it is likely to be correct if the configuration has not been modified):

```
authpriv.*                                      /var/log/secure
```

> Configure `logwatch` or other log monitoring tools to periodically summarize failed connections reported by TCP Wrapper at the facility `authpriv.info`.

By default, TCP Wrapper audits all rejected connections at the facility `authpriv`, level `info`. In the log file, TCP Wrapper rejections will contain the substring:

> *daemon*`[`*pid*`]`: refused connect from *ipaddr*

These lines can be used to detect malicious scans, and to debug failures resulting from an incorrect TCP Wrapper configuration.

If appropriate, it is possible to change the syslog facility and level used by a given TCP Wrapper rule by adding the `severity` option to each desired configuration line in `/etc/hosts.deny`:

> *daemon*: *client* : severity *facility*.*level*

By default, successful connections are not logged by TCP Wrapper. See Section 2.6 for more information about system auditing.

2.5.4.5 Further Resources

For more information about TCP Wrapper, see the `tcpd(8)` and `hosts_access(5)` manpages and the documentation directory `/usr/share/doc/tcp_wrappers-`*version*.

Some information may be available from the Tools section of the author's website, http://www.porcupine.org, and from the RHEL4 Reference Guide [6].

2.5.5 Iptables and Ip6tables

A host-based firewall called *Netfilter* is included as part of the Linux kernel distributed with the system. It is activated by default. This firewall is controlled by the program `iptables`, and the entire capability is frequently referred to by this name. An analogous program called `ip6tables` handles filtering for IPv6.

Unlike TCP Wrappers, which depends on the network server program to support and respect the rules written, Netfilter filtering occurs at the kernel level, before a program can even process the data from the network packet. As such, any program on the system is affected by the rules written.

This section provides basic information about strengthening the iptables and ip6tables configurations included with the system. For more complete information that may allow the construction of a sophisticated ruleset tailored to your environment, please consult the references at the end of this section.

2.5.5.1 Inspect and Activate Default Rules

> View the currently-enforced iptables rules by running the command:
>
> ```
> # iptables -nL --line-numbers
> ```
>
> The command is analogous for the `ip6tables` program.
>
> If the firewall does not appear to be active (i.e., no rules appear), activate it and ensure that it starts at boot by issuing the following commands (and analogously for `ip6tables`):

```
    # service iptables restart
    # chkconfig iptables on
```

CCE 4167-3, 4189-7

The default iptables rules are:

```
Chain INPUT (policy ACCEPT)
num  target       prot opt source              destination
1    RH-Firewall-1-INPUT  all  --  0.0.0.0/0            0.0.0.0/0

Chain FORWARD (policy ACCEPT)
num  target       prot opt source              destination
1    RH-Firewall-1-INPUT  all  --  0.0.0.0/0            0.0.0.0/0

Chain OUTPUT (policy ACCEPT)
num  target       prot opt source              destination

Chain RH-Firewall-1-INPUT (2 references)
num  target     prot opt source              destination
1    ACCEPT     all  --  0.0.0.0/0           0.0.0.0/0
2    ACCEPT     icmp --  0.0.0.0/0           0.0.0.0/0           icmp type 255
3    ACCEPT     esp  --  0.0.0.0/0           0.0.0.0/0
4    ACCEPT     ah   --  0.0.0.0/0           0.0.0.0/0
5    ACCEPT     udp  --  0.0.0.0/0           224.0.0.251         udp dpt:5353
6    ACCEPT     udp  --  0.0.0.0/0           0.0.0.0/0           udp dpt:631
7    ACCEPT     tcp  --  0.0.0.0/0           0.0.0.0/0           tcp dpt:631
8    ACCEPT     all  --  0.0.0.0/0           0.0.0.0/0           state RELATED,ESTABLISHED
9    ACCEPT     tcp  --  0.0.0.0/0           0.0.0.0/0           state NEW tcp dpt:22
10   REJECT     all  --  0.0.0.0/0           0.0.0.0/0           reject-with icmp-host-prohibited
```

The ip6tables default rules are similar, with its rules 2 and 10 reflecting protocol naming and addressing differences. Instead of rule 8, however, ip6tables includes two rules that accept all incoming udp and tcp packets with a particular destination port range. This is because the current Netfilter implementation for IPv6 lacks reliable connection-tracking functionality.

2.5.5.2 Understand the Default Ruleset

Understanding and creating firewall rules can be a challenging activity, filled with corner cases and difficult-to-debug problems. Because of this, administrators should develop a thorough understanding of the default ruleset before carefully modifying it.

The default ruleset is divided into four sections, each of which is called a chain: `INPUT`, `FORWARD`, `OUTPUT`, and `RH-Firewall-1-INPUT`. `INPUT`, `OUTPUT`, and `FORWARD` are built-in chains.

- The `INPUT` chain is activated on packets destined for (i.e., addressed to) the system.

- The `OUTPUT` chain is activated on packets which are originating from the system.

- The `FORWARD` chain is activated for packets that the system will process and send through another interface, if so configured.

- The `RH-Firewall-1-INPUT` chain is a custom (or user-defined) chain, which is used by the `INPUT` and `FORWARD` chains.

A packet starts at the first rule in the appropriate chain and proceeds until it matches a rule. If a match occurs, then control will jump to the specified target. The default ruleset uses the built-in targets `ACCEPT` and `REJECT`, and also the user-defined target/chain `RH-Firewall-1-INPUT`. Jumping to the target `ACCEPT` means to allow the packet through, while `REJECT` means to drop the packet and send an error message to the sending host. A related target called `DROP` means to drop the packet on the floor without even sending an error message.

The default policy for all of the built-in chains (shown after their names in the rule output above) is set to `ACCEPT`. This means that if no rules in the chain match the packets, they are allowed through. Because no rules at all are written for the OUTPUT chain, this means that iptables does not stop any packets originating from the system. The `INPUT` and `FORWARD` chains jump to the user-defined target `RH-Firewall-1-INPUT` for all packets.

`RH-Firewall-1-INPUT` tries to match, in order, the following rules for both iptables and ip6tables:

- Rule 1 appears to accept all packets. However, this appears true only because the rules are not presented in verbose mode. Executing the command

      # iptables -vnL --line-numbers

  reveals that this rule applies only to the loopback (`lo`) interface (see column `in`), while all other rules apply to all interfaces. Thus, packets not coming from the loopback interface do not match and proceed to the next rule.

- Rule 2 explicitly allows all `icmp` packet types; iptables uses the code 255 to mean all icmp types.

- Rule 3 explicitly allows all `esp` packets; these are packets which contain IPsec ESP headers.

- Rule 4 explicitly allows all `ah` packets; these are packets which contain an IPsec authentication header SPI.

- Rule 5 allows inbound communication on udp port 5353 (mDNS), which the avahi daemon uses.

- Rules 6 and 7 allows inbound communication on both tcp and udp port 631, which the cups daemon uses.

- Rule 8, in the iptables rules, allows inbound packets that are part of a session initiated by the system. In ip6tables, rules 8 and 9 allow any inbound packets with a destination port address between 32768 and 61000.

- Rule 9 (10, for ip6tables) allows inbound connections in tcp port 22, which is the SSH protocol.

- Rule 10 (11, for ip6tables) rejects all other packets and sends an error message to the sender. Because this is the last rule and matches any packet, it effectively prevents any packet from reaching the chain's default `ACCEPT` target. Preventing the acceptance of any packet that is not explicitly allowed is proper design for a firewall.

2.5.5.3 Strengthen the Default Ruleset

The default rules can be strengthened. The system scripts that activate the firewall rules expect them to be defined in the configuration files `iptables` and `ip6tables` in the directory `/etc/sysconfig`. Many of the lines in these files are similar to the command line arguments that would be provided to the programs `/sbin/iptables` or `/sbin/ip6tables` – but some are quite different.

The program `system-config-securitylevel` allows additional services to penetrate the default firewall rules and automatically adjusts `/etc/sysconfig/iptables`. This program is only useful if the default ruleset meets your security requirements. Otherwise, this program should not be used to make changes to the firewall configuration because it re-writes the saved configuration file.

The following recommendations describe how to strengthen the default ruleset configuration file. An alternative to editing this configuration file is to create a shell script that makes calls to the `iptables` program to load in rules, and then invokes `service iptables save` to write those loaded rules to `/etc/sysconfig/iptables`.

The following alterations can be made directly to `/etc/sysconfig/iptables` and `/etc/sysconfig/ip6tables`. Instructions apply to both unless otherwise noted. Language and address conventions for regular iptables are used throughout this section; configuration for ip6tables will be either analogous or explicitly covered.

2.5.5.3.1 Change the Default Policies

Change the default policy to `DROP` (from `ACCEPT`) for the `INPUT` and `FORWARD` built-in chains:

```
*filter
:INPUT DROP [0:0]
:FORWARD DROP [0:0]
```

CCE 14264-6

Changing the default policy in this way implements proper design for a firewall, i.e. any packets which are not explicitly permitted should not be accepted.

2.5.5.3.2 Restrict ICMP Message Types

In `/etc/sysconfig/iptables`, the accepted ICMP messages types can be restricted. To accept only ICMP echo reply, destination unreachable, and time exceeded messages, remove the line:

```
-A RH-Firewall-1-INPUT -p icmp --icmp-type any -j ACCEPT
```

and insert the lines:

```
-A RH-Firewall-1-INPUT -p icmp --icmp-type echo-reply -j ACCEPT
-A RH-Firewall-1-INPUT -p icmp --icmp-type destination-unreachable -j ACCEPT
-A RH-Firewall-1-INPUT -p icmp --icmp-type time-exceeded -j ACCEPT
```

To allow the system to respond to pings, also insert the following line:

```
-A RH-Firewall-1-INPUT -p icmp --icmp-type echo-request -j ACCEPT
```

Ping responses can also be limited to certain networks or hosts by using the `-s` option in the previous rule.

Because IPv6 depends so heavily on ICMPv6, it is preferable to deny the ICMPv6 packets you know you don't need (e.g. ping requests) in `/etc/sysconfig/ip6tables`, while letting everything else through:

```
-A RH-Firewall-1-INPUT -p icmpv6 --icmpv6-type echo-request -j DROP
```

If you are going to statically configure the machine's address, it should ignore Router Advertisements which could add another IPv6 address to the interface or alter important network settings:

```
-A RH-Firewall-1-INPUT -p icmpv6 --icmpv6-type router-advertisement -j DROP
```

Restricting other ICMPv6 message types in `/etc/sysconfig/ip6tables` is not recommended because the operation of IPv6 depends heavily on ICMPv6. Thus, more care must be taken when blocking ICMPv6 types.

2.5.5.3.3 Remove IPsec Rules

If the system will not process IPsec traffic, then remove the following rules:

```
      -A RH-Firewall-1-INPUT -p 50 -j ACCEPT
      -A RH-Firewall-1-INPUT -p 51 -j ACCEPT
```

2.5.5.3.4 Log and Drop Packets with Suspicious Source Addresses

Packets with non-routable source addresses should be rejected, as they may indicate spoofing. Because the modified policy will reject non-matching packets, you only need to add these rules if you are interested in also logging these spoofing or suspicious attempts before they are dropped. If you do choose to log various suspicious traffic, add identical rules with a target of DROP after each LOG.

To log and then drop these IPv4 packets, insert the following rules in `/etc/sysconfig/iptables` (excepting any that are intentionally used):

```
      -A INPUT -i eth0 -s 10.0.0.0/8 -j LOG --log-prefix "IP DROP SPOOF A: "
      -A INPUT -i eth0 -s 172.16.0.0/12 -j LOG --log-prefix "IP DROP SPOOF B: "
      -A INPUT -i eth0 -s 192.168.0.0/16 -j LOG --log-prefix "IP DROP SPOOF C: "
      -A INPUT -i eth0 -s 224.0.0.0/4 -j LOG --log-prefix "IP DROP MULTICAST D: "
      -A INPUT -i eth0 -s 240.0.0.0/5 -j LOG --log-prefix "IP DROP SPOOF E: "
      -A INPUT -i eth0 -d 127.0.0.0/8 -j LOG --log-prefix "IP DROP LOOPBACK: "
```

Similarly, you might wish to log packets containing some IPv6 reserved addresses if they are not expected on your network:

```
      -A INPUT -i eth0 -s ::1 -j LOG --log-prefix "IPv6 DROP LOOPBACK: "
      -A INPUT -s 2002:E000::/20 -j LOG --log-prefix "IPv6 6to4 TRAFFIC: "
      -A INPUT -s 2002:7F00::/24 -j LOG --log-prefix "IPv6 6to4 TRAFFIC: "
      -A INPUT -s 2002:0000::/24 -j LOG --log-prefix "IPv6 6to4 TRAFFIC: "
      -A INPUT -s 2002:FF00::/24 -j LOG --log-prefix "IPv6 6to4 TRAFFIC: "
      -A INPUT -s 2002:0A00::/24 -j LOG --log-prefix "IPv6 6to4 TRAFFIC: "
      -A INPUT -s 2002:AC10::/28 -j LOG --log-prefix "IPv6 6to4 TRAFFIC: "
      -A INPUT -s 2002:C0A8::/32 -j LOG --log-prefix "IPv6 6to4 TRAFFIC: "
```

If you are not expecting to see site-local multicast or auto-tunneled traffic, you can log those:

```
      -A INPUT -s FF05::/16 -j LOG --log-prefix "IPv6 SITE-LOCAL MULTICAST: "
      -A INPUT -s ::0.0.0.0/96 -j LOG --log-prefix "IPv4 COMPATIBLE IPv6 ADDR: "
```

If you wish to block multicasts to all link-local nodes (e.g. if you are not using router autoconfiguration and do not plan to have any services that multicast to the entire local network), you can block the link-local all-nodes multicast address (before accepting incoming ICMPv6):

```
      -A INPUT -d FF02::1 -j LOG --log-prefix "Link-local All-Nodes Multicast: "
```

However, if you're going to allow IPv4 compatible IPv6 addresses (of the form ::0.0.0.0/96), you should then consider logging the non-routable IPv4-compatible addresses:

```
      -A INPUT -s ::0.0.0.0/104 -j LOG --log-prefix "IP NON-ROUTABLE ADDR: "
      -A INPUT -s ::127.0.0.0/104 -j LOG --log-prefix "IP DROP LOOPBACK: "
      -A INPUT -s ::224.0.0.0/100 -j LOG --log-prefix "IP DROP MULTICAST D: "
      -A INPUT -s ::255.0.0.0/104 -j LOG --log-prefix "IP BROADCAST: "
```

If you are not expecting to see any IPv4 (or IPv4-compatible) traffic on your network, consider logging it before it gets dropped:

```
    -A INPUT -s ::FFFF:0.0.0.0/96 -j LOG --log-prefix "IPv4 MAPPED IPv6 ADDR: "
    -A INPUT -s 2002::/16 -j LOG --log-prefix "IPv6 6to4 ADDR: "
```

The following rule will log all traffic originating from a site-local address, which is deprecated address space:

```
    -A INPUT -s FEC0::/10 -j LOG --log-prefix "SITE-LOCAL ADDRESS TRAFFIC: "
```

2.5.5.3.5 Log and Drop All Other Packets

To log before dropping all packets that are not explicitly accepted by previous rules, change the final lines from

```
    -A RH-Firewall-1-INPUT -j REJECT --reject-with icmp-host-prohibited
    COMMIT
```

to

```
    -A RH-Firewall-1-INPUT -j LOG
    -A RH-Firewall-1-INPUT -j DROP
    COMMIT
```

The rule to log all dropped packets must be used with care. Chatty but otherwise non-malicious network protocols (e.g. NetBIOS) may result in voluminous logs; insertion of earlier rules to explicitly drop their packets without logging may be appropriate.

2.5.5.4 Further Strengthening

Further strengthening, particularly as a result of customization to a particular environment, is possible for the iptables rules. Consider the following options, though their practicality depends on the network environment and usage scenario:

- **Restrict outgoing traffic.** As shown above, the `OUTPUT` chain's default policy can be changed to `DROP`, and rules can be written to specifically allow only certain types of outbound traffic. Such a policy could prevent casual usage of insecure protocols such as ftp and telnet, or even disrupt spyware. However, it would still not prevent a sophisticated user or program from using a proxy to circumvent the intended effects, and many client programs even try to automatically tunnel through port 80 to avoid such restrictions.

- **SYN flood protection.** SYN flood protection can be provided by iptables, but might run into limiting issues for servers. For example, the `iplimit` match can be used to limit simultaneous connections from a given host or class. Similarly, the `recent` match allows the firewall to deny additional connections from any host within a given period of time (e.g. more than 3 –state NEW connections on port 22 within a minute to prevent dictionary login attacks).

  A more precise option for DoS protection is using TCP SYN cookies. (See Section 2.5.1.2 for more information.)

2.5.5.5 Further Resources

More complex, restrictive, and powerful rulesets can be created, but this requires careful customization that relies on knowledge of the particular environment. The following resources provide more detailed information:

- The `iptables(8)` man page

- The Netfilter Project's documentation at `http://www.netfilter.org`

- The Red Hat Enterprise Linux Reference Guide

2.5.6   Secure Sockets Layer Support

The Secure Sockets Layer (SSL) protocol provides encrypted and authenticated network communications, and many network services include support for it. Using SSL is recommended, especially to avoid any plaintext transmission of sensitive data, even over a local network. The SSL implementation included with the system is called OpenSSL. Recent implementations of SSL may also be referred to as Transport Layer Security (TLS).

SSL uses public key cryptography to provide authentication and encryption. Public key cryptography involves two keys, one called the public key and the other called the private key. These keys are mathematically related such that data encrypted with one key can only be decrypted by the other, and vice versa. As their names suggest, public keys can be distributed to anyone while a private key must remain known only to its owner.

SSL uses *certificates*, which are files that hold cryptographic data: a public key, and a *signature* of that public key. In SSL authentication, a server presents a client with its certificate as a means of demonstrating that it is who it claims it is. If everything goes correctly, the client can verify the server's certificate by determining that the signature inside the certificate could only have been generated by a third party whom the client trusts. This third party is called a Certificate Authority (CA). Each client system should also have certificates from trusted CAs, and the client uses these CA certificates to verify the authenticity of the server's certificate. After authenticating a server using its certificate and a CA certificate, SSL provides encryption by using the server certificate to securely negotiate a shared secret key.

If your server must communicate using SSL with systems that might not be able to securely accept a new CA certificate prior to any SSL communication, then paying an established CA (whose certificates your clients already have) to sign your server certificates is recommended. The steps for doing this vary by vendor. Once the signed certificates have been obtained, configuration of the services is the same whether they were purchased from a vendor or signed by your own CA.

For setting up an internal network and encrypting local traffic, creating your own CA to sign SSL certificates can be appropriate. The major steps in this process are:

1. Create a CA to sign certificates

2. Create SSL certificates for servers using that CA

3. Enable client support by distributing the CA's certificate

2.5.6.1   Create a CA to Sign Certificates

The following instructions apply to OpenSSL since it is included with the system, but creating a CA is possible with any standards-compliant SSL toolkit. The security of certificates depends on the security of the CA that signed them, so performing these steps on a secure machine is critical. The system used as a CA should be physically secure and not connected to any network. It should receive any certificate signing requests (CSRs) via removable media and output certificates onto removable media.

The script `/etc/pki/tls/misc/CA` is included to assist in the process of setting up a CA. This script uses many settings in `/etc/pki/tls/openssl.cnf`. The settings in this file can be changed to suit your needs and allow easier selection of default settings, particularly in the `[req_distinguished_name]` section.

> To create the CA:
>
> ```
> # cd /etc/pki/tls/misc
> # ./CA -newca
> ```
>
> - When prompted, press enter to create a new CA key with the default name `cakey.pem`.
>
> - When prompted, enter a password that will protect the private key, then enter the same password again to verify it.
>
> - At the prompts, fill out as much of the CA information as is relevant for your site. You *must* specify a common name, or generation of the CA certificate will fail.
>
> - Next, you will be prompted for the password, so that the script can re-open the private key in order to write the certificate.

This step performs the following actions:

- creates the directory `/etc/pki/CA` (by default), which contains files necessary for the operation of a certificate authority. These are:

    - `serial`, which contains the current serial number for certificates signed by the CA

    - `index.txt`, which is a text database file that contains information about certificates signed

    - `crl`, which is a directory for holding revoked certificates

    - `private`, a directory which stores the CA's private key

- creates a public-private key pair for the CA in the file `/etc/pki/CA/private/cakey.pem`. The private key must be kept private in order to ensure the security of the certificates the CA will later sign.

- signs the public key (using the corresponding private key, in a process called self-signing) to create the CA certificate, which is then stored in `/etc/pki/CA/cacert.pem`.

When the CA later signs a server certificate using its private key, it means that it is vouching for the authenticity of that server. A client can then use the CA's certificate (which contains its public key) to verify the authenticity of the server certificate. To accomplish this, it is necessary to distribute the CA certificate to any clients as covered in Section 2.5.6.3.

2.5.6.2 Create SSL Certificates for Servers

Creating an SSL certificate for a server involves the following steps:

1. A public-private key pair for the server must be generated.

2. A certificate signing request (CSR) must be created from the key pair.

3. The CSR must be signed by a certificate authority (CA) to create the server certificate. If a CA has been set up as described in Section 2.5.6.1, it can sign the CSR.

4. The server certificate and keys must be installed on the server.

Instructions on how to generate and sign SSL certificates are provided for the following common services:

- Mail server, in Section 3.11.4.6.

- Dovecot, in Section 3.17.2.2.

- Apache, in Section 3.16.4.1.

2.5.6.3 Enable Client Support

The system ships with certificates from well-known commercial CAs. If your server certificates were signed by one of these established CAs, then this step is not necessary since the clients should include the CA certificate already.

If your servers use certificates signed by your own CA, some user applications will warn that the server's certificate cannot be verified because the CA is not recognized. Other applications may simply fail to accept the certificate and refuse to operate, or continue operating without ever having properly verified the server certificate.

To avoid this warning, and properly authenticate the servers, your CA certificate must be exported to every application on every client system that will be connecting to an SSL-enabled server.

2.5.6.3.1 Adding a Trusted CA for Firefox

Firefox needs to have a certificate from the CA that signed the web server's certificate, so that it can authenticate the web server.

> To import a new CA certificate into Firefox 3:
>
> 1. Launch Firefox and choose **Preferences** from the **Edit** menu.
> 2. Click the **Advanced** button.
> 3. Select the **Encryption** tab.
> 4. Click the **View Certificates** button.
> 5. Select the **Authorities** tab.
> 6. Click the **Import** button at the bottom of the screen.
> 7. Navigate to the CA certificate and import it. Determine whether the CA should be used to identify web sites, e-mail users, and software developers and trust it for each accordingly.

2.5.6.3.2 Adding a Trusted CA for Thunderbird

Thunderbird needs to have a certificate from the CA that signed the mail server's certificates, so that it can authenticate the mail server(s).

> To import a new CA certificate into Thunderbird 2:
>
> 1. Launch Thunderbird and choose **Preferences** from the **Edit** menu.
> 2. Click the **Advanced** button.
> 3. Select the **Certificates** tab.
> 4. Click the **View Certificates** button.
> 5. Select the **Authorities** tab.
> 6. Click the **Import** button at the bottom of the screen.
> 7. Navigate to the CA certificate and import it. Determine whether the CA should be used to identify web sites, e-mail users, and software developers and trust it for each accordingly.

2.5.6.3.3 Adding a Trusted CA for Evolution

The Evolution e-mail client needs to have a certificate from the CA that signed the mail server's certificates, so that it can authenticate the mail server(s).

> To import a new CA certificate into Evolution:
>
> 1. Launch Evolution and choose **Preferences** from the **Edit** menu.
> 2. Select **Certificates** from the icon list on the left.
> 3. Click the **Authorities** tab.
> 4. Click the **Import** button.
> 5. Navigate to the CA certificate and import it.

2.5.6.3.4 Remove Certificate Authorities, if Appropriate

> Survey the certificate authorities trusted by Firefox, Thunderbird, Evolution, or other network clients. The list of certificate authorities for each program can be found via GUI, as described in the previous sections.
>
> Remove the certificate authorities which are not appropriate for your network connectivity needs.
>
> This may only make sense for some environments, and may create operational problems for a general purpose Internet-connected system.

2.5.6.4 Further Resources

- The OpenSSL Project home page at `http://www.openssl.org`
- The `openssl(1)` man page
- Jeremy Mates's how-to: `http://sial.org/howto/openssl`

2.5.7 Uncommon Network Protocols

The system includes support for several network protocols which are not commonly used. Although security vulnerabilities in kernel networking code are not frequently discovered, the consequences can be dramatic. Ensuring uncommon network protocols are disabled reduces the system's risk to attacks targeted at its implementation of those protocols.

Although these protocols are not commonly used, avoid disruption in your network environment by ensuring they are not needed prior to disabling them.

2.5.7.1 Disable Support for DCCP

> If the DCCP protocol is not needed, its kernel module can be prevented from loading. To do so, add the following line to `/etc/modprobe.conf`:

```
install dccp /bin/true
```

CCE 14268-7

The Datagram Congestion Control Protocol (DCCP) is a relatively new transport layer protocol, designed to support streaming media and telephony.

2.5.7.2 Disable Support for SCTP

If the SCTP protocol is not needed, its kernel module can be prevented from loading. To do so, add the following line to `/etc/modprobe.conf`:

```
install sctp /bin/true
```

CCE 14132-5

The Stream Control Transmission Protocol (SCTP) is a transport layer protocol, designed to support the idea of message-oriented communication, with several streams of messages within one connection.

2.5.7.3 Disable Support for RDS

If the RDS protocol is not needed, its kernel module can be prevented from loading. To do so, add the following line to `/etc/modprobe.conf`:

```
install rds /bin/true
```

CCE 14027-7

The Reliable Datagram Sockets (RDS) protocol is a transport layer protocol designed to provide reliable high-bandwidth, low-latency communications between nodes in a cluster.

2.5.7.4 Disable Support for TIPC

If the TIPC protocol is not needed, its kernel module can be prevented from loading. To do so, add the following line to `/etc/modprobe.conf`:

```
install tipc /bin/true
```

CCE 14911-2

The Transparent Inter-Process Communication (TIPC) protocol is designed to provide communications between nodes in a cluster.

2.5.8 IPsec

Internet Protocol Security (IPsec) provides the ability to encrypt and authenticate IP communications.

2.5.8.1 Using Openswan for IPsec

2.5.8.1.1 Install the `openswan` Package

> The Openswan software is recommended over the default `ipsec-tools` package for IPsec. Install it with the command:
>
> ```
> # yum install openswan
> ```

2.5.8.1.2 Remove the `ipsec-tools` Package

> Since the `openswan` package provides a superset of its functionality, remove the `ipsec-tools` package:
>
> ```
> # yum erase ipsec-tools
> ```

2.6 Logging and Auditing

Successful local or network attacks on systems do not necessarily leave clear evidence of what happened. It is necessary to build a configuration in advance that collects this evidence, both in order to determine that something anomalous has occurred, and in order to respond appropriately. In addition, a well-configured logging and audit infrastructure will show evidence of any misconfiguration which might leave the system vulnerable to attack.

Logging and auditing take different approaches to collecting data. A logging infrastructure provides a framework for individual programs running on the system to report whatever events are considered interesting: the `sshd` program may report each successful or failed login attempt, while the `sendmail` program may report each time it sends an e-mail on behalf of a local or remote user. An auditing infrastructure, on the other hand, reports each instance of certain low-level events, such as entry to the `setuid` system call, regardless of which program caused the event to occur.

Auditing has the advantage of being more comprehensive, but the disadvantage of reporting a large amount of information, most of which is uninteresting. Logging (particularly using a standard framework like `syslogd`) has the advantage of being compatible with a wide variety of client applications, and of reporting only information considered important by each application, but the disadvantage that the information reported is not consistent between applications.

A robust infrastructure will perform both logging and auditing, and will use *configurable* automated methods of summarizing the reported data, so that system administrators can remove or compress reports of events known to be uninteresting in favor of alert monitoring for events known to be interesting.

This section discusses how to configure logging, log monitoring, and auditing, using tools included with RHEL5. It is recommended that `rsyslog` be used for logging, with `logwatch` providing summarization). `auditd` should be used for auditing, with `aureport` providing summarization.

2.6.1 Configure Logging

This section presents two packages available in RHEL 5 for performing logging, and recommends that `rsyslog` be used.

No matter which logging software is used, a system should send its logs to a remote loghost. An intruder who has compromised the `root` account on a machine may delete the log entries which indicate that the system was attacked before they are seen by an administrator. If system logs are to be useful in detecting malicious activities, it is necessary to send them to a remote server.

CCE 3679-8

2.6.1.1 Configure Syslog

The sysklogd software provides the default logging daemon for RHEL, but has a number of downsides, including a lack of authentication for client or server, lack of encryption, or reliable transport for messages sent over a network. For these reasons, rsyslog is recommended instead (and it is also part of RHEL). It is described next in Section 2.6.1.2. If using the sysklogd software for logging is still necessary, this section discusses how to configure its syslog daemon for best effect.

2.6.1.1.1 Ensure All Important Messages are Captured

<table><tr><td>

Edit the file `/etc/syslog.conf`. Add or correct whichever of the following lines are appropriate for your environment:

```
auth,user.*                                               /var/log/messages
kern.*                                                    /var/log/kern.log
daemon.*                                                  /var/log/daemon.log
syslog.*                                                  /var/log/syslog
lpr,news,uucp,local0,local1,local2,local3,local4,local5,local6.* /var/log/unused.log
```

</td></tr></table>

When a message is sent to syslog for logging, it is sent with a facility name (such as `mail`, `auth`, or `local2`), and a priority (such as `debug`, `notice`, or `emerg`). Each line of syslog's configuration file is a directive which specifies a set of facility/priority pairs, and then gives a filename or host to which log messages of matching types should be sent. In order for a message to match a type, the facility must match, and the priority must be the priority named in the rule *or any higher priority*. (See `syslog.conf(5)` for an ordered list of priorities.)

Older versions of syslog mandated a very restrictive format for the `syslog.conf` file. However, the version of syslog shipped with RHEL5 allows any sort of whitespace (spaces or tabs, not just tabs) to separate the selection criteria from the message disposition, and allows the use of `facility.*` as a wildcard matching a given facility at any priority.

The default RHEL5 syslog configuration stores the facilities `authpriv`, `cron`, and `mail` in named logs. This guide describes the implementation of the following configuration, but any configuration which stores the important facilities and is usable by the administrators will suffice:

- Store each of the facilities `kern`, `daemon`, and `syslog` in its own log, so that it will be easy to access information about messages from those facilities.

- Restrict the information stored in `/var/log/messages` to only the facilities `auth` and `user`, and store all messages from those facilities. Messages can easily become cluttered otherwise.

- Store information about all facilities which should not be in use at this site in a file called `/var/log/unused.log`. If any messages are logged to this file at some future point, this may be an indication that an unknown service is running, and should be investigated. In addition, if `news` and `uucp` are not in use at this site, remove the directive from the default `syslog.conf` which stores those facilities.

Making use of the `local` facilities is also recommended. Specific configuration is beyond the scope of this guide, but applications such as SSH can easily be configured to log to a `local` facility which is not being used for anything else. If this is done, reconfigure `/etc/syslog.conf` to store this facility in an appropriate named log or in `/var/log/messages`, rather than in `/var/log/unused.log`.

2.6.1.1.2   Confirm Existence and Permissions of System Log Files

> For each log file *LOGFILE* referenced in `/etc/syslog.conf` or `/etc/rsyslog.conf`, run the commands:
>
> ```
> # touch LOGFILE
> # chown root:root LOGFILE
> # chmod 0600 LOGFILE
> ```
>
> **CCE 3701-0, 4233-3, 4366-1**

Syslog will refuse to log to a file which does not exist. All messages intended for that file will be silently discarded, so it is important to verify that all log files exist. Some logs may contain sensitive information, so it is better to restrict permissions so that only administrative users can read or write logfiles.

2.6.1.1.3   Send Logs to a Remote Loghost

> Edit `/etc/syslog.conf`. Add or correct the line:
>
> ```
> *.*                         @loghost.example.com
> ```
>
> where *loghost.example.com* is the name of your central log server.
>
> **CCE 4260-6**

It is particularly important that logs be stored on the local host in addition to being sent to the loghost, because syslogd uses the UDP protocol to send messages over a network. UDP does not guarantee reliable delivery, and moderately busy sites *will* lose log messages occasionally, especially in periods of high traffic which may be the result of an attack. In addition, remote syslogd messages are not authenticated, so it is easy for an attacker to introduce spurious messages to the central log server. Also, some problems cause loss of network connectivity, which will prevent the sending of messages to the central server. For all of these reasons, it is better to store log messages both centrally and on each host, so that they can be correlated if necessary.

2.6.1.1.4   Enable `syslogd` to Accept Remote Messages on Loghosts Only

> Is this machine the central log server for your organization? If so, edit the file `/etc/sysconfig/syslog`. Add or correct the following line:
>
> ```
> SYSLOGD_OPTIONS="-m 0 -r -s example.com"
> ```
>
> where *example.com* is the name of your domain.
>
> If the machine is not a log server, edit `/etc/sysconfig/syslog`, and instead add or correct the line:
>
> ```
> SYSLOGD_OPTIONS="-m 0"
> ```
>
> **CCE 3382-9**

By default, RHEL5's syslog does not listen over the network for log messages. The `-r` flag enables `syslogd` to listen over a network, and should be used only if necessary. The `-s` *example.com* flag strips the domain name *example.com* from each sending machine's hostname before logging messages from that host, to reduce the amount of redundant information placed in log files. See the `syslogd(8)` man page for further information.

2.6.1.2 Configure Rsyslog

The `rsyslog` software is recommended as a replacement for the default `sysklogd` daemon. `rsyslog` provides improvements over sysklogd, such as connection-oriented (i.e. TCP) transmission of logs, the option to log to database formats, and the encryption of log data en route to a central logging server.

2.6.1.2.1 Install the `rsyslog` Package

Install the `rsyslog` package manager as follows:

```
# yum install rsyslog
```

2.6.1.2.2 Ensure the `rsyslog` Service is Activated

To ensure that the `rsyslog` service is activated, and that sysklogd's `syslog` daemon will not interfere with it by trying to run, execute the following:

```
# chkconfig syslog off
# chkconfig rsyslog on
```

This will ensure the startup of `rsyslog` on the next system boot. The `/sbin/service` command can be used to change to make these changes happen immediately.

2.6.1.2.3 Ensure Important Messages are Captured

Edit the file `/etc/rsyslog.conf`. Add or correct whichever of the following lines are appropriate for your environment:

```
auth.*,user.*                                              /var/log/messages
kern.*                                                     /var/log/kern.log
daemon.*                                                   /var/log/daemon.log
syslog.*                                                   /var/log/syslog
lpr,news,uucp,local0,local1,local2,local3,local4,local5,local6.* /var/log/unused.log
```

See the man page `rsyslog.conf(5)` for more information.

By default, `rsyslog` *uses a timestamp format that Logwatch does not understand. If your environment uses Logwatch, edit the file* `/etc/rsyslog.conf` *and add or edit the following line:* `$ActionFileDefaultTemplate RSYSLOG_TraditionalFileFormat`

2.6.1.2.4 Confirm Existence and Permissions of Log Files

For each log file *LOGFILE* referenced in `/etc/rsyslog.conf`, run the commands:

```
# touch LOGFILE
# chown root:root LOGFILE
# chmod 0600 LOGFILE
```

2.6.1.2.5 Send Logs to a Remote Host Using Reliable Transport

Edit `/etc/rsyslog.conf`. Add or correct the line:

```
*.*                          @@loghost.example.com
```

where *loghost.example.com* is the name of your central log server. This directive should appear on all systems except a syslog server itself.

The double @ symbol in front of the log host means that TCP will be used to send log messages to the server. Rsyslog supports TCP for log transmission, which ensures more reliable network communication than UDP.

2.6.1.2.6 Enable `rsyslog` to Accept Remote Messages on Loghosts Only

Is this machine the central log server for your organization? If so, edit the file `/etc/rsyslog.conf`. Add or correct the following lines:

```
$ModLoad imtcp.so
$InputTCPServerRun 514
```

These directives instruct rsyslogd to receive messages from the network. Directives that enable receiving messages over the network such as $InputTCPServerRun, $InputUDPServerRun, and $InputRELPServerRun should not appear on client systems.

By default, `rsyslog` does not listen over the network for log messages. The *ModLoad* tells rsyslog to load the `imtcp.so` module so it can listen over a network via TCP, and should be used only if necessary. The *InputTCPServerRun* option instructs `rsyslogd` to listen on the specified TCP port. See the `rsyslogd(8)` man page for further information.

2.6.1.3 Logrotate

2.6.1.3.1 Ensure All Logs are Rotated

Edit the file `/etc/logrotate.d/syslog`. Find the first line, which should look like this (wrapped for clarity):

```
/var/log/messages /var/log/secure /var/log/maillog /var/log/spooler \
  /var/log/boot.log /var/log/cron {
```

Edit this line so that it contains a one-space-separated listing of each log file referenced in `/etc/syslog.conf`.

CCE 4182-2

All logs in use on a system must be rotated regularly, or the log files will consume disk space over time, eventually interfering with system operation. The file `/etc/logrotate.d/syslog` is the configuration file used by the logrotate program to maintain all log files written by syslog. By default, it rotates logs weekly and stores four archival copies of each log. These settings can be modified by editing `/etc/logrotate.conf`, but the defaults are sufficient for purposes of this guide.

Note that `logrotate` is run nightly by the cron job `/etc/cron.daily/logrotate`. If particularly active logs need to be rotated more often than once a day, some other mechanism must be used.

2.6.1.4   Logwatch

2.6.1.4.1   Monitor Suspicious Log Messages using Logwatch

The system includes an extensible program called Logwatch for reporting on unusual items in syslog. Logwatch is valuable because it provides a parser for the syslog entry format and a number of signatures for types of lines which are considered to be mundane or noteworthy. Logwatch has a number of downsides: the signatures can be inaccurate and are not always categorized consistently, and you must be able to program in Perl in order to customize the signature database. However, it is recommended that all Linux sites which do not have time to deploy a third-party log monitoring application run Logwatch in its default configuration. This provides some useful information about system activity in exchange for very little administrator effort.

This guide recommends that Logwatch be run only on the central logserver, if your site has one, in order to focus administrator attention by sending all daily logs in a single e-mail.

2.6.1.4.2   Configure Logwatch on the Central Log Server

Is this machine the central log server? If so, edit the file `/etc/logwatch/conf/logwatch.conf`. Add or correct the following lines:

```
HostLimit = no
SplitHosts = yes
MultiEmail = no
Service = -zz-disk_space
```

Ensure that `logwatch.pl` is run nightly from `cron`. (This is the default):

```
# cd /etc/cron.daily
# ln -s /usr/share/logwatch/scripts/logwatch.pl 0logwatch
```

CCE 4323-2

On a central logserver, you want Logwatch to summarize all syslog entries, including those which did not originate on the logserver itself. The `HostLimit` setting tells Logwatch to report on all hosts, not just the one on which it is running.

If `SplitHosts` is set, Logwatch will separate entries by hostname. This makes the report longer but significantly more usable. If it is not set, then Logwatch will not report which host generated a given log entry, and that information is almost always necessary. If `MultiEmail` is set, then each host's information will be sent in a separate e-mail message. This is a matter of preference.

The `Service` directive `-zz-disk_space` tells Logwatch not to run the `zz-disk_space` report, which reports on free disk space. Since all log monitoring is being done on the central logserver, the disk space listing will always be that of the logserver, regardless of which host is being monitored. This is confusing, so disable that service. Note that this does mean that Logwatch will not monitor disk usage information. Many workarounds are possible, such as running `df` on each host daily via `cron` and sending the output to syslog so that it will be reported to the logserver.

2.6.1.4.3 Disable Logwatch on Clients if a Logserver Exists

> Does your site have a central logserver which has been configured to report on logs received from all systems? If so:
>
> ```
> # rm /etc/cron.daily/0logwatch
> ```

If no logserver exists, it will be necessary for each machine to run Logwatch individually. Using a central logserver provides the security and reliability benefits discussed earlier, and also makes monitoring logs easier and less time-intensive for administrators.

2.6.2 System Accounting with `auditd`

The audit service is provided for system auditing. By default, the service audits about SELinux AVC denials and certain types of security-relevant events such as system logins, account modifications, and authentication events performed by programs such as `sudo`.

Under its default configuration, `auditd` has modest disk space requirements, and should not noticeably impact system performance. The audit service, configured with at least its default rules, is strongly recommended for all sites, regardless of whether they are running SELinux.

DoD or federal networks often have substantial auditing requirements and `auditd` can be configured to meet these requirements.

Typical DoD requirements include:

- Ensure Auditing is Configured to Collect Certain System Events
  - Information on the Use of Print Command (unsuccessful and successful)
  - Startup and Shutdown Events (unsuccessful and successful)
- Ensure the auditing software can record the following for each audit event:
  - Date and time of the event
  - Userid that initiated the event
  - Type of event
  - Success or failure of the event
  - For I&A events, the origin of the request (e.g., terminal ID)
  - For events that introduce an object into a user's address space, and for object deletion events, the name of the object, and in MLS systems, the objects security level.
- Ensure files are backed up no less than weekly onto a different system than the system being audited or backup media.
- Ensure old logs are closed out and new audit logs are started daily

- Ensure the configuration is immutable. With the `-e 2` setting a reboot will be required to change any audit rules.

- Ensure that the audit data files have permissions of 640, or more restrictive.

2.6.2.1 Enable the `auditd` Service

> Ensure that the `auditd` service is enabled (this is the default):
>
> ```
> # chkconfig auditd on
> ```
>
> **CCE 4292-9**

By default, `auditd` logs only SELinux denials, which are helpful for debugging SELinux and discovering intrusion attempts, and certain types of security events, such as modifications to user accounts (`useradd`, `passwd`, etc), login events, and calls to `sudo`.

Data is stored in `/var/log/audit/audit.log`. By default, `auditd` rotates 4 logs by size (5MB), retaining a maximum of 20MB of data in total, and refuses to write entries when the disk is too full. This minimizes the risk of audit data filling its partition and impacting other services. However, it is possible to lose audit data if the system is busy.

2.6.2.2 Configure `auditd` Data Retention

> - Determine *STOREMB*, the amount of audit data (in megabytes) which should be retained in each log file. Edit the file /etc/audit/auditd.conf. Add or modify the following line:
>
>   ```
>   max_log_file = STOREMB
>   ```
>
> - Use a dedicated partition (or logical volume) for log files. It is straightforward to create such a partition or logical volume during system installation time. The partition should be larger than the maximum space which `auditd` will ever use, which is the maximum size of each log file (`max_log_file`) multiplied by the number of log files (`num_logs`). Ensure the partition is mounted on `/var/log/audit`.
>
> - If your site requires that the machine be disabled when auditing cannot be performed, configure `auditd` to halt the system when disk space for auditing runs low. Edit `/etc/audit/auditd.conf`, and add or correct the following lines:
>
>   ```
>   space_left_action = email
>   action_mail_acct = root
>   admin_space_left_action = halt
>   ```
>
> The default action to take when the logs reach their maximum size is to rotate the log files, discarding the oldest one. If it is more important to retain all possible auditing information, even if that opens the possibility of running out of space and taking the action defined by `admin_space_left_action`, add or correct the line:
>
> ```
> max_log_file_action = keep_logs
> ```

By default, `auditd` retains 4 log files of size 5Mb apiece. For a busy system or a system which is thoroughly auditing system activity, this is likely to be insufficient.

The log file size needed will depend heavily on what types of events are being audited. First configure auditing to log all the events of interest. Then monitor the log size manually for awhile to determine what file size will allow you to keep the required data for the correct time period.

Using a dedicated partition for `/var/log/audit` prevents the `auditd` logs from disrupting system functionality if they fill, and, more importantly, prevents other activity in `/var` from filling the partition and stopping the audit trail. (The audit logs are size-limited and therefore unlikely to grow without bound unless configured to do so.)

Some machines may have requirements that no actions occur which cannot be audited. If this is the case, then `auditd` can be configured to halt the machine if it runs out of space.

Note: Since older logs are rotated, configuring `auditd` this way does not prevent older logs from being rotated away before they can be viewed.

If your system is configured to halt when logging cannot be performed, make sure this can never happen under normal circumstances! Ensure that `/var/log/audit` is on its own partition, and that this partition is larger than the maximum amount of data `auditd` will retain normally.

2.6.2.3 Enable Auditing for Processes Which Start Prior to the Audit Daemon

---

To ensure that all processes can be audited, even those which start prior to the audit daemon, add the argument `audit=1` to the kernel line in `/etc/grub.conf`, in the manner below:

```
kernel /vmlinuz-version ro vga=ext root=/dev/VolGroup00/LogVol00 rhgb quiet audit=1
```

CCE 15026-8

Each process on the system carries an "auditable" flag which indicates whether its activities can be audited. Although `auditd` takes care of enabling this for all processes which launch after it does, adding the kernel argument ensures that it is set for every process during boot.

2.6.2.4 Configure `auditd` Rules for Comprehensive Auditing

The `auditd` program can perform comprehensive monitoring of system activity. This section describes recommended configuration settings for comprehensive auditing, but a full description of the auditing system's capabilities is beyond the scope of this guide. The mailing list `linux-audit@redhat.com`[3] may be a good source of further information.

The audit subsystem supports extensive collection of events, including:

- Tracing of arbitrary system calls (identified by name or number) on entry or exit.
- Filtering by PID, UID, call success, system call argument (with some limitations), etc.
- Monitoring of specific files for modifications to the file's contents or metadata.

Auditing rules are controlled in the file `/etc/audit/audit.rules`. Add rules to it to meet the auditing requirements for your organization. Each line in `/etc/audit/audit.rules` represents a series of arguments that can be passed to `auditctl` and can be individually tested as such. See documentation in `/usr/share/doc/audit-version` and in the related man pages for more details.

Recommended audit rules are provided in `/usr/share/doc/audit-version/stig.rules`. In order to activate those rules:

```
# cp /usr/share/doc/audit-version/stig.rules /etc/audit/audit.rules
```

---

[3]List information can be found at http://www.redhat.com/mailman/listinfo/linux-audit

and then edit /etc/audit/audit.rules and comment out the lines containing arch= which are not appropriate for your system's architecture. Then review and understand the following rules, ensuring rules are activated as needed for the appropriate architecture.

After reviewing all the rules, reading the following sections, and editing as needed, activate the new rules:

```
# service auditd restart
```

2.6.2.4.1   Records Events that Modify Date and Time Information

Add the following to /etc/audit/audit.rules, setting *ARCH* to either b32 or b64 as appropriate for your system:

```
-a always,exit -F arch=ARCH -S adjtimex -S settimeofday -S stime -k time-change
-a always,exit -F arch=ARCH -S clock_settime -k time-change
-w /etc/localtime -p wa -k time-change
```

CCE 14051-7

2.6.2.4.2   Record Events that Modify User/Group Information

Add the following to /etc/audit/audit.rules, in order to capture events that modify account changes:

```
-w /etc/group -p wa -k identity
-w /etc/passwd -p wa -k identity
-w /etc/gshadow -p wa -k identity
-w /etc/shadow -p wa -k identity
-w /etc/security/opasswd -p wa -k identity
```

CCE 14829-6

2.6.2.4.3   Record Events that Modify the System's Network Environment

Add the following to /etc/audit/audit.rules, setting *ARCH* to either b32 or b64 as appropriate for your system:

```
-a exit,always -F arch=ARCH -S sethostname -S setdomainname -k system-locale
-w /etc/issue -p wa -k system-locale
-w /etc/issue.net -p wa -k system-locale
-w /etc/hosts -p wa -k system-locale
-w /etc/sysconfig/network -p wa -k system-locale
```

CCE 14816-3

2.6.2.4.4   Record Events that Modify the System's Mandatory Access Controls

Add the following to /etc/audit/audit.rules:

```
-w /etc/selinux/ -p wa -k MAC-policy
```

CCE 14821-3

2.6.2.4.5   Record Attempts to Alter Logon and Logout Events

The audit system already collects login info for all users and root. To watch for attempted manual edits of files involved in storing logon events, add the following to `/etc/audit/audit.rules`:

```
-w /var/log/faillog -p wa -k logins
-w /var/log/lastlog -p wa -k logins
```

CCE 14904-7

2.6.2.4.6   Record Attempts to Alter Process and Session Initiation Information

The audit system already collects process information for all users and root. To watch for attempted manual edits of files involved in storing such process information, add the following to `/etc/audit/audit.rules`:

```
-w /var/run/utmp -p wa -k session
-w /var/log/btmp -p wa -k session
-w /var/log/wtmp -p wa -k session
```

CCE 14679-5

2.6.2.4.7   Ensure `auditd` Collects Discretionary Access Control Permission Modification Events

At a minimum the audit system should collect file permission changes for all users and root. Add the following to `/etc/audit/audit.rules`, setting *ARCH* to either `b32` or `b64` as appropriate for your system:

```
-a always,exit -F arch=ARCH -S chmod -S fchmod -S fchmodat -F auid>=500 \
      -F auid!=4294967295 -k perm_mod
-a always,exit -F arch=ARCH -S chown -S fchown -S fchownat -S lchown -F auid>=500 \
      -F auid!=4294967295 -k perm_mod
-a always,exit -F arch=ARCH -S setxattr -S lsetxattr -S fsetxattr -S removexattr -S \
      lremovexattr -S fremovexattr -F auid>=500 -F auid!=4294967295 -k perm_mod
```

CCE 14058-2

2.6.2.4.8   Ensure `auditd` Collects Unauthorized Access Attempts to Files (unsuccessful)

At a minimum the audit system should collect unauthorized file accesses for all users and root. Add the following to `/etc/audit/audit.rules`, setting *ARCH* to either `b32` or `b64` as appropriate for your system:

```
-a always,exit -F arch=ARCH -S creat -S open -S openat -S truncate -S ftruncate \
      -F exit=-EACCES -F auid>=500 -F auid!=4294967295 -k access
```

```
-a always,exit -F arch=ARCH -S creat -S open -S openat -S truncate -S ftruncate \
      -F exit=-EPERM -F auid>=500 -F auid!=4294967295 -k access
```

                                                                            CCE 14917-9

2.6.2.4.9   Ensure `auditd` Collects Information on the Use of Privileged Commands

At a minimum the audit system should collect the execution of privileged commands for all users and root. This requires adding an audit rule to watch execution of each setuid or setgid program.

First, run the following command for each local partition *PART* to generate rules, one for each setuid or setgid program:

```
# find PART -xdev \( -perm -4000 -o -perm -2000 \) -type f | awk '{print \
      "-a always,exit -F path=" $1 " -F perm=x -F auid>=500 -F auid!=4294967295 \
      -k privileged" }'
```

Next, add those lines to `/etc/audit/audit.rules`.

                                                                            CCE 14296-8

2.6.2.4.10   Ensure `auditd` Collects Information on Exporting to Media (successful)

At a minimum the audit system should collect media exportation events for all users and root. Add the following to `/etc/audit/audit.rules`, setting *ARCH* to either b32 or b64 as appropriate for your system:

```
-a always,exit -F arch=ARCH -S mount -F auid>=500 -F auid!=4294967295 -k export
```

                                                                            CCE 14569-8

2.6.2.4.11   Ensure `auditd` Collects Files Deletion Events by User (successful and unsuccessful)

At a minimum the audit system should collect file deletion events for all users and root. Add the following to `/etc/audit/audit.rules`, setting *ARCH* to either b32 or b64 as appropriate for your system:

```
-a always,exit -F arch=ARCH -S unlink -S unlinkat -S rename -S renameat -F auid>=500 \
      -F auid!=4294967295 -k delete
```

                                                                            CCE 14820-5

2.6.2.4.12   Ensure `auditd` Collects System Administrator Actions

At a minimum the audit system should collect administrator actions for all users and root. Add the following to `/etc/audit/audit.rules`:

```
-w /etc/sudoers -p wa -k actions
```

CCE 14824-7

2.6.2.4.13 Ensure `auditd` Collects Information on Kernel Module Loading and Unloading

Add the following to `/etc/audit/audit.rules` in order to capture kernel module loading and unloading events, setting *ARCH* to either b32 or b64 as appropriate for your system:

```
-w /sbin/insmod -p x -k modules
-w /sbin/rmmod -p x -k modules
-w /sbin/modprobe -p x -k modules
-a always,exit -F arch=ARCH -S init_module -S delete_module -k modules
```

CCE 14688-6

2.6.2.4.14 Make the `auditd` Configuration Immutable

Add the following *as the last rule* in `/etc/audit/audit.rules` in order to make the configuration immutable:

```
-e 2
```

With this setting, a reboot will be required to change any audit rules.

CCE 14692-8

2.6.2.5 Summarize and Review Audit Logs using `aureport`

Familiarize yourself with the `aureport(8)` man page, then design a short series of audit reporting commands suitable for exploring the audit logs on a daily (or more frequent) basis. These commands can be added as a cron job by placing an appropriately named file in `/etc/cron.daily`. See the next section for information on how to ensure that the audit system collects all events needed.

For example, to generate a daily report of every user to login to the machine, the following command could be run from `cron`:

```
# aureport -l -i -ts yesterday -te today
```

To review all audited activity for unusual behavior, a good place to start is to see a summary of which audit rules have been triggering:

```
aureport --key --summary
```

If access violations stand out, review them with:

```
# ausearch --key access --raw | aureport --file --summary
```

To review what executables are doing:

```
# ausearch --key access --raw | aureport -x --summary
```

If access violations have been occurring on a particular file (such as `/etc/shadow`) and you want to determine which user is doing this:

```
# ausearch --key access --file /etc/shadow --raw | aureport --user --summary -i
```

Check for anomalous activity (such as device changing to promiscuous mode, processes ending abnormally, login failure limits being reached) using:

```
# aureport --anomaly
```

The foundation to audit analysis is using keys to classify the events. Information about using `ausearch` to find an SELinux problem can be found in Section 2.4.6.

3. Services

3.1 Disable All Unneeded Services at Boot Time

The best protection against vulnerable software is running less software. This section describes how to review the software which Red Hat Enterprise Linux installs on a system and disable software which is not needed. It then enumerates the software packages installed on a default RHEL5 system and provides guidance about which ones can be safely disabled.

3.1.1 Determine which Services are Enabled at Boot

Run the command:

```
# chkconfig --list | grep :on
```

The first column of this output is the name of a service which is currently enabled at boot. Review each listed service to determine whether it can be disabled.

If it is appropriate to disable some service *srvname*, do so using the command:

```
# chkconfig srvname off
```

Use the guidance below for information about unfamiliar services.

3.1.2 Guidance on Default Services

The table in this section contains a list of all services which are enabled at boot by a default RHEL5 installation. For each service, one of the following recommendations is made:

- **Enable:** The service provides a significant capability with limited risk exposure. Leave the service enabled.

- **Configure:** The service either is required for most systems to function properly or provides an important security function. It should be left enabled by most environments. However, it must be configured securely on all machines, and different options may be needed for workstations than for servers. See the referenced section for recommended configuration of this service.

- **Disable if possible:** The service opens the system to some risk, but may be required by some environments. See the appropriate section of the guide, and disable the service if at all possible.

- **Servers only:** The service provides some function to other machines over the network. If that function is needed in the target environment, the service should remain enabled only on a small number of dedicated servers, and should be disabled on all other machines on the network.

Service name	Action	Reference
acpid	Enable	3.3.15.2
anacron	Disable if possible	3.4
apmd	Disable if possible	3.3.15.1
atd	Configure	3.4
auditd	Configure	2.6.2

Service name	Action	Reference
autofs	Disable if possible	2.2.2.3
avahi-daemon	Disable if possible	3.7
bluetooth	Disable if possible	3.3.14
cpuspeed	Enable	3.3.15.3
crond	Configure	3.4
cups	Disable if possible	3.8
firstboot	Disable if possible	3.3.1
gpm	Disable if possible	3.3.2
haldaemon	Disable if possible	3.3.13.2
hidd	Disable if possible	3.3.14.2
hplip	Disable if possible	3.8.4.1
ip6tables	Configure	2.5.5
iptables	Configure	2.5.5
irqbalance	Enable	3.3.3
isdn	Disable if possible	3.3.4
kdump	Disable if possible	3.3.5
kudzu	Disable if possible	3.3.6
mcstrans	Disable if possible	2.4.3.2 (SELinux)
mdmonitor	Disable if possible	3.3.7
messagebus	Disable if possible	3.3.13.1
microcode_ctl	Disable if possible	3.3.8
netfs	Disable if possible	3.13 (NFS)
network	Enable	3.3.9
nfslock	Disable if possible	3.13 (NFS)
pcscd	Disable if possible	3.3.10
portmap	Disable if possible	3.13 (NFS)
readahead_early	Disable if possible	3.3.12
readahead_later	Disable if possible	3.3.12
restorecond	Enable	2.4.3.3 (SELinux)
rhnsd	Disable if possible	2.1.2.2
rpcgssd	Disable if possible	3.13 (NFS)
rpcidmapd	Disable if possible	3.13 (NFS)
sendmail	Configure	3.11
setroubleshoot	Disable if possible	2.4.3.1 (SELinux)
smartd	Enable	3.3.11
sshd	Servers only	3.5
syslog	Configure	2.6.1.1
xfs	Disable if possible	3.6 (X11)
yum-updatesd	Disable if possible	2.1.2.3.2

3.1.3 Guidance for Unfamiliar Services

If the system is running any services which have not been covered, determine what these services do, and disable them if they are not needed or if they pose a high risk.

If a service *srvname* is unknown, try running:

```
$ rpm -qf /etc/init.d/srvname
```

to discover which RPM package installed the service. Then, run:

```
$ rpm -qi rpmname
```

for a brief description of what that RPM does.

3.2   Obsolete Services

This section discusses a number of network-visible services which have historically caused problems for system security, and for which disabling or severely limiting the service has been the best available guidance for some time. As a result of this consensus, these services are not installed as part of RHEL5 by default.

Organizations which are running these services should prioritize switching to more secure services which provide the needed functionality. If it is absolutely necessary to run one of these services for legacy reasons, care should be taken to restrict the service as much as possible, for instance by configuring host firewall software (see Section 2.5.5) to restrict access to the vulnerable service to only those remote hosts which have a known need to use it.

3.2.1   Inetd and Xinetd

> Is there an operational need to run the deprecated inetd or xinetd software packages? If not, ensure that they are removed from the system:
>
> ```
> # yum erase inetd xinetd
> ```
>
> **CCE 4234-1, 4252-3, 4023-8, 4164-0**

Beginning with Red Hat Enterprise Linux 5, the xinetd service is no longer installed by default. This change represents increased awareness that the dedicated network listener model does not improve security or reliability of services, and that restriction of network listeners is better handled using a granular model such as SELinux than using xinetd's limited security options.

3.2.2   Telnet

> Is there a mission-critical reason for users to access the system via the insecure telnet protocol, rather than the more secure SSH protocol? If not, ensure that the telnet server is removed from the system:
>
> ```
> # yum erase telnet-server
> ```
>
> **CCE 3390-2, 4330-7**

The `telnet` protocol uses unencrypted network communication, which means that data from the login session, including passwords and all other information transmitted during the session, can be stolen by eavesdroppers on the network, and also that outsiders can easily hijack the session to gain authenticated access to the telnet server. Organizations which use `telnet` should be actively working to migrate to a more secure protocol.

See Section 3.5 for information about the SSH service.

3.2.2.1   Remove Telnet Clients

> In order to prevent users from casually attempting to use a telnet server, and thus exposing their credentials over the network, remove the `telnet` package, which contains a telnet client program:

```
    # yum erase telnet
```
If Kerberos is not used, remove the `krb5-workstation` package, which also includes a telnet client:

```
    # yum erase krb5-workstation
```

3.2.3   Rlogin, Rsh, and Rcp

The Berkeley r-commands are legacy services which allow cleartext remote access and have an insecure trust model.

3.2.3.1   Remove the Rsh Server Commands from the System

Is there a mission-critical reason for users to access the system via the insecure `rlogin`, `rsh`, or `rcp` commands rather than the more secure `ssh` and `scp`? If not, ensure that the rsh server is removed from the system:

```
    # yum erase rsh-server
```

CCE 3974-3, 4141-8, 3537-8, 4308-3

SSH was designed to be a drop-in replacement for the r-commands, which suffer from the same hijacking and eavesdropping problems as telnet. There is unlikely to be a case in which these commands cannot be replaced with SSH.

3.2.3.2   Remove `.rhosts` Support from PAM Configuration Files

Check that `pam_rhosts` authentication is not used by any PAM services. Run the command:

```
    # grep -l pam_rhosts /etc/pam.d/*
```

This command should return no output.

The RHEL5 default is not to rely on `.rhosts` or `/etc/hosts.equiv` for any PAM-based services, so, on an uncustomized system, this command should return no output. If any files do use `pam_rhosts`, modify them to make use of a more secure authentication method instead. For more information about PAM, see Section 2.3.3.

3.2.3.3   Remove the Rsh Client Commands from the System

In order to prevent users from casually attempting to make use of an rsh server and thus exposing their credentials over the network, remove the `rsh` package, which contains client programs for many of r-commands described above:

```
    # yum erase rsh
```

Users should be trained to use the SSH client, and never attempt to connect to an rsh or telnet server. The `krb5-workstation` package also contains r-command client programs and should be removed as described in Section 3.2.2.1, if Kerberos is not in use.

3.2.4 NIS

> The NIS client service `ypbind` is not activated by default. In the event that it was activated at some point, disable it by executing the command:
>
> ```
> # chkconfig ypbind off
> ```
>
> The NIS server package is not installed by default. In the event that it was installed at some point, remove it from the system by executing the command:
>
> ```
> # yum erase ypserv
> ```
>
> **CCE 3705-1, 4348-9**

The Network Information Service (NIS), also known as "Yellow Pages" (YP), and its successor NIS+ have been made obsolete by Kerberos, LDAP, and other modern centralized authentication services. NIS should not be used because it suffers from security problems inherent in its design, such as inadequate protection of important authentication information.

3.2.5 TFTP Server

> Is there an operational need to run the deprecated TFTP server software? If not, ensure that it is removed from the system:
>
> ```
> # yum erase tftp-server
> ```
>
> **CCE 4273-9, 3916-4**

TFTP is a lightweight version of the FTP protocol which has traditionally been used to configure networking equipment. However, TFTP provides little security, and modern versions of networking operating systems frequently support configuration via SSH or other more secure protocols. A TFTP server should be run only if no more secure method of supporting existing equipment can be found.

3.2.6 Talk

The Talk software makes it possible for a user to send messages to the terminal session of another user on another system. The `talk-server` package is not installed by default, although the `talk` client package is. Both are obsolete and can be removed.

3.2.6.1 Remove `talk-server` Package

> To remove the talk daemons from the system, run the following command:
>
> ```
> # yum erase talk-server
> ```

3.2.6.2   Remove `talk` Package

> To remove the talk daemons from the system, run the following command:
>
> ```
> # yum erase talk
> ```

3.3   Base Services

This section addresses the base services that are configured to start up on boot in a RHEL5 default installation. Some of these services listen on the network and should be treated with particular discretion. The other services are local system utilities that may or may not be extraneous. Each of these services should be disabled if not required.

3.3.1   Installation Helper Service (`firstboot`)

Firstboot is a daemon specific to the Red Hat installation process. It handles "one-time" configuration following successful installation of the operating system. As such, there is no reason for this service to remain enabled.

> Disable firstboot by issuing the command:
>
> ```
> # chkconfig firstboot off
> ```
>
> **CCE 3412-4**

3.3.2   Console Mouse Service (gpm)

GPM is the service that controls the *text console* mouse pointer. (The X Windows mouse pointer is unaffected by this service.)

> If mouse functionality in the console is not required, disable this service:
>
> ```
> # chkconfig gpm off
> ```
>
> **CCE 4229-1**

Although it is preferable to run as few services as possible, the console mouse pointer can be useful for preventing administrator mistakes in runlevel 3 by enabling copy-and-paste operations.

3.3.3   Interrupt Distribution on Multiprocessor Systems (`irqbalance`)

The goal of the irqbalance service is to optimize the balance between power savings and performance through distribution of hardware interrupts across multiple processors.

> In a server environment with multiple processors, this provides a useful service and should be left enabled. If a machine has only one processor, the service may be disabled:
>
> ```
> # chkconfig irqbalance off
> ```

CCE 4123-6

3.3.4   ISDN Support (`isdn`)

The ISDN service facilitates Internet connectivity in the presence of an ISDN modem.

If an ISDN modem is not being used, disable this service:

```
# chkconfig isdn off
```

CCE 14825-4

3.3.4.1   Remove the isdn4k-utils Package if Possible

If the `isdn` service will not be used, then the `isdn4k-utils` package can be deleted:

```
# yum erase isdn4k-utils
```

The package also contains a setuid program as discussed in Section 2.2.3.4.

3.3.5   Kdump Kernel Crash Analyzer (`kdump`)

Kdump is a new kernel crash dump analyzer. It uses kexec to boot a secondary kernel ("capture" kernel) following a system crash. The kernel dump from the system crash is loaded into the capture kernel for analysis.

Unless the system is used for kernel development or testing, disable the service:

```
# chkconfig kdump off
```

CCE 3425-6

3.3.6   Kudzu Hardware Probing Utility (`kudzu`)

Is there a mission-critical reason for console users to add new hardware to the system? If not:

```
# chkconfig kudzu off
```

CCE 4211-9

Kudzu, Red Hat's hardware detection program, represents an unnecessary security risk as it allows unprivileged users to perform hardware configuration without authorization. Unless this specific functionality is required, Kudzu should be disabled.

3.3.7   Software RAID Monitor (`mdmonitor`)

The mdmonitor service is used for monitoring a *software* RAID (hardware RAID setups do not use this service). This service is extraneous unless software RAID is in use (which is not common).

If software RAID monitoring is not required, disable this service:

```
# chkconfig mdmonitor off
```

CCE 3854-7

3.3.8   IA32 Microcode Utility (`microcode_ctl`)

`microcode_ctl` is a microcode utility for use with Intel IA32 processors (Pentium Pro, PII, Celeron, PIII, Xeon, Pentium 4, etc)

If the system is not running an Intel IA32 processor, disable this service:

```
# chkconfig microcode_ctl off
```

CCE 4356-2

3.3.9   Network Service (`network`)

The network service allows associated network interfaces to access the network. This section contains general guidance for controlling the operation of the service. For kernel parameters which affect networking, see Section 2.5.1. For detailed configuration of IPv6, see Section 2.5.3.

CCE 4369-5

3.3.9.1   Disable All Networking if Not Needed

If the system is a standalone machine with no need for network access or even communication over the loopback device, then disable this service:

```
# chkconfig network off
```

3.3.9.2   Disable All External Network Interfaces if Not Needed

If the system does not require network communications but still needs to use the loopback interface, remove all files of the form `ifcfg-interface` except for `ifcfg-lo` from `/etc/sysconfig/network-scripts`:

```
# rm /etc/sysconfig/network-scripts/ifcfg-interface
```

3.3.9.3 Disable Zeroconf Networking

Zeroconf networking allows the system to assign itself an IP address and engage in IP communication without a statically-assigned address or even a DHCP server. Automatic address assignment via Zeroconf (or DHCP) is not recommended.

> To disable Zeroconf automatic route assignment in the 169.245.0.0 subnet, add or correct the following line in /etc/sysconfig/network:
>
> ```
> NOZEROCONF=yes
> ```
>
> **CCE 14054-1**

Zeroconf addresses are in the network 169.254.0.0. The networking scripts add entries to the system's routing table for these addresses. Zeroconf address assignment commonly occurs when the system is configured to use DHCP but fails to receive an address assignment from the DHCP server.

3.3.10 Smart Card Support (pcscd)

The pcscd service provides support for Smart Cards and Smart Card Readers.

> If Smart Cards are not in use on the system, disable this service:
>
> ```
> # chkconfig pcscd off
> ```
>
> **CCE 4100-4**

3.3.11 SMART Disk Monitoring Support (smartd)

SMART (Self-Monitoring, Analysis, and Reporting Technology) is a feature of hard drives that allows them to detect symptoms of disk failure and relay an appropriate warning. This technology is considered to bring relatively low security risk, and can be useful.

> Leave this service running if the system's hard drives are SMART-capable. Otherwise, disable it:
>
> ```
> # chkconfig smartd off
> ```
>
> **CCE 3455-3**

3.3.12 Boot Caching (readahead_early/readahead_later)

The following services provide one-time caching of files belonging to some boot services, with the goal of allowing the system to boot faster.

> It is recommended that this service be disabled on most machines:
>
> ```
> # chkconfig readahead_early off
> # chkconfig readahead_later off
> ```
>
> **CCE 4421-4, 4302-6**

The `readahead` services do not substantially increase a system's risk exposure, but they also do not provide great benefit. Unless the system is running a specialized application for which the file caching substantially improves system boot time, this guide recommends disabling the services.

3.3.13   Application Support Services

The following services are software projects of freedesktop.org that are meant to provide system integration through a series of common APIs for applications. They are heavily integrated into the X Windows environment. If the system is not using X Windows, these services can typically be disabled.

3.3.13.1   D-Bus IPC Service (`messagebus`)

D-Bus is an IPC mechanism that provides a common channel for inter-process communication.

If no services which require D-Bus are in use, disable this service:

```
# chkconfig messagebus off
```

CCE 3822-4

A number of default services make use of D-Bus, including X Windows (Section 3.6), Bluetooth (Section 3.3.14) and Avahi (Section 3.7). This guide recommends that D-Bus and all its dependencies be disabled unless there is a mission-critical need for them.

Stricter configuration of D-Bus is possible and documented in the man page `dbus-daemon(1)`. D-Bus maintains two separate configuration files, located in `/etc/dbus-1/`, one for system-specific configuration and the other for session-specific configuration.

3.3.13.2   HAL Daemon (`haldaemon`)

The haldaemon service provides a dynamic way of managing device interfaces. It automates device configuration and provides an API for making devices accessible to applications through the D-Bus interface.

CCE 4364-6

3.3.13.2.1   Disable HAL Daemon if Possible

HAL provides valuable attack surfaces to attackers as an intermediary to privileged operations and should be disabled unless necessary:

```
# chkconfig haldaemon off
```

3.3.13.2.2   Configure HAL Daemon if Necessary

HAL provides a limited user the ability to mount system devices. This is primarily used by X utilities such as `gnome-volume-manager` to perform automounting of removable media.

HAL configuration is currently only possible through a series of fdi files located in `/usr/share/hal/fdi/`

Note: The HAL future road map includes a mandatory framework for managing administrative privileges called PolicyKit.

> To prevent users from accessing devices through HAL, create the file
>
> `/etc/hal/fdi/policy/99-policy-all-drives.fdi`
>
> with the contents:
>
> ```xml
> <?xml version="1.0" encoding="UTF-8"?>
> <deviceinfo version="0.2">
>   <device>
>     <match key="info.capabilities" contains="volume">
>       <merge key="volume.ignore" type="bool">true</merge>
>     </match>
>   </device>
> </deviceinfo>
> ```

The above code matches any device labeled with the `volume` capability (any device capable of being mounted will be labeled this way) and sets the corresponding `volume.ignore` key to `true`, indicating that the volume should be ignored. This both makes the volume invisible to the UI, and denies mount attempts by unprivileged users.

3.3.14 Bluetooth Support

Bluetooth provides a way to transfer information between devices such as mobile phones, laptops, PCs, printers, digital cameras, and video game consoles over a short-range wireless link. Any wireless communication presents a serious security risk to sensitive or classified systems. Section 2.5.2 contains information on the related topic of wireless networking.

Removal of hardware is the only way to ensure that the Bluetooth wireless capability remains disabled. If it is completely impractical to remove the Bluetooth hardware module, and site policy still allows the device to enter sensitive spaces, every effort to disable the capability via software should be made. In general, acquisition policy should include provisions to prevent the purchase of equipment that will be used in sensitive spaces and includes Bluetooth capabilities.

3.3.14.1 Bluetooth Host Controller Interface Daemon (`bluetooth`)

The bluetooth service enables the system to use Bluetooth devices.

> If the system requires no Bluetooth devices, disable this service:
>
> ```
> # chkconfig bluetooth off
> ```
>
> **CCE 4355-4**

3.3.14.2 Bluetooth Input Devices (`hidd`)

The hidd service provides support for Bluetooth input devices.

If the system has no Bluetooth input devices (e.g. wireless keyboard or mouse), disable this service:

```
# chkconfig hidd off
```

CCE 4377-8

3.3.14.3   Disable Bluetooth Kernel Modules

The kernel's module loading system can be configured to prevent loading of the Bluetooth module.

Add the following to `/etc/modprobe.conf` to prevent the loading of the Bluetooth module:

```
alias net-pf-31 off
alias bluetooth off
```

CCE 14948-4

The unexpected name, `net-pf-31`, is a result of how the kernel requests modules for network protocol families; it is simply an alias for the bluetooth module.

3.3.15   Power Management Support

The following services provide an interface to power management functions. These functions include monitoring battery power, system hibernate/suspend, CPU throttling, and various power-save utilities.

3.3.15.1   Advanced Power Management Subsystem (`apmd`)

The apmd service provides last generation power management support.

If the system is capable of ACPI support, or if power management is not necessary, disable this service:

```
# chkconfig apmd off
```

CCE 4289-5

APM is being replaced by ACPI and should be considered deprecated. As such, it can be disabled if ACPI is supported by your hardware and kernel. If the file `/proc/acpi/info` exists and contains ACPI version information, then APM can safely be disabled without loss of functionality.

3.3.15.2   Advanced Configuration and Power Interface (`acpid`)

The acpid service provides next generation power management support.

Unless power management features are not necessary, leave this service enabled.

CCE 4298-6

3.3.15.3 CPU Throttling (`cpuspeed`)

The cpuspeed service uses hardware support to throttle the CPU when the system is idle.

> Unless CPU power optimization is unnecessary, leave this service enabled.
>
> **CCE 4051-9**

3.3.16 Infrared Communications (`irda`)

The `irda` service provides short-range wireless communications for systems with infrared hardware support. The need for IR communication is uncommon and is being superceded by Bluetooth for many applications. As with any wireless communications, it presents an attacker with the ability to communicate with the system and should be disabled unless required.

3.3.16.1 Disable the irda Service if Possible

> Disable the `irda` service unless there is a compelling need for it:
>
> ```
> # chkconfig irda off
> ```

3.3.16.2 Remove the irda-utils Package if Possible

> If the `irda` service will not be used, then the `irda-utils` package can be deleted:
>
> ```
> # yum erase irda-utils
> ```

3.3.17 Raw Devices (`rawdevices`)

The `rawdevices` service assigns raw devices to block devices and is commonly used by database systems. As such, it should not be activated on systems such as desktops.

3.3.17.1 Disable the Raw Devices Daemon if Possible

> Disable the `rawdevices` service unless there is a compelling need for it:
>
> ```
> # chkconfig rawdevices off
> ```

3.4 Cron and At Daemons

The `cron` and `at` services are used to allow commands to be executed at a later time. The `cron` service is required by almost all systems to perform necessary maintenance tasks, while `at` may or may not be required on a given system. Both daemons should be configured defensively.

3.4.1   Disable `anacron` if Possible

> Is this a machine which is designed to run all the time, such as a server or a workstation which is left on at night? If so:
>
> ```
> # yum erase anacron
> ```
>
> CCE 4406-5, 4428-9

The anacron subsystem is designed to provide cron functionality for machines which may be shut down during the normal times that system cron jobs run, frequently in the middle of the night. Laptops and workstations which are shut down at night should keep anacron enabled, so that standard system cron jobs will run when the machine boots.

However, on machines which do not need this additional functionality, anacron represents another piece of privileged software which could contain vulnerabilities. Therefore, it should be removed when possible to reduce system risk.

3.4.2   Restrict Permissions on Files Used by `cron`

> 1. Restrict the permissions on the primary system crontab file:
>
>    ```
>    # chown root:root /etc/crontab
>    # chmod 600 /etc/crontab
>    ```
>
> 2. If anacron has not been removed, restrict the permissions on its primary configuration file:
>
>    ```
>    # chown root:root /etc/anacrontab
>    # chmod 600 /etc/anacrontab
>    ```
>
> 3. Restrict the permission on all system crontab directories:
>
>    ```
>    # cd /etc
>    # chown -R root:root cron.hourly cron.daily cron.weekly cron.monthly cron.d
>    # chmod -R go-rwx    cron.hourly cron.daily cron.weekly cron.monthly cron.d
>    ```
>
> 4. Restrict the permissions on the spool directory for user crontab files:
>
>    ```
>    # chown root:root /var/spool/cron
>    # chmod -R go-rwx /var/spool/cron
>    ```
>
> CCE 4322-4, 4450-3, 4331-5, 3851-3, 4379-4, 4388-5, 4054-3, 4441-2, 4212-7, 4380-2, 3833-1, 3604-6, 4106-1, 3983-4, 3626-9, 4022-0, 4304-2, 4203-6, 4251-5, 3481-9, 4250-7

Cron and anacron make use of a number of configuration files and directories. The system crontabs need only be edited by root, and user crontabs are edited using the setuid root `crontab` command. If unprivileged users can modify system cron configuration files, they may be able to gain elevated privileges, so all unnecessary access to these files should be disabled.

3.4.3   Disable at if Possible

> Unless the at daemon is required, disable it with the following command:
>
> ```
> # chkconfig atd off
> ```
>
> **CCE 14466-7**

Many of the periodic or delayed execution features of the at daemon can be provided through the cron daemon instead.

3.4.4   Restrict at and cron to Authorized Users

> 1. Remove the cron.deny file:
>
>    ```
>    # rm /etc/cron.deny
>    ```
>
> 2. Edit /etc/cron.allow, adding one line for each user allowed to use the crontab command to create cron jobs.
>
> 3. Remove the at.deny file:
>
>    ```
>    # rm /etc/at.deny
>    ```
>
> 4. Edit /etc/at.allow, adding one line for each user allowed to use the at command to create at jobs.

The /etc/cron.allow and /etc/at.allow files contain lists of users who are allowed to use cron and at to delay execution of processes. If these files exist and if the corresponding files /etc/cron.deny and /etc/at.deny do not exist, then only users listed in the relevant allow files can run the crontab and at commands to submit jobs to be run at scheduled intervals.

On many systems, only the system administrator needs the ability to schedule jobs. Note that even if a given user is not listed in cron.allow, cron jobs can still be run as that user. The cron.allow file controls only administrative access to the crontab command for scheduling and modifying cron jobs.

3.5   SSH Server

The SSH protocol is recommended for remote login and remote file transfer. SSH provides confidentiality and integrity for data exchanged between two systems, as well as server authentication, through the use of public key cryptography. The implementation included with the system is called OpenSSH, and more detailed documentation is available from its website, http://www.openssh.org. Its server program is called **sshd** and provided by the RPM package openssh-server.

3.5.1   Disable OpenSSH Server if Possible

Unless the system needs to provide the remote login and file transfer capabilities of SSH, disable and remove the OpenSSH server and its configuration.

3.5.1.1 Disable and Remove OpenSSH Software

> Disable and remove `openssh-server` with the commands:
>
>   # chkconfig sshd off
>   # yum erase openssh-server
>
> **CCE 4268-9, 4272-1**

Users of the system will still be able to use the SSH client program **/usr/bin/ssh** to access SSH servers on other systems.

3.5.1.2 Remove SSH Server `iptables` Firewall Exception

> Edit the files /etc/sysconfig/iptables and /etc/sysconfig/ip6tables (if IPv6 is in use). In each file, locate and delete the line:
>
>   -A RH-Firewall-1-INPUT -m state --state NEW -m tcp -p tcp --dport 22 -j ACCEPT
>
> **CCE 4295-2**

By default, inbound connections to SSH's port are allowed. If the SSH server is not being used, this exception should be removed from the firewall configuration. See Section 2.5.5 for more information about Iptables.

3.5.2 Configure OpenSSH Server if Necessary

If the system needs to act as an SSH server, then certain changes should be made to the OpenSSH daemon configuration file /etc/ssh/sshd_config. The following recommendations can be applied to this file. See the sshd_config(5) man page for more detailed information.

3.5.2.1 Ensure Only Protocol 2 Connections Allowed

Only SSH protocol version 2 connections should be permitted. Version 1 of the protocol contains security vulnerabilities. The default setting shipped in the configuration file is correct, but it is important enough to check.

> Verify that the following line appears:
>
>   Protocol 2
>
> **CCE 4325-7**

3.5.2.2 Limit Users' SSH Access

> By default, the SSH configuration allows any user to access the system. In order to allow all users to login via SSH but deny only a few users, add or correct the following line:
>
>   DenyUsers USER1 USER2

Alternatively, if it is appropriate to allow *only* a few users access to the system via SSH, add or correct the following line:

```
AllowUsers USER1 USER2
```

3.5.2.3 Set Idle Timeout Interval for User Logins

SSH allows administrators to set an idle timeout interval. After this interval has passed, the idle user will be automatically logged out.

Find and edit the following lines in `/etc/ssh/sshd_config` as follows:

```
ClientAliveInterval interval
ClientAliveCountMax 0
```

The timeout *interval* is given in seconds. To have a timeout of 5 minutes, set *interval* to 300.

CCE 14061-6

If a shorter timeout has already been set for the login shell, as in Section 2.3.5.5, that value will preempt any SSH setting made here. Keep in mind that some processes may stop SSH from correctly detecting that the user is idle.

3.5.2.4 Disable `.rhosts` Files

SSH can emulate the behavior of the obsolete `rsh` command in allowing users to enable insecure access to their accounts via `.rhosts` files.

To ensure that this behavior is disabled, add or correct the following line:

```
IgnoreRhosts yes
```

CCE 4475-0

3.5.2.5 Disable Host-Based Authentication

SSH's cryptographic host-based authentication is slightly more secure than `.rhosts` authentication, since hosts are cryptographically authenticated. However, it is not recommended that hosts unilaterally trust one another, even within an organization.

To disable host-based authentication, add or correct the following line:

```
HostbasedAuthentication no
```

CCE 4370-3

3.5.2.6 Disable `root` Login via SSH

The `root` user should never be allowed to login directly over a network, as this both reduces auditable information about who ran privileged commands on the system and allows direct attack attempts on `root`'s password.

> To disable root login via SSH, add or correct the following line:
>
> ```
> PermitRootLogin no
> ```
>
> **CCE 4387-7**

3.5.2.7 Disable Empty Passwords

> To explicitly disallow remote login from accounts with empty passwords, add or correct the following line:
>
> ```
> PermitEmptyPasswords no
> ```
>
> **CCE 3660-8**

Measures should also be taken to disable accounts with empty passwords system-wide, as described in Section 2.3.1.5.1.

3.5.2.8 Enable a Warning Banner

Section 2.3.7 contains information on how to create an appropriate warning banner.

> To enable a warning banner, add or correct the following line:
>
> ```
> Banner /etc/issue
> ```
>
> **CCE 4431-3**

3.5.2.9 Do Not Allow Users to Set Environment Options

> To prevent users from being able to present environment options to the SSH daemon and potentially bypass some access restrictions, add or correct the following line:
>
> ```
> PermitUserEnvironment no
> ```
>
> **CCE 14716-5**

3.5.2.10 Use Only Approved Ciphers in Counter Mode

> Limit the ciphers to those which are FIPS-approved and only use ciphers in counter (CTR) mode. The following line demonstrates use of FIPS-approved ciphers in CTR mode:
>
> ```
> Ciphers aes128-ctr,aes192-ctr,aes256-ctr
> ```
>
> **CCE 14491-5**

The man page `sshd_config(5)` contains a list of the ciphers supported for the current release of the SSH daemon.

3.5.2.11 Strengthen Firewall Configuration if Possible

If the SSH server must only accept connections from the local network, then strengthen the default firewall rule for the SSH service.

> Determine an appropriate network block, *netwk*, and network mask, *mask*, representing the machines on your network which must be allowed to access this SSH server.
>
> Edit the files `/etc/sysconfig/iptables` and `/etc/sysconfig/ip6tables` (if IPv6 is in use). In each file, locate the line:
>
> ```
> -A RH-Firewall-1-INPUT -m state --state NEW -m tcp -p tcp --dport 22 -j ACCEPT
> ```
>
> and replace it with:
>
> ```
> -A RH-Firewall-1-INPUT -s netwk/mask -m state --state NEW -p tcp --dport 22 -j ACCEPT
> ```
>
> If your site uses IPv6, and you are editing `ip6tables`, use the line:
>
> ```
> -A RH-Firewall-1-INPUT -s ipv6netwk::/ipv6mask -m tcp -p tcp --dport 22 -j ACCEPT
> ```
>
> instead because Netfilter does not yet reliably support stateful filtering for IPv6.

See Section 2.5.5 for more information about Iptables configuration.

3.6 X Window System

The X Window System implementation included with the system is called X.org.

3.6.1 Disable X Windows if Possible

Unless there is a mission-critical reason for the machine to run a GUI login screen, prevent X from starting automatically at boot. There is usually no reason to run X Windows on a dedicated server machine, since administrators can login via SSH or on the text console.

3.6.1.1 Disable X Windows at System Boot

> Edit the file `/etc/inittab`, and correct the line `id:5:initdefault:` to:
>
> ```
> id:3:initdefault:
> ```
>
> **CCE 4462-8**

This action changes the default boot runlevel of the system from 5 to 3. These two runlevels should be identical except that runlevel 5 starts X on boot, while runlevel 3 does not.

3.6.1.2 Remove X Windows from the System if Possible

> Remove the X11 RPMs from the system:

```
        # yum groupremove "X Window System"

                                                                          CCE 4422-2
```

As long as X.org remains installed on the system, users can still run X Windows by typing `startx` at the shell prompt. This may run X Windows using configuration settings which are less secure than the system defaults. Therefore, if the machine is a dedicated server which does not need to provide graphical logins at all, it is safest to remove the X.org software entirely.

The command given here will remove over 100 packages. It should safely and effectively remove X from machines which do not need it.

3.6.1.3   Lock Down X Windows `startx` Configuration if Necessary

If X is not to be started at boot time but the software must remain installed, users will be able to run X manually using the `startx` command. In some cases, this runs X with a configuration which is less safe than the default. Follow these instructions to mitigate risk from this configuration.

3.6.1.3.1   Disable X Font Server

```
Disable the xfs helper service:

    # chkconfig xfs off

                                                                          CCE 4448-7
```

The system's X.org requires the X Font Server service (`xfs`) to function. The `xfs` service will be started automatically if X.org is activated via `startx`. Therefore, it is safe to prevent `xfs` from starting at boot when X is disabled, even if users are allowed to run X manually.

3.6.1.3.2   Disable X Window System Listening

```
To prevent X.org from listening for remote connections, create the file /etc/X11/xinit/xserverrc and fill
it with the following line:

    exec X :0 -nolisten tcp $@

                                                                          CCE 4074-1
```

One of X.org's features is the ability to provide remote graphical display. This feature should be disabled unless it is required. If the system uses runlevel 5, which is the default, the GDM display manager starts X safely, with remote listening disabled. However, if X is started from the command line with the `startx` command, then the server will listen for new connections on X's default port, 6000.

See the `xinit(1)`, `startx(1)`, and `Xserver(1)` man pages for more information.

3.6.2   Configure X Windows if Necessary

If there is a mission-critical reason for this machine to run a GUI, improve the security of the default X configuration by following the guidance in this section.

3.6.2.1 Create Warning Banners for GUI Login Users

> Edit the file /etc/gdm/custom.conf. Locate the [greeter] section, and correct that section to contain the lines:
>
> ```
> [greeter]
> InfoMsgFile=/etc/issue
> ```
>
> **CCE 3717-6**

See Section 2.3.7 for an explanation of banner file use. This setting will cause the system greeting banner to be displayed in a box prior to GUI login. If the default banner font is inappropriate, it can be changed by specifying the InfoMsgFont directive as well, for instance:

```
InfoMsgFont=Sans 12
```

3.7 Avahi Server

The Avahi daemon implements the DNS Service Discovery and Multicast DNS protocols, which provide service and host discovery on a network. It allows a system to automatically identify resources on the network, such as printers or web servers. This capability is also known as mDNSresponder and is a major part of Zeroconf networking. By default, it is enabled.

3.7.1 Disable Avahi Server if Possible

Because the Avahi daemon service keeps an open network port, it is subject to network attacks. Disabling it is particularly important to reduce the system's vulnerability to such attacks.

3.7.1.1 Disable Avahi Server Software

> Issue the command:
>
> ```
> # chkconfig avahi-daemon off
> ```
>
> **CCE 4365-3**

3.7.1.2 Remove Avahi Server `iptables` Firewall Exception

> Edit the files /etc/sysconfig/iptables and /etc/sysconfig/ip6tables (if IPv6 is in use). In each file, locate and delete the line:
>
> ```
> -A RH-Firewall-1-INPUT -p udp --dport 5353 -d 224.0.0.251 -j ACCEPT
> ```

By default, inbound connections to Avahi's port are allowed. If the Avahi server is not being used, this exception should be removed from the firewall configuration. See Section 2.5.5 for more information about the Iptables firewall.

3.7.2 Configure Avahi if Necessary

If your system requires the Avahi daemon, its configuration can be restricted to improve security. The Avahi daemon configuration file is `/etc/avahi/avahi-daemon.conf`. The following security recommendations should be applied to this file. See the `avahi-daemon.conf`(5) man page or documentation at http://www.avahi.org for more detailed information about the configuration options.

3.7.2.1 Serve Only via Required Protocol

The default setting in the configuration file allows Avahi to use both IPv4 and IPv6 sockets.

> If you are using only IPv4, edit `/etc/avahi/avahi-daemon.conf` and ensure the following line exists in the [`server`] section:
>
> ```
> use-ipv6=no
> ```
>
> Similarly, if you are using only IPv6, disable IPv4 sockets with the line:
>
> ```
> use-ipv4=no
> ```
>
> **CCE 4136-8, 4409-9**

3.7.2.2 Check Responses' TTL Field

Avahi can be set to ignore IP packets unless their TTL field is 255.

> To make Avahi ignore packets unless the TTL field is 255, edit `/etc/avahi/avahi-daemon.conf` and ensure the following line appears in the [`server`] section:
>
> ```
> check-response-ttl=yes
> ```
>
> **CCE 4426-3**

This helps to ensure that only mDNS responses from the local network are processed, because the TTL field in a packet is decremented from its initial value of 255 whenever it is routed from one network to another. Although a properly-configured router or firewall should not allow mDNS packets into the local network at all, this option provides another check to ensure they are not trusted.

3.7.2.3 Prevent Other Programs from Using Avahi's Port

Avahi can stop other mDNS stacks from running on the host by preventing other processes from binding to port 5353.

> To prevent other mDNS stacks from running, edit `/etc/avahi/avahi-daemon.conf` and ensure the following line appears in the [`server`] section:
>
> ```
> disallow-other-stacks=yes
> ```
>
> **CCE 4193-9**

This is designed to help ensure that only Avahi is responsible for mDNS traffic coming from that port on the system.

3.7.2.4 Disable Publishing if Possible

The default setting in the configuration file allows the `avahi-daemon` to send information about the local host, such as its address records and the services it offers, to the local network.

> To stop sending this information but still allow Avahi to query the network for services, ensure the configuration file includes the following line in the `[publish]` section:
>
> ```
> disable-publishing=yes
> ```
>
> **CCE 4444-6**

This line may be particularly useful if Avahi is needed for printer discovery, but not to advertise services. This configuration is highly recommended for client systems that should not advertise their services (or existence).

3.7.2.5 Restrict Published Information

If it is necessary to publish some information to the network, it should not be joined by any extraneous information, or by information supplied by a non-trusted source on the system.

> Prevent user applications from using Avahi to publish services by adding or correcting the following line in the `[publish]` section:
>
> ```
> disable-user-service-publishing=yes
> ```
>
> Implement as many of the following lines as possible, to restrict the information published by Avahi:
>
> ```
> publish-addresses=no
> publish-hinfo=no
> publish-workstation=no
> publish-domain=no
> ```
>
> Inspect the files in the directory `/etc/avahi/services/`. Unless there is an operational need to publish information about each of these services, delete the corresponding file.
>
> **CCE 4352-1, 4433-9, 4451-1, 4341-4, 4358-8**

These options should be used even if publishing is disabled entirely via `disable-publishing`, since that option prevents publishing attempts from succeeding, while these options prevent the attempts from being made in the first place. Using both approaches is recommended for completeness.

3.8 Print Support

The Common Unix Printing System (CUPS) service provides both local and network printing support. A system running the CUPS service can accept print jobs from other systems, process them, and send them to the appropriate printer. It also provides an interface for remote administration through a web browser. The CUPS service is installed and activated by default. The project homepage and more detailed documentation are available at `http://www.cups.org`.

The HP Linux Imaging and Printing service (HPLIP) is a separate package that provides support for some of the additional features that HP printers provide that CUPS may not necessarily support. It relies upon the CUPS service.

3.8.1   Disable the CUPS Service if Possible

> Do you need the ability to print from this machine or to allow others to print to it? If not:
>
> ```
> # chkconfig cups off
> ```
>
> CCE 4112-9, 3755-6

3.8.2   Disable Firewall Access to Printing Service if Possible

> Does this system need to operate as a network print server? If not, edit the files `/etc/sysconfig/iptables` and `/etc/sysconfig/ip6tables` (if IPv6 is in use). In each file, locate and delete the lines:
>
> ```
> -A RH-Firewall-1-INPUT -p udp -m udp --dport 631 -j ACCEPT
> -A RH-Firewall-1-INPUT -p tcp -m tcp --dport 631 -j ACCEPT
> ```
>
> CCE 3649-1

By default, inbound connections to the Internet Printing Protocol port are allowed. If the print server does not need to be accessed, either because the machine is not running the print service at all or because the machine is not providing a remote network printer to other machines, this exception should be removed from the firewall configuration. See Section 2.5.5 for more information about the Iptables firewall.

3.8.3   Configure the CUPS Service if Necessary

CUPS provides the ability to easily share local printers with other machines over the network. It does this by allowing machines to share lists of available printers. Additionally, each machine that runs the CUPS service can potentially act as a print server. Whenever possible, the printer sharing and print server capabilities of CUPS should be limited or disabled. The following recommendations should demonstrate how to do just that.

3.8.3.1   Limit Printer Browsing

By default, CUPS listens on the network for printer list broadcasts on UDP port 631. This functionality is called printer browsing.

3.8.3.1.1   Disable Printer Browsing Entirely if Possible

> To disable printer browsing entirely, edit the CUPS configuration file, located at `/etc/cups/cupsd.conf`:
>
> ```
> Browsing Off
> BrowseAllow none
> ```
>
> CCE 4420-6, 4407-3

The CUPS print service can be configured to broadcast a list of available printers to the network. Other machines on the network, also running the CUPS print service, can be configured to listen to these broadcasts and add and configure these printers for immediate use. By disabling this browsing capability, the machine will no longer generate or receive such broadcasts.

3.8.3.1.2 Limit Printer Browsing to a Particular Subnet if Necessary

It is possible to disable outgoing printer list broadcasts without affecting incoming broadcasts from other machines. To do so, open the CUPS configuration file, located at `/etc/cups/cupsd.conf`. Look for the line that begins with `BrowseAddress` and remove it. The line will look like the following:

```
BrowseAddress @LOCAL
```

If the intent is not to block printer sharing, but to limit it to a particular set of machines, you can limit the UDP printer broadcasts to trusted network addresses.

```
BrowseAddress ip-address:631
```

Likewise, to ignore incoming UDP printer list broadcasts, or to limit the set of machines to listen to, use the `BrowseAllow` and `BrowseDeny` directives.

```
BrowseDeny all
BrowseAllow ip-address
```

This combination will deny incoming broadcasts from any machine except those that are explicitly allowed with `BrowseAllow`.

By default, when printer sharing is enabled, CUPS will broadcast to every network that its host machine is connected to through all available network interfaces on port 631. It will also listen to incoming broadcasts from other machines on the network. Either list one `BrowseAddress` line for each client machine and one `BrowseAllow` line for each print server or use one of the supported shorthand notations that the CUPS service recognizes. Please see the `cupsd.conf(5)` man page or the documentation provided at http://www.cups.org for more information on other ways to format these directives.

3.8.3.2 Disable Print Server Capabilities if Possible

Disabling the print server capabilities in this manner will also disable the Web Administration interface.

To prevent remote users from potentially connecting to and using locally configured printers, disable the CUPS print server sharing capabilities. To do so, limit how the server will listen for print jobs by removing the more generic `port` directive from `/etc/cups/cupsd.conf`:

```
Port 631
```

and replacing it with the `Listen` directive:

```
Listen localhost:631
```

This will prevent remote users from printing to locally configured printers while still allowing local users on the machine to print normally.

By default, locally configured printers will not be shared over the network, but if this functionality has somehow been enabled, these recommendations will disable it again. Be sure to disable outgoing printer list broadcasts, or remote users will still be able to see the locally configured printers, even if they cannot actually print to them. To limit print serving to a particular set of users, use the `Policy` directive.

3.8.3.3 Limit Access to the Web Administration Interface

> By default, access to the CUPS web administration interface is limited to the local machine. It is recommended that this not be changed, especially since the authentication mechanisms that CUPS provides are limited in their effectiveness. If it is absolutely necessary to allow remote users to administer locally installed printers, be sure to limit that access as much as possible by taking advantage of the `Location` and `Policy` directive blocks.
>
> For example, to enable remote access for *ip-address* for user *username*, modify each of the Location and Policy directive blocks as follows:
>
> ```
> <Location />
> AuthType Basic
> Require user username
>
> Order allow,deny
> Allow localhost
> Allow ip-address
> </Location>
> ```
>
> As with the `BrowseAllow` directive, use one `Allow` directive for each machine that needs access or use one of the available CUPS directive definition shortcuts to enable access from a class of machines at once. The `Require user` directive can take a list of individual users, a group of users (prefixed with @), or the shorthand `valid-user`.

Host-based authentication has known limitations, especially since IP addresses are easy to spoof. Requiring users to authenticate themselves can alleviate this problem, but it cannot eliminate it. Do not use the root account to manage and administer printers. Create a separate account for this purpose and limit access to valid users with `Require valid-user` or `Require user` *printeradmin*.

3.8.3.4 Take Further Security Measures When Appropriate

Whenever possible, limit outside networks' access to port 631. Consider using CUPS directives that limit the number of incoming clients, such as `MaxClients` or `MaxClientsPerHost`. Additionally, there are a series of `Policy` and `Location` directives intended to limit which users can perform different printing tasks. When used together, these may help to mitigate the possibility of a denial of service attack. See `cupsd.conf(5)` for a full list of possible directives.

3.8.4 The HP Linux Imaging and Printing (HPLIP) Toolkit

The HPLIP package is an HP printing support utility that is installed and enabled in a default installation. The HPLIP package is comprised of two separate components. The first is the main HPLIP service and the second is a smaller subcomponent called HPIJS. HPLIP is a feature-oriented network service that provides higher level printing support (such as bi-directional I/O, scanning, photo card, and toolbox functionality). HPIJS is a lower level basic printing driver that provides basic support for non-PostScript HP printers.

3.8.4.1   Disable HPLIP Service if Possible

Since the HPIJS driver will still function without the added HPLIP service, HPLIP should be disabled unless the specific higher level functions that HPLIP provides are needed by a non-PostScript HP printer on the system.

```
# chkconfig hplip off
```

CCE 4425-5

Note: If installing the HPLIP package from scratch, it should be noted that HPIJS can be installed directly without HPLIP. Please see the FAQ at the HPLIP web site at `http://hplip.sourceforge.net/faqs.html` for more information on how to do this.

3.9   DHCP

The Dynamic Host Configuration Protocol (DHCP) allows systems to request and obtain an IP address and many other parameters from a server.

In general, sites use DHCP either to allow a large pool of mobile or unknown machines to share a limited number of IP addresses, or to standardize installations by avoiding static, individual IP address configuration on hosts. It is recommended that sites avoid DHCP as much as possible. Since DHCP authentication is not well-supported, DHCP clients are open to attacks from rogue DHCP servers. Such servers can give clients incorrect information (e.g. malicious DNS server addresses) which could lead to their compromise.

If a machine must act as a DHCP client or server, configure it defensively using the guidance in this section. This guide recommends configuring networking on clients by manually editing the appropriate files under `/etc/sysconfig`. It is also possible to use the graphical front-end programs `system-config-network` and `system-config-network-tui`, but these programs rewrite configuration files from scratch based on their defaults – destroying any manual changes – and should therefore be used with caution.

3.9.1   Disable DHCP Client if Possible

For each interface *IFACE* on the system (e.g. eth0), edit `/etc/sysconfig/network-scripts/ifcfg-`*IFACE* and make the following changes:

1. Correct the `BOOTPROTO` line to read:

   ```
   BOOTPROTO=static
   ```

2. Add or correct the following lines, substituting the appropriate values based on your site's addressing scheme:

   ```
   NETMASK=255.255.255.0
   IPADDR=192.168.1.2
   GATEWAY=192.168.1.1
   ```

CCE 4191-3

DHCP is the default network configuration method provided by the system installer, so it may be enabled on many systems.

3.9.2   Configure DHCP Client if Necessary

If DHCP must be used, then certain configuration changes can minimize the amount of information it receives and applies from the network, and thus the amount of incorrect information a rogue DHCP server could successfully distribute.

For more information on configuring `dhclient`, see the `dhclient(8)` and `dhclient.conf(5)` man pages.

3.9.2.1   Minimize the DHCP-Configured Options

Create the file `/etc/dhclient.conf`, and add an appropriate setting for each of the ten configuration settings which can be obtained via DHCP. For each setting, *setting*, do one of the following:

- If the setting should *not* be configured remotely by the DHCP server, select an appropriate static value, and add the line:

    ```
    supersede setting value;
    ```

- If the setting should be configured remotely by the DHCP server, add the lines:

    ```
    request setting;
    require setting;
    ```

For example, suppose the DHCP server should provide only the IP address itself and the subnet mask. Then the entire file should look like:

```
supersede domain-name "example.com";
supersede domain-name-servers 192.168.1.2;
supersede nis-domain "";
supersede nis-servers "";
supersede ntp-servers "ntp.example.com";
supersede routers 192.168.1.1;
supersede time-offset -18000;

request subnet-mask;
require subnet-mask;
```

By default, the DHCP client program, `dhclient`, requests and applies ten configuration options (in addition to the IP address) from the DHCP server: `subnet-mask`, `broadcast-address`, `time-offset`, `routers`, `domain-name`, `domain-name-servers`, `host-name`, `nis-domain`, `nis-servers`, and `ntp-servers`.

Many of the options requested and applied by `dhclient` may be the same for every system on a network. It is recommended that almost all configuration options be assigned statically, and only options which must vary on a host-by-host basis be assigned via DHCP. This limits the damage which can be done by a rogue DHCP server.

If appropriate for your site, it is also possible to supersede the `host-name` directive in `/etc/dhclient.conf`, establishing a static hostname for the machine. However, `dhclient` does not use the host name option provided by the DHCP server (instead using the value provided by a reverse DNS lookup).

Note: In this example, the options `nis-servers` and `nis-domain` are set to empty strings, on the assumption that the deprecated NIS protocol is not in use. (See Section 3.2.4.) It is necessary to supersede settings for unused services so that they cannot be set by a hostile DHCP server. If an option is set to an empty string, `dhclient` will typically not attempt to configure the service.

3.9.3 Disable DHCP Server if Possible

If the `dhcp` package has been installed on a machine which does not need to operate as a DHCP server, disable the daemon:

```
# chkconfig dhcpd off
```

If possible, remove the software as well:

```
# yum erase dhcp
```

CCE 4336-4, 4464-4

The DHCP server `dhcpd` is not installed or activated by default. If the software was installed and activated, but the system does not need to act as a DHCP server, it should be disabled and removed. Unmanaged DHCP servers will provide faulty information to clients, interfering with the operation of a legitimate site DHCP server if there is one, or causing misconfigured machines to exhibit unpredictable behavior if there is not.

3.9.4 Configure the DHCP Server if Necessary

If the system must act as a DHCP server, the configuration information it serves should be minimized. Also, support for other protocols and DNS-updating schemes should be explicitly disabled unless needed.

The configuration file for `dhcpd` is called `/etc/dhcpd.conf`. The file begins with a number of global configuration options. The remainder of the file is divided into sections, one for each block of addresses offered by `dhcpd`, each of which contains configuration options specific to that address block.

3.9.4.1 Do Not Use Dynamic DNS

To prevent the DHCP server from receiving DNS information from clients, edit `/etc/dhcpd.conf`, and add or correct the following global option:

```
ddns-update-style none;
```

CCE 4257-2

The Dynamic DNS protocol is used to remotely update the data served by a DNS server. DHCP servers can use Dynamic DNS to publish information about their clients. This setup carries security risks, and its use is not recommended.

If Dynamic DNS must be used despite the risks it poses, it is critical that Dynamic DNS transactions be protected using TSIG or some other cryptographic authentication mechanism. See Section 3.14 for more information about DNS servers, including further information about TSIG and Dynamic DNS. Also see `dhcpd.conf(5)` for more information about protecting the DHCP server from passing along malicious DNS data from its clients.

Note: The `ddns-update-style` option controls only whether the DHCP server will attempt to act as a Dynamic DNS client. As long as the DNS server itself is correctly configured to reject DDNS attempts, an incorrect `ddns-update-style` setting on the client is harmless (but should be fixed as a best practice).

3.9.4.2 Deny Decline Messages

> Edit `/etc/dhcpd.conf` and add or correct the following global option to prevent the DHCP server from responding the DHCPDECLINE messages, if possible:
>
>   deny declines;
>
> **CCE 4403-2**

The DHCPDECLINE message can be sent by a DHCP client to indicate that it does not consider the lease offered by the server to be valid. By issuing many DHCPDECLINE messages, a malicious client can exhaust the DHCP server's pool of IP addresses, causing the DHCP server to forget old address allocations.

3.9.4.3 Deny BOOTP Queries

> Unless your network needs to support older BOOTP clients, disable support for the `bootp` protocol by adding or correcting the global option:
>
>   deny bootp;
>
> **CCE 4345-5**

The `bootp` option tells `dhcpd` to respond to BOOTP queries. If support for this simpler protocol is not needed, it should be disabled to remove attack vectors against the DHCP server.

3.9.4.4 Minimize Served Information

> Edit `/etc/dhcpd.conf`. Examine each address range section within the file, and ensure that the following options are *not* defined unless there is an operational need to provide this information via DHCP:
>
>   option domain-name
>   option domain-name-servers
>   option nis-domain
>   option nis-servers
>   option ntp-servers
>   option routers
>   option time-offset
>
> **CCE 3724-2, 4243-2, 4389-3, 3913-1, 4169-9, 4318-2, 4319-0**

Because the configuration information provided by the DHCP server could be maliciously provided to clients by a rogue DHCP server, the amount of information provided via DHCP should be minimized. Remove these definitions from the DHCP server configuration to ensure that legitimate clients do not unnecessarily rely on DHCP for this information.

Note: By default, the RHEL5 client installation uses DHCP to request much of the above information from the DHCP server. In particular, `domain-name`, `domain-name-servers`, and `routers` are configured via DHCP. These settings are typically necessary for proper network functionality, but are also usually static across machines at a given site. See Section 3.9.2.1 for a description of how to configure static site information within the DHCP client configuration.

3.9.4.5 Configure Logging

> Ensure that the following line exists in `/etc/syslog.conf`:
>
>   daemon.*   /var/log/daemon.log
>
> Configure `logwatch` or other log monitoring tools to summarize error conditions reported by the `dhcpd` process.
>
> **CCE 3733-3**

By default, `dhcpd` logs notices to the `daemon` facility. Sending all `daemon` messages to a dedicated log file is part of the syslog configuration outlined in Section 2.6.1.1.1.

3.9.4.6 Further Resources

- The man pages `dhcpd.conf(5)` and `dhcpd(8)`

- ISC web page `http://isc.org/products/DHCP`

3.10   Network Time Protocol

The Network Time Protocol is used to manage the system clock over a network. Computer clocks are not very accurate, so time will drift on unmanaged systems. Central time protocols can be used both to ensure that time is consistent among a network of machines, and that their time is consistent with the outside world.

Local time synchronization is recommended for all networks. If every machine on your network reliably reports the same time as every other machine, then it is much easier to correlate log messages in case of an attack. In addition, a number of cryptographic protocols (such as Kerberos) use timestamps to prevent certain types of attacks. If your network does not have synchronized time, these protocols may be unreliable or even unusable.

Depending on the specifics of the network, global time accuracy may be just as important as local synchronization, or not very important at all. If your network is connected to the Internet, it is recommended that you make use of a public timeserver, since globally accurate timestamps may be necessary if you need to investigate or respond to an attack which originated outside of your network.

Whether or not you use an outside timeserver, configure the network to have a small number of machines operating as NTP servers, and the remainder obtaining time information from those internal servers.

3.10.1   Select NTP Software

The Network Time Protocol (RFC 1305) is designed to synchronize time with a very high degree of accuracy even on an unreliable network. NTP is therefore a complex protocol. The Simple Network Time Protocol (RFC 4330) implements a subset of NTP which is intended to be good enough to meet the time requirements of most networks.

The primary implementation of NTP comes from `ntp.org`, and is shipped with RHEL5 as the `ntp` RPM. An alternative is OpenNTPD, which is an implementation of SNTP, and which can be obtained as source code from `http://www.openntpd.org`. OpenNTPD may be simpler to configure than the reference NTP implementation, at the cost of the need to install and maintain third-party software.

This guide does not recommend the use of a particular NTP/SNTP software package, but does recommend that some NTP software be selected and installed on all machines. The remainder of this section describes how to securely configure NTP clients and servers, and discusses both the reference NTP implementation and OpenNTPD.

3.10.2   Configure Reference NTP if Appropriate

The `ntp` RPM implements the reference NTP server.

3.10.2.1   Configure an NTP Client

There are a number of options for configuring clients to work with the reference NTP server. It is possible to run `ntpd` as a service (i.e., continuously) on each host, configuring clients so that the `ntp` protocol ignores all network access. This still introduces an additional network listener on client machines, and is therefore not recommended.

This guide instead recommends running `ntpd` periodically via `cron`. It is also possible to run `ntpdate` via `cron` with the -u option, but it is being obsoleted in favor of `ntpd`.

Alternately, even if the server is running the reference NTP implementation, it is possible for clients to access it using SNTP. See Section 3.10.3.2 for information about configuring SNTP clients.

3.10.2.1.1   Set Up Client NTP Configuration File

> A valid configuration file for the client system's `ntpd` must exist at `/etc/ntp.conf`. Ensure that `/etc/ntp.conf` contains the following line, where *ntp-server* is the hostname or IP address of the site NTP server:
>
> ```
> server ntp-server
> ```

Note: The `ntpd` software also includes authentication and encryption support which allows for clients to verify the identity of the server, and thus guarantee the integrity of time data with high probability. See `ntpd` documentation at http://www.ntp.org for more details on implementing this recommended feature.

3.10.2.1.2   Run `ntpd` using Cron

> Create a file `/etc/cron.d/ntpd` containing the following crontab:
>
> ```
> 15 * * * * root /usr/sbin/ntpd -q -u ntp:ntp
> ```
>
> The -q option instructs `ntpd` to exit just after setting the clock, and the -u option instructs it to run as the specified user.
>
> **Note:** When setting the clock for the first time, execute the above command with the -g option, as `ntpd` will refuse to set the clock if it is significantly different from the source.

This crontab will execute `ntpd` to synchronize the time to the NTP server at 15 minutes past every hour. (It is possible to choose a different minute, or to vary the minute between machines in order to avoid heavy traffic to the NTP server.) Hourly synchronization should be sufficiently frequent that clock drift will not be noticeable.

3.10.2.2 Configure an NTP Server

The site's NTP server contacts a central NTP server, probably either one provided by your ISP or a public time server, to obtain accurate time data. The server then allows other machines on your network to request the time data.

The NTP server configuration file is located at `/etc/ntp.conf`.

3.10.2.2.1 Enable the NTP Daemon

If this machine is an NTP server, ensure that `ntpd` is enabled at boot time:

```
# chkconfig ntpd on
```

CCE 4376-0

3.10.2.2.2 Deny All Access to `ntpd` by Default

Edit the file `/etc/ntp.conf`. Prepend or correct the following line:

```
restrict default ignore
```

CCE 4134-3

Since `ntpd` is a complex software package which listens for network connections and runs as root, it must be protected from network access by unauthorized machines. This setting uses `ntpd`'s internal authorization to deny all access to any machine, server or client, which is not specifically authorized by other policy settings.

3.10.2.2.3 Specify a Remote NTP Server for Time Data

Find the IP address, *server-ip*, of an appropriate remote NTP server. Edit the file `/etc/ntp.conf`, and add or correct the following lines:

```
restrict server-ip mask 255.255.255.255 nomodify notrap noquery
server server-ip
```

CCE 4385-1

If your site does not require time data to be accurate, but merely to be synchronized among local machines, this step can be omitted, and the NTP server will default to providing time data from the local clock. However, it is a good idea to periodically synchronize the clock to some source of accurate time, even if it is not appropriate to do so automatically.

The previous step disabled all remote access to this NTP server's state data. This NTP server must contact a remote server to obtain accurate data, so NTP's configuration must allow that remote data to be used to modify the system clock. The `restrict` line changes the default access permissions for that remote server. The `server` line specifies the remote server as the preferred NTP server for time data. If you intend to synchronize to more than one server, specify `restrict` and `server` lines for each server.

Note: It would be possible to specify a hostname, rather than an IP address, for the `server` field. However, the `restrict` setting applies only to network blocks of IP addresses, so it is considered more maintainable to use the IP address in both fields.

3.10.2.2.4   Allow Legitimate NTP Clients to Access the Server

Determine an appropriate network block, *netwk*, and network mask, *mask*, representing the machines on your network which will synchronize to this server. Edit `/etc/ntp.conf` and add the line:

```
restrict netwk mask mask nomodify notrap
```

Edit `/etc/sysconfig/iptables`. Add the following line, ensuring that it appears *before* the final `LOG` and `DROP` lines for the `RH-Firewall-1-INPUT` chain:

```
-A RH-Firewall-1-INPUT -s netwk/mask -m state --state NEW -p udp --dport 123 -j ACCEPT
```

If the clients are spread across more than one netblock, separate `restrict` and `ACCEPT` lines should be added for each netblock.

The iptables configuration is needed because the default iptables configuration does not allow inbound access to any services. See Section 2.5.5 for more information about iptables.

Note: The reference NTP implementation will refuse to serve time data to clients until enough time has elapsed that the server host's time can be assumed to have settled to an accurate value. While testing, wait ten minutes after starting `ntpd` before attempting to synchronize clients.

3.10.3   Configure OpenNTPD if Appropriate

OpenNTPD is an implementation of the SNTP protocol which is provided as a simple alternative to the reference NTP server. Advantages of OpenNTPD include simplicity of configuration and a smaller codebase, though it also lacks many of the management and other protocol features used by the reference NTP server. This simplicity comes at the cost of degraded time accuracy, but SNTP is probably accurate enough for most sites with typical monitoring requirements.

3.10.3.1   Obtain NTP Software

If your site intends to use the OpenNTPD implementation, it is necessary to compile and install the software. (If your site intends to use the reference NTP implementation, no installation is necessary.)

1. Obtain the software by downloading an appropriate source version, `openntpd-version.tar.gz`, from `http://www.openntpd.org/portable.html`.

2. Unpack the source code:

   ```
   $ tar xzf openntpd-version.tar.gz
   ```

3. Configure and compile the source. (By default, the code will be compiled for installation into `/usr/local`):

   ```
   $ cd openntpd-version
   $ ./configure --with-privsep-user=ntp
   $ make
   ```

4. As `root`, install the resulting program into `/usr/local`:

   ```
   # make install
   ```

   CCE 4032-9

The configuration option `--with-privsep-user=ntp` tells OpenNTPD to use the existing system account `ntp` for the non-root portion of its operation.

3.10.3.2 Configure an SNTP Client

OpenNTPD runs only in daemon mode — there is no command line suitable to be run from `cron`. However, this is considered reasonably safe for client use because the daemon does not listen on any network ports by default, and because OpenNTPD is a small codebase with no remote management interface or other complex features.

However, it is possible to run a time-stepping program, such as `rdate(1)`, from `cron` instead of configuring the daemon as outlined in this section.

3.10.3.2.1 Enable the NTP Daemon

Edit the file `/etc/rc.local`. Add or correct the following line:

```
/usr/local/sbin/ntpd -s
```

CCE 4424-8

3.10.3.2.2 Configure the Client NTP Daemon to Use the Local Server

Edit the file `/usr/local/etc/ntpd.conf`. Add or correct the following line:

```
server local-server.example.com
```

where *local-server.example.com* is the hostname of the site's local NTP or SNTP server.

CCE 3487-6

3.10.3.3 Configure an SNTP Server

The SNTP server obtains time data from a remote server, and then listens on a network interface for time queries from local machines.

3.10.3.3.1 Enable the NTP Daemon

Edit the file `/etc/rc.local`. Add or correct the following line:

```
/usr/local/sbin/ntpd -s
```

Since OpenNTPD is third-party software, it does not have a standard startup script, so the daemon is started at boot using the `local` facility.

3.10.3.3.2 Listen for Client Connections

Edit the file `/usr/local/etc/ntpd.conf`. Add or correct the following line:

```
listen on ipaddr
```

where *ipaddr* is the primary IP address of this server.

By default, `ntpd` does not listen for any connections over a network. Listening must be actively enabled on NTP servers so that clients may obtain time data.

3.10.3.3.3 Allow Legitimate NTP Clients to Access the Server

Determine an appropriate network block, *netwk*, and network mask, *mask*, representing the machines on your network which will synchronize to this server.

Edit `/etc/sysconfig/iptables`. Add the following line, ensuring that it appears *before* the final `LOG` and `DROP` lines for the `RH-Firewall-1-INPUT` chain:

```
-A RH-Firewall-1-INPUT -s netwk/mask -m state --state NEW -p udp --dport 123 -j ACCEPT
```

The iptables configuration is needed because the default iptables configuration does not allow inbound access to any services. See Section 2.5.5 for more information about iptables.

3.10.3.3.4 Specify a Remote NTP Server for Time Data

Find the hostname, *server-host*, of an appropriate remote NTP server. Edit the file `/usr/local/etc/ntpd.conf`, and add or correct the following line:

```
server server-host
```

This setting configures `ntpd` to obtain time data from the remote host. To use multiple time servers, add one line for each server.

3.11   Mail Transfer Agent

Mail servers are used to send and receive mail over a network on behalf of site users. Mail is a very common service, and MTAs are frequent targets of network attack. Ensure that machines are not running MTAs unnecessarily, and configure needed MTAs as defensively as possible.

CCE 4416-4

3.11.1   Select Mail Server Software and Configuration

Follow one of the following options for configuring e-mail on the machine, depending on the system's role in the network:

> - If this machine does not need to operate as a mail server, follow the remaining instructions in this section to select either Sendmail or Postfix and see Section 3.11.2 for information on how to ensure this software run only in a submission-only mode. MTA software must still be installed in order to ensure local mail delivery for services such as cron.
>
> - If the machine must operate as a mail server, follow the remaining instructions in this section to select either Sendmail or Postfix and then read the strategies for MTA configuration in Section 3.11.3 for information about configuration options. Then apply both the MTA-independent operating system configuration guidance in Section 3.11.4, and the specific guidance for your MTA in Section 3.11.6 or Section 3.11.5.

Very few machines at any site should be configured to receive mail over a network. However, it may be necessary for most machines at a given site to send e-mail, for instance so that `cron` jobs can report output to an administrator. Postfix and Sendmail support a submission-only mode in which mail can be sent from the machine to a central site MTA (or directly delivered to a local account), but the machine cannot receive mail over a network.

If a Mail Transfer Agent (MTA) is needed, the system default is Sendmail. Postfix, which was written with security in mind, is also available and is preferred. Postfix can be more effectively contained by SELinux as its modular design has resulted in separate processes performing specific actions. More information on these MTAs is available from their respective websites, http://www.sendmail.org and http://www.postfix.org.

The `alternatives` system in RHEL will automatically take care of directing dependent software on the system to use either Postfix or Sendmail if only one is installed. See its man page `alternatives(8)` for more information.

3.11.1.1 Select Postfix as Mail Server Software

By default, systems are installed with Sendmail as the MTA software. To use Postfix instead, run the following commands:

```
# yum install postfix
# yum erase sendmail
```

Postfix is preferred because it was designed with security in mind and can be more effectively contained by SELinux.

CCE 14495-6, 14068-1

Choosing Postfix over Sendmail can also be achieved at system installation time via kickstart, by adding the following lines to the kickstart file in its `%packages` section:

```
postfix
-sendmail
```

3.11.1.2 Select Sendmail as Mail Server Software

By default, systems are installed with Sendmail as the MTA software and so no action is required if Sendmail must be used as the MTA, although Postfix is recommended. If, however, Postfix was installed in addition to Sendmail or in place of it, but there is a compelling need to use Sendmail, run the following commands:

```
# yum install sendmail
# yum erase postfix
```

3.11.2   Configure SMTP For Mail Clients

This section discusses settings for Postfix and Sendmail in a submission-only e-mail configuration.

3.11.2.1   Configure Postfix for Submission-Only Mode

3.11.2.1.1   Disable Listening on the Network

> Edit the file `/etc/postfix/main.cf`. Ensure that only the following `inet_interfaces` line appears:
>
>   inet_interfaces = localhost
>
> **CCE 15018-5**

This ensures that Postfix will only accept mail messages from processes running on the local system, and not from the network.

3.11.2.2   Configure Sendmail for Submission-Only Mode

3.11.2.2.1   Disable the Listening Sendmail Daemon

> Edit the file `/etc/sysconfig/sendmail`. Add or modify the line:
>
>   DAEMON=no
>
> **CCE 4293-7**

The MTA performs two functions: listening over a network for incoming SMTP e-mail requests, and sending mail from the local machine. Since outbound mail may be delayed due to network outages or other problems, the outbound MTA runs in a queue-only mode, in which it periodically attempts to resend any delayed mail. Setting `DAEMON=no` tells `sendmail` to execute only the queue runner on this machine, and never to receive SMTP mail requests.

3.11.2.2.2   Configure Mail Submission if Appropriate

> If it is appropriate to configure mail submission with a central MTA, edit `/etc/mail/submit.cf`. Locate the line beginning with `D{MTAHost}`, and modify it to read:
>
>   D{MTAHost}*mailserver*
>
> where *mailserver* is the hostname of the server to which this machine should forward its outgoing mail.

This suggestion is provided as a simple way to migrate away from a configuration in which each machine at a site runs its own MTA, to a configuration in which client machines do not run listening daemons. If this modification is made to `/etc/mail/submit.cf`, then, when a local process on a machine attempts to send mail, the message will be forwarded to the machine *mailserver* for processing.

Modifying `/etc/mail/submit.cf` directly is only appropriate if your site does not perform any other mailserver customization on clients. If other customization is done, use your usual Sendmail change procedure to define the MTA host.

Note: In addition to making this change on the client, it may also be necessary to reconfigure the MTA on *mailserver* so that it will relay mail on behalf of this host.

3.11.3 Strategies for MTA Security

This section discusses several types of MTA configuration which should be performed in order to protect against attacks involving the mail system. Though configuration syntax will differ depending on which MTA is in use (see Section 3.11.5 for Sendmail configuration syntax and Section 3.11.6 for Postfix), these strategies are generally advisable for any MTA, including ones not covered by this guide.

3.11.3.1 Use Resource Limits to Mitigate Denial of Service

It is often desirable to constrain an attacker's ability to consume a mail server's resources simply by sending otherwise valid mail at a high rate, whether maliciously or accidentally. Relevant resource limits include constraints on: the number of MTA daemons which may run at one time, the rate at which incoming messages may be received, the size and complexity of each message, or the amount of mail queue space which must remain free in order for mail to be delivered.

That last parameter deserves additional explanation. Most MTAs require queue space for temporary files in order to process existing messages in their queues. Therefore, if the queue filesystem is allowed to fill completely in a denial of service, the MTA will not be able to clear its own queue even when the malicious traffic has stopped. This will delay recovery from an attack.

3.11.3.2 Configure SMTP Greeting Banner

When remote mail senders connect to the MTA on port 25, they are greeted by an initial banner as part of the SMTP dialogue. This banner is necessary, but it frequently gives away too much information, including the MTA software which is in use, and sometimes also its version number. Remote mail senders do not need this information in order to send mail, so the banner should be changed to reveal only the hostname (which is already known and may be useful) and the word ESMTP, to indicate that the modern SMTP protocol variant is supported.

3.11.3.3 Control Mail Relaying

The sending of Unsolicited Bulk E-mail, referred to variously as UBE, UCE, or spam, is a major problem on the Internet today. The security implications of spam are that it operates as a Denial of Service attack on legitimate e-mail use. Strategies for fighting spam receipt at your site are complex and quickly evolving, and thus far beyond the scope of this guide. The problem of relaying unauthorized e-mail, however, can and should be addressed by any network-connected site.

Most MTAs perform two functions: to accept mail from remote sites on behalf of local users, and to allow local users to send mail to remote sites. The former function is relatively easy — mail whose recipient address is local can be assumed to be destined for a local user. The latter function is more complex. Since it is typically considered neither secure nor desirable for users to log in to the MTA host itself to send mail, the MTA must be able to remotely accept mail addressed to anyone from the user's workstation. If the MTA is running very old software or is configured poorly, it can be possible for attackers to take advantage of this feature, using your MTA to relay their spam from one remote site to another. This is undesirable for many reasons, not least that your site will quickly be blacklisted as a spam source, leaving you unable to send legitimate e-mail to your correspondents.

The simplest solution described in this guide is to configure the MTA to relay mail only from the local site's address range, and some variant on this is the default for most modern MTAs.

That solution may be insufficient for sites whose users need to send mail from remote machines, for instance while travelling, as well as for sites where mail submission must be accepted from network ranges which are not considered secure, either because authorized machines are unmanaged or because it is possible to connect unauthorized machines to the network.

If remote or mobile hosts are authorized to relay, or if local clients exist in insecure netblocks, the SMTP AUTH protocol should be used to require mail senders to authenticate before submitting messages. For better protection and to allow support for a wide range of authentication mechanisms without sending passwords over a network in clear text, SMTP AUTH transactions should be encrypted using SSL.

Another approach is to require mail to be submitted on port 587, the designated Message Submission Port. Use of a separate port allows the mail relay function to be entirely separated from the mail delivery function. This may become a best practice in the future, but description of how to configure the Message Submission Port is currently beyond the scope of this guide. See RFC 2476 for information about this configuration.

3.11.4   Configure Operating System to Protect Mail Server

The guidance in this section is appropriate for any host which is operating as a site MTA, whether the mail server runs using Sendmail, Postfix, or some other software.

3.11.4.1   Use Separate Hosts for External and Internal Mail if Possible

The mail server is a frequent target of network attack from the outside. However, since all site users receive mail, the mail server must be open to some connection from each inside users. It is strongly recommended that these functions be separated, by having an externally visible mail server which processes all incoming and outgoing mail, then forwards internal mail to a separate machine from which users can access it.

3.11.4.2   Protect the MTA Host from User Access

The mail server contains privileged data belonging to all users and performs a vital network function. Preventing users from logging into this server is a precaution against privilege escalation or denial of service attacks which might compromise the mail service. Take steps to ensure that only system administrators are allowed shell access to the MTA host.

3.11.4.3   Restrict Remote Access to the Mail Spool

If users directly connect to this machine to receive mail, ensure that there is a single, well-secured mechanism for access to the directory `/var/spool/mail` (the directory `/var/mail` is a symlink to this).

Allowing unrestricted access to `/var/spool/mail` can be dangerous, since this directory contains sensitive information belonging to all users. Protocols such as NFS, which have an insecure authorization mechanism by default, should be considered insufficient for these purposes. See Section 3.17 for details on secure configuration of POP3 or IMAP, which are the preferred ways to provide user access to mail.

3.11.4.4   Configure `iptables` to Allow Access to the Mail Server

> Edit `/etc/sysconfig/iptables`. Add the following line, ensuring that it appears *before* the final `LOG` and `DROP` lines for the `RH-Firewall-1-INPUT` chain:
>
> ```
> -A RH-Firewall-1-INPUT -m state --state NEW -p tcp --dport 25 -j ACCEPT
> ```

The default Iptables configuration does not allow inbound access to the SMTP service. This modification allows that access, while keeping other ports on the server in their default protected state. See Section 2.5.5 for more information about Iptables.

3.11.4.5   Verify System Logging and Log Permissions for Mail

> Edit the file `/etc/syslog.conf`. Add or correct the following line if necessary (this is the default):
>
> ```
> mail.*                                    -/var/log/maillog
> ```
>
> Run the following commands to ensure correct permissions on the mail log:
>
> ```
> # chown root:root /var/log/maillog
> # chmod 600 /var/log/maillog
> ```

The mail server logs contain a record of every e-mail which is sent or received on the system, which is considered sensitive information by most sites. It is necessary that these logs be collected for purposes of debugging and statistics, but their contents should be protected from unauthorized access.

3.11.4.6   Configure SSL Certificates for Use with SMTP AUTH

If SMTP AUTH is to be used (see Section 3.11.3.3 for a description of possible anti-relaying mechanisms), the use of SSL to protect credentials in transit is strongly recommended. There are also configurations for which it may be desirable to encrypt all mail in transit from one MTA to another, though such configurations are beyond the scope of this guide. In either event, the steps for creating and installing an SSL certificate are independent of the MTA in use, and are described here.

3.11.4.6.1   Create an SSL Certificate

Note: This step must be performed on your CA system, not on the MTA host itself. If you will have a commercial CA sign certificates, then this step should be performed on a separate, physically secure system devoted to that purpose.

> Change into the CA certificate directory:
>
> ```
> # cd /etc/pki/tls/certs
> ```
>
> Generate a key pair for the mail server:
>
> ```
> # openssl genrsa -out mailserverkey.pem 2048
> ```
>
> Next, generate a certificate signing request (CSR) for the CA to sign, making sure to supply your mail server's fully qualified domain name as the Common Name:

```
# openssl req -new -key mailserverkey.pem -out mailserver.csr
```

Next, the mail server CSR must be signed to create the mail server certificate. You can either send the CSR to an established CA or sign it with your CA.

To sign `mailserver.csr` using your CA:

```
# openssl ca -in mailserver.csr -out mailservercert.pem
```

This step creates a private key, `mailserverkey.pem`, and a public certificate, `mailservercert.pem`. The mail server will use these to prove its identity by demonstrating that it has a certificate which has been signed by a CA. Mail clients at your site should be willing to send their mail only to a server they can authenticate.

3.11.4.6.2   Install the SSL Certificate

Create the PKI directory for mail certificates, if it does not already exist:

```
# mkdir /etc/pki/tls/mail
# chown root:root /etc/pki/tls/mail
# chmod 755 /etc/pki/tls/mail
```

Using removable media or some other secure transmission format, install the files generated in the previous step onto the mail server:

- `/etc/pki/tls/mail/serverkey.pem`: the private key `mailserverkey.pem`

- `/etc/pki/tls/mail/servercert.pem`: the certificate file `mailservercert.pem`

Verify the ownership and permissions of these files:

```
# chown root:root /etc/pki/tls/mail/serverkey.pem
# chown root:root /etc/pki/tls/mail/servercert.pem
# chmod 600 /etc/pki/tls/mail/serverkey.pem
# chmod 644 /etc/pki/tls/mail/servercert.pem
```

Verify that the CA's public certificate file has been installed as `/etc/pki/tls/CA/cacert.pem`, and has the correct permissions:

```
# chown root:root /etc/pki/tls/CA/cacert.pem
# chmod 644 /etc/pki/tls/CA/cacert.pem
```

3.11.5   Configure Sendmail Server if Necessary

When `sendmail` is configured to act as a server for incoming mail, it listens on port 25 for connections, and responds to those connections using the configuration in `/etc/mail/sendmail.cf`. This file has a somewhat opaque format, and modifying it directly is generally not recommended. Instead, the following procedure should be used to modify the `sendmail` configuration:

1. Install the `sendmail-cf` RPM, which is required in order to compile a new configuration file:

   ```
   # yum install sendmail-cf
   ```

2. Edit the M4 source file `/etc/mail/sendmail.mc` as directed by the configuration step you are applying.

3. Inside the directory /etc/mail/, use `make` to build the configuration according to the Makefile provided by Sendmail:

```
# cd /etc/mail
# make sendmail.cf
```

3.11.5.1   Limit Denial of Service Attacks

> Edit /etc/mail/sendmail.mc, and add or correct the following options:
>
> ```
> define(`confMAX_DAEMON_CHILDREN',`40')dnl
> define(`confCONNECTION_RATE_THROTTLE', `3')dnl
> define(`confMIN_FREE_BLOCKS',`20971520')dnl
> define(`confMAX_HEADERS_LENGTH',`51200')dnl
> define(`confMAX_MESSAGE_SIZE',`10485760')dnl
> define(`confMAX_RCPTS_PER_MESSAGE',`100')dnl
> ```

Note: The values given here are examples, and may need to be modified for any particular site, especially one with high e-mail volume.

These configuration options serve to make it more difficult for attackers to consume resources on the MTA host. (See Section 3.11.3.1 for details on why this is done.) The MAX_DAEMON_CHILDREN option limits the number of sendmail processes which may be deployed to handle incoming connections at any one time, while CONNECTION_RATE_THROTTLE limits the number of connections per second which each listener may receive. The MIN_FREE_BLOCKS option stops e-mail receipt when the queue filesystem is close to full. The MAX_HEADERS_LENGTH (bytes), MAX_MESSAGE_SIZE (bytes), and MAX_RCPTS_PER_MESSAGE (distinct recipients) options place bounds on the legal sizes of messages received via SMTP.

3.11.5.2   Configure SMTP Greeting Banner

> Edit /etc/mail/sendmail.mc, and add or correct the following line, substituting an appropriate greeting string for $j:
>
> ```
> define(`confSMTP_LOGIN_MSG', `$j')dnl
> and recompile sendmail's configuration.
> ```

The default greeting banner discloses that the listening mail process is Sendmail rather than some other MTA, and also provides the version number. See Section 2.3.7 for more about warning banners, and Section 3.11.3.2 for strategies regarding SMTP greeting banners in particular.

The Sendmail variable $j contains the hostname of the mail server, which may be an appropriate greeting string for most environments.

3.11.5.3   Control Mail Relaying

This guide will discuss two mechanisms for controlling mail relaying in Sendmail. The /etc/mail/relay-domains file contains a list of hostnames that are allowed to relay mail. Follow the guidance in Section 3.11.5.3.1 to configure relaying for trusted machines.

If there are machines which must be allowed to relay mail, but which cannot be trusted to relay unconditionally, configure SMTP AUTH with TLS support using the guidance in Sections 3.11.5.3.2 and following.

3.11.5.3.1 Configure Trusted Networks and Hosts

- If all machines which share a common domain or subdomain name may relay, then edit `/etc/mail/relay-domains`, adding a line for each domain or subdomain, e.g.:

    ```
    example.com
    trusted-subnet.school.edu
    ...
    ```

- If the machines which are allowed to relay must be specified on a per-host basis, then edit `/etc/mail/relay-domains`, adding a line for each such host:

    ```
    host1.example.com
    host5.subnet.example.com
    smtp.trusted-subnet.school.edu
    ```

    Then edit `/etc/mail/sendmail.mc`, add or correct the line:

    ```
    FEATURE(`relay_hosts_only')dnl
    ```

    and recompile sendmail's configuration.

The file `/etc/mail/relay-domains` must contain only the set of machines for which this MTA should unconditionally relay mail. This configures both inbound and outbound relaying, that is, hosts mentioned in `relay-domains` may send mail through the MTA, and the MTA will also accept inbound mail addressed to such hosts. This is a trust relationship — if spammers gain access to these machines, your site will effectively become an open relay. It is recommended that only machines which are managed by you or by another trusted organization be placed in `relay-domains`, and that users of all other machines be required to use SMTP AUTH to send mail.

Note: The `relay-domains` file must be configured to contain either a list of domains (in which case every host in each of those domains will be allowed to relay) or a list of hosts (in which case each individual relaying host must be listed and the `sendmail.cf` must be reconfigured to interpret the `relay-domains` file in the desired way).

3.11.5.3.2 Require SMTP AUTH Before Relaying from Untrusted Clients

By default, Sendmail uses the Cyrus-SASL library to provide authentication.

To enable the use of SASL authentication for relaying, edit `/etc/mail/sendmail.mc` and add or correct the following settings:

```
TRUST_AUTH_MECH(`LOGIN PLAIN')
define(`confAUTH_MECHANISMS', `LOGIN PLAIN')
```

and recompile `sendmail.cf`.

Then edit `/usr/lib/sasl2/Sendmail.conf` and add or correct the following lines:

```
pwcheck_method: saslauthd
```

Enable the `saslauthd` daemon:

```
# chkconfig saslauthd on
```

The `AUTH_MECHANISMS` configuration option tells sendmail to allow the specified authentication mechanisms to be used during the SMTP dialogue. The two listed mechanisms use SASL to test a password provided by the user. Since these mechanisms transmit plaintext passwords, they should be protected using TLS as described in the next section.

The `TRUST_AUTH_MECH` command tells sendmail that senders who successfully authenticate using the specified mechanism may relay mail through this MTA even if their addresses are not in `relay-domains`.

The file `/usr/lib/sasl/Sendmail.conf` is the Cyrus-SASL configuration file for Sendmail. The `pwcheck_method` directive tells SASL how to find passwords. The simplest method, described here, is to run a separate authentication daemon, `saslauthd`, which is able to communicate with the system authentication service. On Red Hat, `saslauthd` uses PAM by default, which should work in most cases. If you have a centralized authentication system which does not work via PAM, look at the `saslauthd(8)` manpage to determine how to configure `saslauthd` for your environment.

3.11.5.3.3 Require TLS for SMTP AUTH

Edit `/etc/mail/sendmail.mc`, add or correct the following lines:

```
define(`confAUTH_OPTIONS', `A p')dnl
define(`confCACERT_PATH', `/etc/pki/tls/CA')dnl
define(`confCACERT', `/etc/pki/tls/CA/cacert.pem')dnl
define(`confSERVER_CERT', `/etc/pki/tls/mail/servercert.pem')dnl
define(`confSERVER_KEY', `/etc/pki/tls/mail/serverkey.pem')dnl
```

and recompile `sendmail.cf`.

These options, combined with the previous settings, tell Sendmail to protect all SMTP AUTH transactions using TLS. The first four options describe the location of the necessary TLS certificate and key files.

The `AUTH_OPTIONS` parameter configures the SMTP AUTH dialogue. The `A` option is enabled by default, and simply says that authentication is allowed if an appropriate mechanism can be found. The `p` option tells Sendmail to protect against passive attacks. The `PLAIN` and `LOGIN` authentication mechanisms, recommended by this guide for compatibility with PAM, send passwords in the clear. (Cleartext password transmissions are vulnerable to passive attack.) Therefore, if `p` is set, the SMTP daemon will not make the `AUTH` command available until after the client has used the `STARTTLS` command to encrypt the session. If other authentication mechanisms were enabled which did not send passwords in the clear, then TLS would not necessarily be required.

3.11.6 Configure Postfix if Necessary

Postfix stores its configuration files in the directory `/etc/postfix` by default. The primary configuration file is `/etc/postfix/main.cf`. Other files will be introduced as needed.

3.11.6.1 Limit Denial of Service Attacks

Edit `/etc/postfix/main.cf`. Add or correct the following lines:

```
default_process_limit = 100
smtpd_client_connection_count_limit = 10
smtpd_client_connection_rate_limit = 30
queue_minfree = 20971520
```

```
header_size_limit = 51200
message_size_limit = 10485760
smtpd_recipient_limit = 100
```

Note: The values given here are examples, and may need to be modified for any particular site. By default, the Postfix `anvil` process gathers mail receipt statistics. To get information about about what connection rates are typical at your site, look in `/var/log/maillog` for lines with the daemon name `postfix/anvil`.

These configuration options serve to make it more difficult for attackers to consume resources on the MTA host. (See Section 3.11.3.1 for details on why this is done.) The `default_process_limit` parameter controls how many `smtpd` processes can exist at a time, while `smtpd_client_connection_count_limit` controls the number of those which can be occupied by any one remote sender, and `smtpd_client_connection_rate_limit` controls the number of connections any one client can make per minute. By default, local hosts (those in `mynetworks`) are exempted from per-client rate limiting.

The `queue_minfree` parameter establishes a free space threshold, in order to stop e-mail receipt before the queue filesystem is entirely full. The `header_size_limit`, `message_size_limit`, and `smtpd_recipient_limit` parameters place bounds on the legal sizes of messages received via SMTP.

3.11.6.2   Configure SMTP Greeting Banner

Edit `/etc/postfix/main.cf`, and add or correct the following line, substituting some other wording for the banner information if you prefer:

```
smtpd_banner = $myhostname ESMTP
```

The default greeting banner discloses that the listening mail process is Postfix. See Section 2.3.7 for more about warning banners, and Section 3.11.3.2 for strategies regarding SMTP greeting banners in particular.

3.11.6.3   Control Mail Relaying

Postfix's mail relay controls are implemented with the help of the `smtpd_recipient_restrictions` option, which controls the restrictions placed on the SMTP dialogue once the sender and recipient envelope addresses are known.

The guidance in Sections 3.11.6.3.1–3.11.6.3.2 should be applied to all machines. If there are machines which must be allowed to relay mail, but which cannot be trusted to relay unconditionally, configure SMTP AUTH with SSL support using the guidance in Sections 3.11.6.3.3 and following.

3.11.6.3.1   Configure Trusted Networks and Hosts

Edit `/etc/postfix/main.cf`, and configure the contents of the `mynetworks` variable in one of the following ways:

- If any machine in the subnet containing the MTA may be trusted to relay messages, add or correct the line:

  ```
  mynetworks_style = subnet
  ```

- If only the MTA host itself is trusted to relay messages, add or correct:

```
        mynetworks_style = host
```

- If the set of machines which can relay is more complicated, manually specify an entry for each netblock or IP address which is trusted to relay by setting the **mynetworks** variable directly:

```
mynetworks = 10.0.0.0/16 , 192.168.1.0/24 , 127.0.0.1
```

The **mynetworks** variable must contain only the set of machines for which this MTA should unconditionally relay mail. This is a trust relationship — if spammers gain access to these machines, your site will effectively become an open relay. It is recommended that only machines which are managed by you or by another trusted organization be placed in **mynetworks**, and users of all other machines be required to use SMTP AUTH to send mail.

3.11.6.3.2 Allow Unlimited Relaying for Trusted Networks Only

Edit `/etc/postfix/main.cf`, and add or correct the **smtpd_recipient_restrictions** definition so that it contains at least:

```
smtpd_recipient_restrictions =
    ...
  permit_mynetworks,
  reject_unauth_destination,
    ...
```

The full contents of **smtpd_recipient_restrictions** will vary by site, since this is a common place to put spam restrictions and other site-specific options. The **permit_mynetworks** option allows all mail to be relayed from the machines in **mynetworks**. Then, the **reject_unauth_destination** option denies all mail whose destination address is not local, preventing any other machines from relaying. These two options should always appear in this order, and should usually follow one another immediately unless SMTP AUTH is used.

3.11.6.3.3 Require SMTP AUTH Before Relaying from Untrusted Clients

SMTP authentication allows remote clients to relay mail safely by requiring them to authenticate before submitting mail. Postfix's SMTP AUTH uses an authentication library called SASL, which is not part of Postfix itself. This section describes how to configure authentication using the Cyrus-SASL implementation. See below for a discussion of other options.

To enable the use of SASL authentication, edit `/etc/postfix/main.cf` and add or correct the following settings:

```
smtpd_sasl_auth_enable = yes
smtpd_recipient_restrictions =
    ...
  permit_mynetworks,
  permit_sasl_authenticated,
  reject_unauth_destination,
    ...
```

Then edit `/usr/lib/sasl/smtpd.conf` and add or correct the following line with the correct authentication mechanism for SASL to use:

```
    pwcheck_method: saslauthd
```

Enable the `saslauthd` daemon:

```
    # chkconfig saslauthd on
```

Postfix can use either the Cyrus library or Dovecot as a source for SASL authentication. If this host is running Dovecot for some other reason, it is recommended that Dovecot's SASL support be used instead of running the Cyrus code as well. See http://www.postfix.org/SASL_README.html for instructions on implementing that configuration, which is not described in this guide.

In Postfix's configuration, the directive `smtpd_sasl_auth_enable` tells `smtpd` to allow the use of the SMTP AUTH command during the SMTP dialogue, and to support that command by getting authentication information from SASL. The `smtpd_recipient_restrictions` directive is changed so that, if the client is not connecting from a trusted address, it is allowed to attempt authentication (`permit_sasl_authenticated`) in order to relay mail.

The file `/usr/lib/sasl/smtpd.conf` is the Cyrus-SASL configuration file. The `pwcheck_method` directive tells SASL how to find passwords. The simplest method, described above, is to run a separate authentication daemon, `saslauthd`, which is able to communicate with the system authentication system. On RHEL5, `saslauthd` uses PAM by default, which should work in most cases. If you have a centralized authentication system which does not work via PAM, look at the `saslauthd(8)` manpage to find out how to configure `saslauthd` for your environment.

3.11.6.4 Require TLS for SMTP AUTH

Edit `/etc/postfix/main.cf`, and add or correct the following lines:

```
    smtpd_tls_CApath = /etc/pki/tls/CA
    smtpd_tls_CAfile = /etc/pki/tls/CA/cacert.pem
    smtpd_tls_cert_file = /etc/pki/tls/mail/servercert.pem
    smtpd_tls_key_file = /etc/pki/tls/mail/serverkey.pem
    smtpd_tls_security_level = may
    smtpd_tls_auth_only = yes
```

These options tell Postfix to protect all SMTP AUTH transactions using TLS. The first four options describe the locations of the necessary TLS key files.

The `smtpd_tls_security_level` directive tells `smtpd` to allow the STARTTLS command during the SMTP protocol exchange, but not to require it for mail senders. (Unless your site receives mail only from other trusted sites whose sysadmins can be asked to maintain a copy of your site certificate, you do not want to require TLS for all SMTP exchanges.)

The `smtpd_tls_auth_only` directive tells `smtpd` to require the STARTTLS command before allowing the client to attempt to authenticate for relaying using SMTP AUTH. It may not be possible to use this directive if you must allow relaying from non-TLS-capable client software. If this is the case, simply omit that line.

3.12 LDAP

LDAP is a popular directory service, that is, a standardized way of looking up information from a central database. It is relatively simple to configure a RHEL5 machine to obtain authentication information from an LDAP server. If your network uses LDAP for authentication, be sure to configure both clients and servers securely.

3.12.1   Use OpenLDAP to Provide LDAP Service if Possible

The system's default LDAP client/server program is called OpenLDAP. Its documentation is available at the project web page: `http://www.openldap.org`.

3.12.2   Configure OpenLDAP Clients

Before configuring any machine to be an LDAP client, ensure that a working LDAP server is present on the network. See Section 3.12.3 for instructions on configuring an LDAP server.

This guide recommends configuring OpenLDAP clients by manually editing the appropriate configuration files. RHEL5 provides an automated configuration tool called `authconfig` and a graphical wrapper for `authconfig` called `system-config-authentication`. However, these tools do not give sufficient flexibility over configuration. The `authconfig` tools do not allow you to specify locations of SSL certificate files, which is useful when trying to use SSL cleanly across several protocols. They are also overly aggressive in placing services such as netgroups and automounter maps under LDAP control, where it is safer to use LDAP only for services to which it is relevant in your environment.

3.12.2.1   Configure the Appropriate LDAP Parameters for the Domain

Assume the fully qualified host name of your LDAP server is *ldap.example.com* and the base DN of your domain is *dc=example,dc=com* (it is conventional to use the domain name as a base DN). Edit `/etc/ldap.conf`, and add or correct the following lines:

```
base dc=example,dc=com
uri ldap://ldap.example.com/
```

Then edit `/etc/openldap/ldap.conf`, and add or correct the following lines:

```
BASE dc=example,dc=com
URI ldap://ldap.example.com/
```

The machine whose hostname is given here must be configured as an LDAP server, serving data identified by the base DN used here. See Section 3.12.3 for details on configuring an LDAP server.

3.12.2.2   Configure LDAP to Use TLS for All Transactions

1. Ensure a copy of the site's CA certificate has been placed in the file `/etc/pki/tls/CA/cacert.pem`.

2. Configure LDAP to enforce TLS use and to trust certificates signed by the site's CA. First, edit the file `/etc/ldap.conf`, and add or correct the following lines:

```
ssl start_tls
tls_checkpeer yes
tls_cacertdir /etc/pki/tls/CA
tls_cacertfile /etc/pki/tls/CA/cacert.pem
```

Then edit `/etc/openldap/ldap.conf`, and add or correct the following lines:

```
        TLS_CACERTDIR /etc/pki/tls/CA
        TLS_CACERT /etc/pki/tls/CA/cacert.pem
```

CCE 14894-0

Section 2.5.6 describes the system-wide configuration of SSL for your enterprise. It is possible to place your certificate information under some directory other than `/etc/pki/tls`, but using a consistent directory structure across all SSL services at your site is recommended. The LDAP server must be configured with a certificate signed by the CA certificate named here.

3.12.2.3 Configure Authentication Services to Use OpenLDAP

Edit the file `/etc/ldap.conf`, and add or correct the following lines:

```
pam_password md5
```

Edit the file `/etc/nsswitch.conf`, and add or correct the following lines:

```
passwd: files ldap
shadow: files ldap
group: files ldap
```

Edit the file `/etc/pam.d/system-auth-ac`. Make the following changes, which will add references to LDAP in each of the four sections of the file:

- Immediately before the last line in the `auth` section (the one containing `pam_deny.so`), insert the line:

    ```
    auth        sufficient        pam_ldap.so use_first_pass
    ```

- Modify the first line in the `account` section by adding the option `broken_shadow`. The line should then read:

    ```
    account     required        pam_unix.so broken_shadow
    ```

- Immediately before the last line in the `account` section (the one containing `pam_permit.so`), insert the line:

    ```
    account     [default=bad success=ok user_unknown=ignore] pam_ldap.so
    ```

- Immediately before the last line in the `password` section (the one containing `pam_deny.so`), insert the line:

    ```
    password    sufficient        pam_ldap.so use_authtok
    ```

- At the end of the file (after the last line in the `session` section), append the line:

    ```
    session     optional        pam_ldap.so
    ```

The first modification tells LDAP to expect passwords in MD5 hash format, rather than clear text.

Red Hat systems use the file `/etc/nsswitch.conf` to determine the appropriate sources to search for certain kinds of data, such as usernames, groups, hostnames, netgroups, or protocols. It is possible to manage many other types of data using LDAP, but this guide recommends that only usernames (`passwd` data), passwords (`shadow` data), and groups (`group` data) be managed using LDAP. If your site uses netgroups, it may be appropriate to manage these via LDAP as well.

However, data which almost never changes, such as the contents of the `/etc/services` file, is a poor choice for central administration, since it introduces risk with little benefit. It is recommended that the automounter not be used at all, so LDAP control of automounter maps is unlikely to be appropriate.

The file `/etc/pam.d/system-auth-ac` is used by PAM to control access to most authenticated services. The syntax of the PAM configuration file is somewhat cryptic. The lines recommended here have the combined effect of using LDAP to find authentication data for users who cannot be found in the local `/etc/passwd` file. This means that, for instance, it is still possible to use a local `root` password. The details of options such as `broken_shadow`, `use_authtok`, and `use_first_pass` may be looked up in the man pages for the various PAM modules. Their basic effect is to attempt to authenticate given a password against both the local `/etc/shadow` and the central LDAP server, without forcing the user to type the password more than once. PAM configuration is discussed further in Section 2.3.3.

3.12.3   Configure OpenLDAP Server

This section contains guidance on how to configure an OpenLDAP server to securely provide information for use in a centralized authentication service. This is not a comprehensive guide to maintaining an OpenLDAP server, but may be helpful in transitioning to an OpenLDAP infrastructure nonetheless.

3.12.3.1   Install OpenLDAP Server RPM

Is this machine the OpenLDAP server? If so:

```
# yum install openldap-servers
# chkconfig ldap on
```

CCE 3501-4

The `openldap-servers` RPM is not installed by default on RHEL5 machines. It is needed only by the OpenLDAP server, not by the clients which use LDAP for authentication.

3.12.3.2   Configure Domain-Specific Parameters

Edit the file `/etc/openldap/slapd.conf`. Add or correct the following lines:

```
suffix "dc=example,dc=com"
rootdn "cn=Manager,dc=example,dc=com"
```

where *dc=example,dc=com* is the same root you will use on the LDAP clients.

These are basic LDAP configuration directives. The `suffix` parameter gives the root name of all information served by this LDAP server, and should be some name related to your domain. The `rootdn` parameter names LDAP's privileged user, who is allowed to read or write all data managed by this LDAP server.

3.12.3.3   Configure an LDAP Root Password

Ensure that the configuration file has reasonable permissions before putting the hashed root password in that file:

```
# chown root:ldap /etc/openldap/slapd.conf
# chmod 640 /etc/openldap/slapd.conf
```

Generate a hashed password using the `slappasswd` utility:

```
# slappasswd
New password:
Re-enter new password:
```

This will output a hashed password string. Edit the file `/etc/openldap/slapd.conf`, and add or correct the line:

```
rootpw     {SSHA}hashed-password-string
```

Be sure to select a secure password for the LDAP root user, since this user has permission to read and write all LDAP data, so a compromise of the LDAP root password will probably enable a full compromise of your site. Protect configuration files containing the hashed password the same way you would protect other files, such as `/etc/shadow`, which contain hashed authentication data. In addition, be sure to use a reasonably strong hash function, such as SHA-1,[1] rather than an insecure scheme such as crypt.

3.12.3.4   Configure the LDAP Server to Require TLS for All Transactions

Because LDAP queries and responses, particularly those containing authentication information or other sensitive data, must be protected from disclosure or modification while in transit over the network, this guide recommends using SSL to protect all transactions. In order to do this, it is necessary to have a site-wide SSL infrastructure in which a CA certificate is used to verify that other certificates, such as that presented by the LDAP server to its clients, are authentic.

Therefore, this procedure involves using the CA system to create a certificate for the LDAP server, then installing that certificate on the LDAP server and configuring `slapd` to require its use. See Section 2.5.6 for details about the process of creating SSL certificates for use by servers at your site.

3.12.3.4.1   Create the Certificate for the LDAP Server

Note: This step must be performed on the CA system, not on the LDAP server itself.

Change into the CA certificate directory:

```
# cd /etc/pki/tls/certs
```

Generate a key pair for the LDAP server:

```
# openssl genrsa -out ldapserverkey.pem 2048
```

Next, generate a certificate signing request (CSR) for the CA to sign:

```
# openssl req -new -key ldapserverkey.pem -out ldapserver.csr
```

Sign the `ldapserver.csr` request:

```
# openssl ca -in ldapserver.csr -out ldapservercert.pem
```

---

[1]If you are using SHA-1, the hashed password string will begin with "{SHA}" or "{SSHA}".

This step creates a private key, `ldapserverkey.pem`, and a public certificate, `ldapservercert.pem`. The LDAP server will use these to prove its identity by demonstrating that it has a certificate which has been signed by the site CA. LDAP clients at your site should only be willing to accept authentication data from a verified LDAP server.

3.12.3.4.2 Install the Certificate on the LDAP Server

Create the PKI directory for LDAP certificates if it does not already exist:

```
# mkdir /etc/pki/tls/ldap
# chown root:root /etc/pki/tls/ldap
# chmod 755 /etc/pki/tls/ldap
```

Using removable media or some other secure transmission format, install the files generated in the previous step onto the LDAP server:

- `/etc/pki/tls/ldap/serverkey.pem`: the private key `ldapserverkey.pem`

- `/etc/pki/tls/ldap/servercert.pem`: the certificate file `ldapservercert.pem`

Verify the ownership and permissions of these files:

```
# chown root:ldap /etc/pki/tls/ldap/serverkey.pem
# chown root:ldap /etc/pki/tls/ldap/servercert.pem
# chmod 640 /etc/pki/tls/ldap/serverkey.pem
# chmod 640 /etc/pki/tls/ldap/servercert.pem
```

Verify that the CA's public certificate file has been installed as `/etc/pki/tls/CA/cacert.pem`, and has the correct permissions:

```
# mkdir /etc/pki/tls/CA
# chown root:root /etc/pki/tls/CA/cacert.pem
# chmod 644 /etc/pki/tls/CA/cacert.pem
```

CCE 4360-4, 4378-6, 4492-5, 4263-0, 3502-2, 4449-5, 4361-2, 4427-1, 4321-6, 4339-8, 4105-3, 3718-4

As a result of these steps, the LDAP server will have access to its own private certificate and the key with which that certificate is encrypted, and to the public certificate file belonging to the CA. Note that it would be possible for the key to be protected further, so that processes running as `ldap` could not read it. If this were done, the LDAP server process would need to be restarted manually whenever the server rebooted.

3.12.3.4.3 Configure `slapd` to Use the Certificates

Edit the file `/etc/openldap/slapd.conf`. Add or correct the following lines:

```
TLSCACertificateFile /etc/pki/tls/CA/cacert.pem
TLSCertificateFile /etc/pki/tls/ldap/servercert.pem
TLSCertificateKeyFile /etc/pki/tls/ldap/serverkey.pem

security simple_bind=128
```

The first set of lines tell `slapd` where to find the appropriate SSL certificates to present to clients when they request an encrypted transaction. The last setting tells `slapd` never to allow clients to present credentials (i.e.

passwords) in an unencrypted session. It is a good security principle never to allow unencrypted passwords to traverse a network, so ensure that LDAP mandates this.

3.12.3.5 Install Account Information into the LDAP Database

There are many ways to maintain an OpenLDAP database. Methods include:

- Input entries in `ldif(5)` format into a file */path/to/new_entries* , and use `slapadd` to import those entries while `slapd` is *not* running:

  ```
  # slapadd -l /path/to/new_entries
  ```

- Write a script to create and modify LDAP entries by connecting to the LDAP server normally. The Perl `Net::LDAP` module is appropriate for this, there is a Python API called `python-ldap`, and functionality is likely available for other scripting languages as well.

- Use an LDAP front-end program which provides an interface for editing the database. If the front-end program is web-based or otherwise accessible over a network, ensure that authentication information is protected via SSL between the administrator's client and the program, as well as between the program and the LDAP database.

Any of these methods or others may be appropriate for your site. This guide does not provide a recommendation, and there will be no further discussion of the syntax of entering LDAP data into the database.

3.12.3.5.1 Create Top-level LDAP Structure for Domain

```
Create a structure for the domain itself with at least the following attributes:

    dn: dc=example,dc=com
    objectClass: dcObject
    objectClass: organization
    dc: example
    o: Organization Description
```

This is a placeholder for the root of the domain's LDAP tree. Without this entry, LDAP will not be able to find any other entries for the domain.

3.12.3.5.2 Create LDAP Structures for Users and Groups

```
Create LDAP structures for people (users) and for groups with at least the following attributes:

    dn: ou=people,dc=example,dc=com
    ou: people
    structuralObjectClass: organizationalUnit
    objectClass: organizationalUnit

    dn: ou=groups,dc=example,dc=com
    ou: groups
    structuralObjectClass: organizationalUnit
    objectClass: organizationalUnit
```

Posix users and groups are the two top-level items which will be needed in order to use LDAP for authentication. These organizational units are used to identify the two categories within LDAP.

3.12.3.5.3   Create Unix Accounts

For each Unix user, create an LDAP entry with at least the following attributes (others may be appropriate for your site as well), using variable values appropriate to that user.

```
dn: uid=username,ou=people,dc=example,dc=com
structuralObjectClass: inetOrgPerson
objectClass: inetOrgPerson
objectClass: posixAccount
objectClass: shadowAccount
cn: fullname
sn: surname
gecos: fullname
gidNumber: primary-group-id
homeDirectory: /home/username
loginShell: /path/to/shell
uid: username
uidNumber: uid
userPassword: {MD5}md5-hashed-password
```

If your site implements password expiration in which passwords must be changed every N days (see Section 2.3.1.7), then each entry should also have the attribute:

```
shadowMax: N
```

In general, the LDAP schemas for users use `uid` to refer to the text username, and `uidNumber` for the numeric UID. This usage may be slightly confusing when compared to the standard Unix usage.

You should not create entries for the `root` account or for system accounts which are unique to individual systems, but only for user accounts which are to be shared across machines, and which have authentication information (such as a password) associated with them.

3.12.3.5.4   Create Unix Groups

For each Unix group, create an LDAP entry with at least the following attributes:

```
dn: cn=groupname,ou=groups,dc=example,dc=com
cn: groupname
structuralObjectClass: posixGroup
objectClass: posixGroup
gidNumber: gid
memberUid: username1
memberUid: username2
...
memberUid: usernameN
```

Note that each user has a primary group, identified by the `gidNumber` field in the user's account entry. That group must be created, but it is *not* necessary to list the user as a `memberUid` of the group. This behavior should be familiar to administrators, since it is identical to the handling of the `/etc/passwd` and `/etc/group` files.

Do not create entries for the `root` group or for system groups, but only for groups which contain human users or which are shared across systems.

3.12.3.5.5   Create Groups to Administer LDAP

If a group of LDAP administrators, *admins*, is desired, that group must be created somewhat differently. The specification should have these attributes:

```
dn: cn=admins,ou=groups,dc=example,dc=com
cn: admins
structuralObjectClass: groupOfUniqueNames
objectClass: groupOfUniqueNames
uniqueMember: cn=Manager,dc=example,dc=com
uniqueMember: uid=admin1-username,ou=people,dc=example,dc=com
uniqueMember: uid=admin2-username,ou=people,dc=example,dc=com
...
uniqueMember: uid=adminN-username,ou=people,dc=example,dc=com
```

LDAP cannot use Posix groups for its own internal authentication — it needs to compare the username specified in an authenticated bind to some internal `groupOfUniqueNames`. If you do not specify an LDAP administrators' group, then all LDAP management will need to be done using the LDAP root user (`Manager`). For reasons of auditing and error detection, it is recommended that LDAP administrators have unique identities. (See Section 2.3.1.3 for similar reasoning applied to the use of `sudo` for privileged system commands.)

3.12.3.6   Configure `slapd` to Protect Authentication Information

Edit the file `/etc/openldap/slapd.conf`. Add or correct the following access specifications:

1. Protect the user's password by allowing the user himself or the LDAP administrators to change it, allowing the anonymous user to authenticate against it, and allowing no other access:

```
access to attrs=userPassword
  by self write
  by group/groupOfUniqueNames/uniqueMember="cn=admins,ou=groups,dc=example,dc=com" write
  by anonymous auth
  by * none
access to attrs=shadowLastChange
  by self write
  by group/groupOfUniqueNames/uniqueMember="cn=admins,ou=groups,dc=example,dc=com" write
  by * read
```

2. Allow anyone to read other information, and allow the administrators to change it:

```
access to *
  by group/groupOfUniqueNames/uniqueMember="cn=admins,ou=groups,dc=example,dc=com" write
  by * read
```

Access rules are applied in the order encountered, so more specific rules should appear first. In particular, the rule restricting access to `userPassword` must appear before the rule allowing access to all data. The `shadowLastChange` attribute is a timestamp, and is only critical if your site implements password expiration. If your site does not have an LDAP administrators group, the LDAP root user (called `Manager` in this guide) will be able to change data without an explicit access statement.

3.12.3.7 Correct Permissions on LDAP Server Files

Correct the permissions on the ldap server's files:

```
# chown ldap:root /var/lib/ldap/*
```

CCE 4484-2, 4502-1

Some manual methods of inserting information into the LDAP database may leave these files with incorrect permissions. This will prevent `slapd` from starting correctly.

3.12.3.8 Configure `iptables` to Allow Access to the LDAP Server

Determine an appropriate network block, *netwk*, and network mask, *mask*, representing the machines on your network which will synchronize to this server.

Edit `/etc/sysconfig/iptables`. Add the following lines, ensuring that they appear *before* the final `LOG` and `DROP` lines for the `RH-Firewall-1-INPUT` chain:

```
-A RH-Firewall-1-INPUT -s netwk/mask -m state --state NEW -p tcp --dport 389 -j ACCEPT
-A RH-Firewall-1-INPUT -s netwk/mask -m state --state NEW -p tcp --dport 636 -j ACCEPT
```

The default Iptables configuration does not allow inbound access to any services. These modifications allow access to the LDAP primary (389) and encrypted-only (636) ports, while keeping all other ports on the server in their default protected state. See Section 2.5.5 for more information about Iptables.

Note: Even if the LDAP server restricts connections so that only encrypted queries are allowed, it will probably be necessary to allow traffic to the default port 389. This is true because many LDAP clients implement encryption by connecting to the primary port and issuing the `STARTTLS` command.

3.12.3.9 Configure Logging for LDAP

1. Edit the file `/etc/syslog.conf`. Add or correct the following line:

   ```
   local4.*                                    /var/log/ldap.log
   ```

2. Create the log file with safe permissions:

   ```
   # touch /var/log/ldap.log
   # chown root:root /var/log/ldap.log
   # chmod 0600 /var/log/ldap.log
   ```

3. Edit the file `/etc/logrotate.d/syslog` and add the pathname

   ```
   /var/log/ldap.log
   ```

   to the space-separated list in the first line.

> 4. Edit the LDAP configuration file `/etc/openldap/slapd.conf` and set a reasonable set of default log parameters, such as:
>
>     ```
>     loglevel stats2
>     ```

OpenLDAP sends its log data to the syslog facility `local4` at priority `debug`. By default, RHEL5 does not store this facility at all. The syslog configuration suggested here will store any output logged by `slapd` in the file `/var/log/ldap.log`, and will include that file in the standard log rotation for syslog files.

By default, LDAP's logging is quite verbose. The `loglevel` parameter is a space-separated list of items to be logged. Specifying `stats2` will reduce the log output somewhat, but this level will still produce some logging every time an LDAP query is made. (This may be appropriate, depending on your site's auditing requirements.) In order to capture only `slapd` startup messages, specify `loglevel none`.

See `slapd.conf(5)` for detailed information about the `loglevel` parameter. See Section 2.6.1.1 for more information about syslog.

3.13   NFS and RPC

The Network File System is the most popular distributed filesystem for the Unix environment, and is very widely deployed. Unfortunately, NFS was not designed with security in mind, and has a number of weaknesses, both in terms of the protocol itself and because any NFS installation must expose several daemons, running on both servers and clients, to network attack.

This section discusses the circumstances under which it is possible to disable NFS and its dependencies, and then details steps which should be taken to secure, as much as possible, NFS's configuration. This section is relevant to machines operating as NFS clients, as well as to those operating as NFS servers.

3.13.1   Disable All NFS Services if Possible

The steps in Section 3.13.1 will prevent a machine from operating as either an NFS client or an NFS server. Only perform these steps on machines which do not need NFS at all.

> Is there a mission-critical reason for this machine to operate as *either* an NFS client or an NFS server?
>
> If not, follow all instructions in the remainder of Section 3.13.1 to disable subsystems required by NFS.

NFS is a commonly used mechanism for sharing data between machines in an organization. However, its use opens many potential security holes. If NFS is not universally needed in your organization, improve the security posture of any machine which does not require NFS by disabling it entirely.

3.13.1.1   Disable Services Used Only by NFS

> If NFS is not needed, perform the following steps to disable NFS client daemons:

```
# chkconfig nfslock off
# chkconfig rpcgssd off
# chkconfig rpcidmapd off
```

CCE 4396-8, 3535-2, 3568-3

The `nfslock`, `rpcgssd`, and `rpcidmapd` daemons all perform NFS client functions.

All of these daemons run with elevated privileges, and many listen for network connections. If they are not needed, they should be disabled to improve system security posture.

3.13.1.2 Disable `netfs` if Possible

Determine whether any network filesystems handled by `netfs` are mounted on this system:

```
# mount -t nfs,nfs4,smbfs,cifs,ncpfs
```

If this command returns no output, disable `netfs` to improve system security:

```
# chkconfig netfs off
```

CCE 4533-6

The `netfs` script manages the boot-time mounting of several types of networked filesystems, of which NFS and Samba (see Section 3.18) are the most common. If these filesystem types are not in use, the script can be disabled, protecting the system somewhat against accidental or malicious changes to /etc/fstab and against flaws in the `netfs` script itself.

3.13.1.3 Disable RPC Portmapper if Possible

If:

- NFS is not needed

- The site does not rely on NIS for authentication information, and

- The machine does not run any other RPC-based service

then disable the RPC portmapper service:

```
# chkconfig portmap off
```

CCE 4550-0

By design, the RPC model does not require particular services to listen on fixed ports, but instead uses a daemon, `portmap`, to tell prospective clients which ports to use to contact the services they are trying to reach. This model weakens system security by introducing another privileged daemon which may be directly attacked, and is unnecessary because RPC was never adopted by enough services to risk using up all the ports on a system.

Unfortunately, the portmapper is central to RPC design, so it cannot be disabled if your site is using any RPC-based services, including NFS, NIS (see Section 3.2.4 for information about NIS, which is not recommended), or any third-party or custom RPC-based program. If none of these programs are in use, however, `portmap` should be disabled to improve system security.

In order to get more information about whether `portmap` may be disabled on a given host, query the local portmapper using the command:

```
# rpcinfo -p
```

If the only services listed are `portmapper` and `status`, it is safe to disable the portmapper. If other services are listed and your site is not running NFS or NIS, investigate these services and disable them if possible.

3.13.2   Configure All Machines which Use NFS

The steps in this section are appropriate for all machines which run NFS, whether they operate as clients or as servers.

3.13.2.1   Make Each Machine a Client or a Server, not Both

If NFS must be used, it should be deployed in the simplest configuration possible to avoid maintainability problems which may lead to unnecessary security exposure. Due to the reliability and security problems caused by NFS, it is not a good idea for machines which act as NFS servers to also mount filesystems via NFS. At the least, crossed mounts (the situation in which each of two servers mounts a filesystem from the other) should never be used.

3.13.2.2   Restrict Access to the Portmapper

Edit the file `/etc/hosts.deny`. Add or correct the line:

```
portmap: ALL
```

Edit the file `/etc/hosts.allow`. Add or correct the line:

```
portmap: IPADDR1 , IPADDR2 , ...
```

where each *IPADDR* is the IP address of a server or client with which this machine shares NFS filesystems. If the machine is an NFS server, it may be simpler to use an IP netblock specification, such as `10.3.2.` (this is the TCP Wrappers syntax representing the netblock `10.3.2.0/24`), or a hostname specification, such as `.subdomain.example.com`. The use of hostnames is not recommended.

The `/etc/hosts.allow` and `/etc/hosts.deny` files are used by TCP Wrappers to determine whether specified remote hosts are allowed to access certain services. The default portmapper shipped with RHEL5 has TCP Wrappers support built in, so this specification can be used to provide some protection against network attacks on the portmapper. (See Section 2.5.4 for more information about TCP Wrappers.)

Note: This step protects only the `portmap` service itself. It is still possible for attackers to guess the port numbers of NFS services and attack those services directly, even if they are denied access to the portmapper.

3.13.2.3   Configure NFS Services to Use Fixed Ports

Edit the file `/etc/sysconfig/nfs`. Add or correct the following lines:

```
LOCKD_TCPPORT=lockd-port
LOCKD_UDPPORT=lockd-port
```

```
    MOUNTD_PORT=mountd-port
    RQUOTAD_PORT=rquotad-port
    STATD_PORT=statd-port
    STATD_OUTGOING_PORT=statd-outgoing-port
```

where each *X-port* is a port which is not used by any other service on your network.

CCE 4559-1, 4015-4, 3667-3, 4310-9, 4438-8, 3579-0

Firewalling should be done at each host and at the border firewalls to protect the NFS daemons from remote access, since NFS servers should never be accessible from outside the organization. However, by default, the portmapper assigns each NFS service to a port dynamically at service startup time. Dynamic ports cannot be protected by port filtering firewalls such as `iptables` (Section 2.5.5).

Therefore, restrict each service to always use a given port, so that firewalling can be done effectively. Note that, because of the way RPC is implemented, it is not possible to disable the portmapper even if ports are assigned statically to all RPC services.

3.13.3 Configure NFS Clients

The steps in this section are appropriate for machines which operate as NFS clients.

3.13.3.1 Disable NFS Server Daemons

```
# chkconfig nfs off
# chkconfig rpcsvcgssd off
```

CCE 4473-5, 4491-7

There is no need to run the NFS server daemons except on a small number of properly secured machines designated as NFS servers. Ensure that these daemons are turned off on clients.

3.13.3.2 Mount Remote Filesystems with Restrictive Options

Edit the file `/etc/fstab`. For each filesystem whose type (column 3) is `nfs` or `nfs4`, add the text `,nodev,nosuid` to the list of mount options in column 4. If appropriate, also add `,noexec`.

CCE 4368-7, 4024-6, 4526-0

See Section 2.2.1.2 for a description of the effects of these options. In general, execution of files mounted via NFS should be considered risky because of the possibility that an adversary could intercept the request and substitute a malicious file. Allowing setuid files to be executed from remote servers is particularly risky, both for this reason and because it requires the clients to extend root-level trust to the NFS server.

3.13.4 Configure NFS Servers

The steps in this section are appropriate for machines which operate as NFS servers.

3.13.4.1   Configure the Exports File Restrictively

Linux's NFS implementation uses the file `/etc/exports` to control what filesystems and directories may be accessed via NFS. (See the `exports(5)` manpage for more information about the format of this file.)

The syntax of the `exports` file is not necessarily checked fully on reload, and syntax errors can leave your NFS configuration more open than intended. Therefore, exercise caution when modifying the file.

The syntax of each line in `/etc/exports` is

> */DIR   ipaddr1(opt1,opt2) ipaddr2(opt3)*

where */DIR* is a directory or filesystem to export, *ipaddrN* is an IP address, netblock, hostname, domain, or netgroup to which to export, and *optN* is an option.

3.13.4.1.1   Use Access Lists to Enforce Authorization Restrictions on Mounts

> Edit `/etc/exports`. Ensure that each export line contains a set of IP addresses or hosts which are allowed to access that export.

If no IP addresses or hostnames are specified on an export line, then that export is available to any remote host which requests it. All lines of the exports file should specify the hosts (or subnets, if needed) which are allowed to access the exported directory, so that unknown or remote hosts will be denied.

3.13.4.1.2   Use Root-Squashing on All Exports

> Edit `/etc/exports`. Ensure that *no* line contains the option `no_root_squash`.
>
> **CCE 4544-3**

If a filesystem is exported using root squashing, requests from root on the client are considered to be unprivileged (mapped to a user such as `nobody`). This provides some mild protection against remote abuse of an NFS server. Root squashing is enabled by default, and should not be disabled.

3.13.4.1.3   Restrict NFS Clients to Privileged Ports

> Edit `/etc/exports`. Ensure that *no* line contains the option `insecure`.
>
> **CCE 4465-1**

By default, Linux's NFS implementation requires that all client requests be made from ports less than 1024. If your organization has control over machines connected to its network, and if NFS requests are prohibited at the border firewall, this offers some protection against malicious requests from unprivileged users. Therefore, the default should not be changed.

3.13.4.1.4 Export Filesystems Read-Only if Possible

> Edit `/etc/exports`. Ensure that every line contains the option `ro` and *does not* contain the option `rw`, unless there is an operational need for remote clients to modify that filesystem.
>
> **CCE 4350-5**

If a filesystem is being exported so that users can view the files in a convenient fashion, but there is no need for users to edit those files, exporting the filesystem read-only removes an attack vector against the server. The default filesystem export mode is `ro`, so do not specify `rw` without a good reason.

3.13.4.2 Allow Legitimate NFS Clients to Access the Server

> Determine an appropriate network block, `netwk`, and network mask, `mask`, representing the machines on your network which must mount NFS filesystems from this server.
>
> Edit `/etc/sysconfig/iptables`. Add the following lines, ensuring that they appear *before* the final `LOG` and `DROP` lines for the `RH-Firewall-1-INPUT` chain:
>
> ```
> -A RH-Firewall-1-INPUT -s netwk/mask -m state --state NEW -p udp --dport 111 -j ACCEPT
> -A RH-Firewall-1-INPUT -s netwk/mask -m state --state NEW -p tcp --dport 111 -j ACCEPT
> -A RH-Firewall-1-INPUT -s netwk/mask -m state --state NEW -p tcp --dport 2049 -j ACCEPT
>
> -A RH-Firewall-1-INPUT -s netwk/mask -m state --state NEW -p tcp --dport lockd-port -j ACCEPT
> -A RH-Firewall-1-INPUT -s netwk/mask -m state --state NEW -p udp --dport lockd-port -j ACCEPT
> -A RH-Firewall-1-INPUT -s netwk/mask -m state --state NEW -p tcp --dport mountd-port -j ACCEPT
> -A RH-Firewall-1-INPUT -s netwk/mask -m state --state NEW -p udp --dport mountd-port -j ACCEPT
> -A RH-Firewall-1-INPUT -s netwk/mask -m state --state NEW -p tcp --dport rquotad-port -j ACCEPT
> -A RH-Firewall-1-INPUT -s netwk/mask -m state --state NEW -p udp --dport rquotad-port -j ACCEPT
> -A RH-Firewall-1-INPUT -s netwk/mask -m state --state NEW -p tcp --dport statd-port -j ACCEPT
> -A RH-Firewall-1-INPUT -s netwk/mask -m state --state NEW -p udp --dport statd-port -j ACCEPT
> ```
>
> where the variable port numbers match those selected in Section 3.13.2.3

The default iptables configuration does not allow inbound access to any services. This modification will allow the specified block of remote hosts to initiate connections to the set of NFS daemons, while keeping all other ports on the server in their default protected state. See Section 2.5.5 for more information about iptables.

3.14 DNS Server

Most organizations have an operational need to run at least one nameserver. However, there are many common attacks involving DNS, be configured defensively.

3.14.1 Disable DNS Server if Possible

> Is there an operational need for this machine to act as a DNS server for this site?
>
> If not, disable the software and remove it from the system:

```
# chkconfig named off
# yum erase bind
```

CCE 3578-2, 4219-2

DNS software should be disabled on any machine which does not need to be a nameserver. Note that the BIND DNS server software is not installed on RHEL5 by default. The remainder of this section discusses secure configuration of machines which must be nameservers.

3.14.2   Run the BIND9 Software if DNS Service is Needed

It is highly recommended that the BIND9 software be used to provide DNS service. BIND is the Internet standard Unix nameserver, and, while it has had security problems in the past, it is also well-maintained and Red Hat is likely to quickly issue updates in response to any problems discovered in the future. In addition, BIND version 9 has new security features and more secure default settings than earlier versions. In particular, BIND version 4 is no longer recommended for production use, and BIND4 servers should be upgraded to a newer version as soon as possible.

3.14.3   Isolate DNS from Other Services

This section discusses mechanisms for preventing the DNS server from interfering with other services. This is done both to protect the remainder of the network should a nameserver be compromised, and to make direct attacks on nameservers more difficult.

3.14.3.1   Run DNS Software on Dedicated Servers if Possible

Since DNS is a high-risk service which must frequently be made available to the entire Internet, it is strongly recommended that no other services be offered by machines which act as organizational DNS servers.

3.14.3.2   Run DNS Software in a `chroot` Jail

Install the `bind-chroot` package:

```
# yum install bind-chroot
```

Place a valid `named.conf` file inside the chroot jail:

```
# cp /etc/named.conf /var/named/chroot/etc/named.conf
# chown root:root /var/named/chroot/etc/named.conf
# chmod 644 /var/named/chroot/etc/named.conf
```

Create and populate an appropriate zone directory within the jail, based on the options directive. If your `named.conf` includes:

```
options {
  directory "/path/to/DIRNAME";
  ...
}
```

> then copy that directory and its contents from the original zone directory:
>
> ```
> # cp -r /path/to/DIRNAME /var/named/chroot/DIRNAME
> ```
>
> Edit the file /etc/sysconfig/named. Add or correct the line:
>
> ```
> ROOTDIR=/var/named/chroot
> ```
>
> **CCE 3985-9, 4487-5, 4258-0**

Chroot jails are not foolproof. However, they serve to make it more difficult for a compromised program to be used to attack the entire host. They do this by restricting a program's ability to traverse the directory upward, so that files outside the jail are not visible to the chrooted process. Since RHEL5 supports a standard mechanism for placing BIND in a chroot jail, you should take advantage of this feature.

Note: If you are running BIND in a chroot jail, then you should use the jailed `named.conf` as the primary nameserver configuration file. That is, when this guide recommends editing `/etc/named.conf`, you should instead edit `/var/named/chroot/etc/named.conf`.

3.14.3.3   Configure Firewalls to Protect the DNS Server

> Edit the file /etc/sysconfig/iptables. Add the following lines, ensuring that they appear *before* the final `LOG` and `DROP` lines for the `RH-Firewall-1-INPUT` chain:
>
> ```
> -A RH-Firewall-1-INPUT -m state --state NEW -p udp --dport 53 -j ACCEPT
> -A RH-Firewall-1-INPUT -m state --state NEW -p tcp --dport 53 -j ACCEPT
> ```

These lines are necessary in order to allow remote machines to contact the DNS server. If this server is only available to the local network, it may be appropriate to insert a `-s` flag into this rule to allow traffic only from packets on the local network. See Section 3.5.1.2 for an example of such a modification.

See Section 2.5.5 for general information about iptables.

3.14.4   Protect DNS Data from Tampering or Attack

This section discusses DNS configuration options which make it more difficult for attackers to gain access to private DNS data or to modify DNS data.

3.14.4.1   Run Separate DNS Servers for External and Internal Queries if Possible

> Is it possible to run external and internal nameservers on separate machines? If so, follow the configuration guidance in this section. If not, see Section 3.14.4.2 for an alternate approach using BIND9.
>
> On the external nameserver, edit /etc/named.conf. Add or correct the following directives:
>
> ```
> options {
>   allow-query { any; };
>   recursion no;
>   ...
> };
> ```

```
    zone "example.com" IN {
      ...
    };
```

On the internal nameserver, edit /etc/named.conf. Add or correct the following directives, where *SUBNET*
is the numerical IP representation of your organization in the form xxx.xxx.xxx.xxx/xx:

```
    acl internal {
      SUBNET;
      localhost;
    };

    options {
      allow-query { internal; };
      ...
    };

    zone "internal.example.com" IN {
      ...
    };
```

Enterprise nameservers generally serve two functions. One is to provide public information about the machines
in a domain for the benefit of outside users who wish to contact those machines, for instance in order to send mail
to users in the enterprise, or to visit the enterprise's external web page. The other is to provide nameservice to
client machines within the enterprise. Client machines require both private information about enterprise machines
(which may be different from the public information served to the rest of the world) and public information about
machines outside the enterprise, which is used to send mail or visit websites outside of the organization.

In order to provide the public nameservice function, it is necessary to share data with untrusted machines which
request it — otherwise, the enterprise cannot be conveniently contacted by outside users. However, internal data
should be protected from disclosure, and serving irrelevant public name queries for outside domains leaves the
DNS server open to cache poisoning and other attacks. Therefore, local network nameservice functions *should
not* be provided to untrusted machines.

Separate machines should be used to fill these two functions whenever possible.

3.14.4.2   Use Views to Partition External and Internal Information if Necessary

If it is not possible to run external and internal nameservers on separate physical machines, run BIND9 and
simulate this feature using views.

Edit /etc/named.conf. Add or correct the following directives (where *SUBNET* is the numerical IP representation of your organization in the form xxx.xxx.xxx.xxx/xx):

```
    acl internal {
      SUBNET;
      localhost;
    };

    view "internal-view" {
      match-clients { internal; };
```

```
    zone "." IN {
      type hint;
      file "db.cache";
    };

    zone "internal.example.com" IN {
      ...
    };
};

view "external-view" {
  match-clients { any; };
  recursion no;

  zone "example.com" IN {
    ...
  };
};
```

The view feature is provided by BIND9 as a way to allow a single nameserver to make different sets of data available to different sets of clients. If possible, it is always better to run external and internal nameservers on separate machines, so that even complete compromise of the external server cannot be used to obtain internal data or confuse internal DNS clients. However, this is not always feasible, and use of a feature like views is preferable to leaving internal DNS data entirely unprotected.

Note: As shown in the example, database files which are required for recursion, such as the root hints file, must be available to any clients which are allowed to make recursive queries. Under typical circumstances, this includes only the internal clients which are allowed to use this server as a general-purpose nameserver.

3.14.4.3 Disable Zone Transfers from the Nameserver if Possible

Is it necessary for a secondary nameserver to receive zone data via zone transfer from the primary server? If not, follow the instructions in this section. If so, see the next section for instructions on protecting zone transfers.

Edit /etc/named.conf. Add or correct the following directive:

```
options {
  allow-transfer { none; };
  ...
}
```

If both the primary and secondary nameserver are under your control, or if you have only one nameserver, it may be possible to use an external configuration management mechanism to distribute zone updates. In that case, it is not necessary to allow zone transfers within BIND itself, so they should be disabled to avoid the potential for abuse.

3.14.4.4 Authenticate Zone Transfers if Necessary

If it is necessary for a secondary nameserver to receive zone data via zone transfer from the primary server, follow the instructions here.

Use `dnssec-keygen` to create a symmetric key file in the current directory:

```
# cd /tmp
# dnssec-keygen -a HMAC-MD5 -b 128 -n HOST dns.example.com
Kdns.example.com.+aaa+iiiii
```

This output is the name of a file containing the new key. Read the file to find the base64-encoded key string:

```
# cat Kdns.example.com.+NNN+MMMMM.key
dns.example.com IN KEY 512 3 157 base64-key-string
```

Edit `/etc/named.conf` on the primary nameserver. Add the directives:

```
key zone-transfer-key {
  algorithm hmac-md5;
  secret "base64-key-string";
};

zone "example.com" IN {
  type master;
  allow-transfer { key zone-transfer-key; };
  ...
}
```

Edit `/etc/named.conf` on the secondary nameserver. Add the directives:

```
key zone-transfer-key {
  algorithm hmac-md5;
  secret "base64-key-string";
};

server IP-OF-MASTER {
  keys { zone-transfer-key; };
};

zone "example.com" IN {
  type slave;
  masters { IP-OF-MASTER; };
  ...
};
```

The BIND transaction signature (TSIG) functionality allows primary and secondary nameservers to use a shared secret to verify authorization to perform zone transfers. This method is more secure than using IP-based limiting to restrict nameserver access, since IP addresses can be easily spoofed.

However, if you cannot configure TSIG between your servers because, for instance, the secondary nameserver is not under your control and its administrators are unwilling to configure TSIG, you can configure an `allow-transfer` directive with numerical IP addresses or ACLs as a last resort.

Note: The purpose of the `dnssec-keygen` command is to create the shared secret string *base64-key-string*. Once this secret has been obtained and inserted into `named.conf` on the primary and secondary servers, the key files K*dns.example.com.+NNN+MMMMM*.key and K*dns.example.com.+NNN+MMMMM*.private are no longer needed, and may safely be deleted.

3.14.4.5   Disable Dynamic Updates if Possible

Is there a mission-critical reason to enable the risky dynamic update functionality? If not:

Edit /etc/named.conf. For each zone specification, correct the following directive if necessary:

```
zone "example.com" IN {
  allow-update { none; };
  ...
}
```

CCE 4399-2

Dynamic updates allow remote servers to add, delete, or modify any entries in your zone file. Therefore, they should be considered highly risky, and disabled unless there is a very good reason for their use.

If dynamic updates must be allowed, IP-based ACLs are insufficient protection, since they are easily spoofed. Instead, use TSIG keys (see the previous section for an example), and consider using the update-policy directive to restrict changes to only the precise type of change needed.

3.15   FTP Server

FTP is a common method for allowing remote access to files. Like telnet, the FTP protocol is unencrypted, which means that passwords and other data transmitted during the session can be captured and that the session is vulnerable to hijacking. Therefore, running the FTP server software is not recommended.

However, there are some FTP server configurations which may be appropriate for some environments, particularly those which allow only read-only anonymous access as a means of downloading data available to the public.

3.15.1   Disable vsftpd if Possible

Is there a mission-critical reason for the machine to act as an FTP server?

If not, disable the software and remove it from the system:

```
# chkconfig vsftpd off
# yum erase vsftpd
```

CCE 3919-8, 14881-7

3.15.2   Use vsftpd to Provide FTP Service if Necessary

If this machine must operate as an FTP server, install the vsftpd package via the standard channels:

```
# yum install vsftpd
```

After RHEL 2.1, Red Hat switched from distributing wu-ftpd with RHEL to distributing vsftpd. For security and for consistency with future Red Hat releases, the use of vsftpd is recommended.

3.15.3 Configure `vsftpd` Securely

The primary vsftpd configuration file is `/etc/vsftpd.conf`, if that file exists, or `/etc/vsftpd/vsftpd.conf` if it does not. For the remainder of this section, the phrase "the configuration file" will refer to whichever of those files is appropriate for your environment.

3.15.3.1 Enable Logging of All FTP Transactions

Edit the vsftpd configuration file. Add or correct the following configuration options:

```
xferlog_std_format=NO
log_ftp_protocol=YES
```

CCE 4549-2

The modifications above ensure that all commands sent to the ftp server are logged using the verbose vsftpd log format. The default vsftpd log file is `/var/log/vsftpd.log`.

Note: If verbose logging to `vsftpd.log` is done, sparse logging of downloads to `/var/log/xferlog` will *not* also occur. However, the information about what files were downloaded is included in the information logged to `vsftpd.log`.

3.15.3.2 Create Warning Banners for All FTP Users

Edit the vsftpd configuration file. Add or correct the following configuration options:

```
banner_file=/etc/issue
```

CCE 4554-2

See Section 2.3.7 for an explanation of banner file use. This setting will cause the system greeting banner to be used for FTP connections as well.

3.15.3.3 Restrict the Set of Users Allowed to Access FTP

This section describes how to disable non-anonymous (password-based) FTP logins, or, if it is not possible to do this entirely due to legacy applications, how to restrict insecure FTP login to only those users who have an identified need for this access.

3.15.3.3.1 Restrict Access to Anonymous Users if Possible

Is there a mission-critical reason for users to transfer files to/from their own accounts using FTP, rather than using a secure protocol like SCP/SFTP? If not:

Edit the vsftpd configuration file. Add or correct the following configuration option:

```
        local_enable=NO
```

If non-anonymous FTP logins are necessary, follow the guidance in the remainder of this section to secure these logins as much as possible.

CCE 4443-8

The use of non-anonymous FTP logins is strongly discouraged. Since SSH clients and servers are widely available, and since SSH provides support for a transfer mode which resembles FTP in user interface, there is no good reason to allow password-based FTP access. See Section 3.5 for more information about SSH.

3.15.3.3.2 Limit Users Allowed FTP Access if Necessary

If there is a mission-critical reason for users to access their accounts via the insecure FTP protocol, limit the set of users who are allowed this access.

Edit the vsftpd configuration file. Add or correct the following configuration options:

```
        userlist_enable=YES
        userlist_file=/etc/vsftp.ftpusers
        userlist_deny=NO
```

Edit the file `/etc/vsftp.ftpusers`. For each user *USERNAME* who should be allowed to access the system via ftp, add a line containing that user's name.

        USERNAME

If anonymous access is also required, add the anonymous usernames to `/etc/vsftp.ftpusers` as well:

```
        anonymous
        ftp
```

Historically, the file `/etc/ftpusers` contained a list of users who were *not* allowed to access the system via ftp. It was used to prevent system users such as the root user from logging in via the insecure ftp protocol.

However, when the configuration option `userlist_deny=NO` is set, vsftpd interprets ftpusers as the set of users who *are* allowed to login via ftp. Since it should be possible for most users to access their accounts via secure protocols, it is recommended that this setting be used, so that non-anonymous ftp access can be limited to legacy users who have been explicitly identified.

3.15.3.4 Disable FTP Uploads if Possible

Is there a mission-critical reason for users to upload files via FTP? If not:

Edit the vsftpd configuration file. Add or correct the following configuration options:

```
        write_enable=NO
```

If FTP uploads are necessary, follow the guidance in the remainder of this section to secure these transactions as much as possible.

CCE 4461-0

Anonymous FTP can be a convenient way to make files available for universal download. However, it is less common to have a need to allow unauthenticated users to place files on the FTP server. If this must be done, it is necessary to ensure that files cannot be uploaded and downloaded from the same directory.

3.15.3.5   Place the FTP Home Directory on its Own Partition

> By default, the anonymous FTP root is the home directory of the `ftp` user account. The `df` command can be used to verify that this directory is on its own partition.

If there is a mission-critical reason for anonymous users to upload files, precautions must be taken to prevent these users from filling a disk used by other services.

3.15.3.6   Configure Firewalls to Protect the FTP Server

> Edit the file `/etc/sysconfig/iptables`. Add the following lines, ensuring that they appear *before* the final `LOG` and `DROP` lines for the `RH-Firewall-1-INPUT` chain:
>
> ```
>     -A RH-Firewall-1-INPUT -m state --state NEW -p tcp --dport 21 -j ACCEPT
> ```
>
> Edit the file `/etc/sysconfig/iptables-config`. Ensure that the space-separated list of modules contains the FTP connection tracking module:
>
> ```
>     IPTABLES_MODULES="ip_conntrack_ftp"
> ```

These settings configure iptables to allow connections to an FTP server. The first line allows initial connections to the FTP server port.

FTP is an older protocol which is not very compatible with firewalls. During the initial FTP dialogue, the client and server negotiate an arbitrary port to be used for data transfer. The `ip_conntrack_ftp` module is used by iptables to listen to that dialogue and allow connections to the data ports which FTP negotiates. This allows an FTP server to operate on a machine which is running a firewall.

3.16   Web Server

The web server is responsible for providing access to content via the HTTP protocol. Web servers represent a significant security risk because:

- The HTTP port is commonly probed by malicious sources
- Web server software is very complex, and includes a long history of vulnerabilities
- The HTTP protocol is unencrypted and vulnerable to passive monitoring

The system's default web server software is Apache 2 and is provided in the RPM package `httpd`.

3.16.1   Disable Apache if Possible

> If Apache was installed and activated, but the system does not need to act as a web server, then it should be disabled and removed from the system:

```
# chkconfig httpd off
# yum erase httpd
```

CCE 4338-0, 4514-6

3.16.2 Install Apache if Necessary

If the Apache web server must be run, follow these guidelines to install it defensively. Then follow the guidelines in the remainder of Section 3.16 to configure the web server machine and software as securely as possible.

3.16.2.1 Install Apache Software Safely

Install the Apache 2 package from the standard Red Hat distribution channel:

```
# yum install httpd
```

CCE 4346-3

Note: This method of installation is recommended over installing the "Web Server" package group during the system installation process. The Web Server package group includes many packages which are likely extraneous, while the command-line method installs only the required `httpd` package itself.

3.16.2.2 Confirm Minimal Built-in Modules

The default Apache installation minimizes the number of modules that are compiled directly into the binary (`core prefork http_core mod_so`). This minimizes risk by limiting the capabilities allowed by the webserver.

Query the set of compiled-in modules using the following command:

```
$ httpd -l
```

If the number of compiled-in modules is significantly larger than the aforementioned set, this guide recommends reinstallating Apache with a reduced configuration.

3.16.3 Secure the Apache Configuration

The Apache configuration file is `/etc/httpd/conf/httpd.conf`. Apply the recommendations in the remainder of this section to this file.

3.16.3.1 Restrict Information Leakage

The `ServerTokens` and `ServerSignature` directives determine how much information the web server discloses about the configuration of the system. `ServerTokens Prod` restricts information in page headers, returning only the word "Apache." `ServerSignature Off` keeps Apache from displaying the server version on error pages. It is a good security practice to limit the information provided to clients.

> Add or correct the following directives in `/etc/httpd/conf/httpd.conf` so that as little information as possible is released:
>
> ```
> ServerTokens Prod
> ServerSignature Off
> ```
>
> **CCE 4474-3, 3756-4**

3.16.3.2 Minimize Loadable Modules

A default installation of Apache includes a plethora of "dynamically shared objects" (DSO) that are loaded at run-time. Unlike the aforementioned "compiled-in" modules, a DSO can be disabled in the configuration file by removing the corresponding `LoadModule` directive.

Note: A DSO only provides additional functionality if associated directives are included in the Apache configuration file. It should also be noted that removing a DSO will produce errors on Apache startup if the configuration file contains directives that apply to that module. Refer to `http://httpd.apache.org/docs/` for details on which directives are associated with each DSO.

Follow each DSO removal, the configuration can be tested with the following command to check if everything still works:

```
# service httpd configtest
```

The purpose of each of the modules loaded by default will now be addressed one at a time. If none of a module's directives are being used, remove it.

3.16.3.2.1 Apache Core Modules

> These modules comprise a basic subset of modules that are likely needed for base Apache functionality; ensure they are not commented out in `/etc/httpd/conf/httpd.conf`:
>
> ```
> LoadModule auth_basic_module modules/mod_auth_basic.so
> LoadModule authn_default_module modules/mod_authn_default.so
> LoadModule authz_host_module modules/mod_authz_host.so
> LoadModule authz_user_module modules/mod_authz_user.so
> LoadModule authz_groupfile_module modules/mod_authz_groupfile.so
> LoadModule authz_default_module modules/mod_authz_default.so
> LoadModule log_config_module modules/mod_log_config.so
> LoadModule logio_module modules/mod_logio.so
> LoadModule setenvif_module modules/mod_setenvif.so
> LoadModule mime_module modules/mod_mome.so
> LoadModule autoindex_module modules/mod_autoindex.so
> LoadModule negotiation_module modules/mod_negotiation.so
> LoadModule dir_module modules/mod_dir.so
> LoadModule alias_module modules/mod_alias.so
> ```

3.16.3.2.2 HTTP Basic Authentication

The following modules are necessary if this web server will provide content that will be restricted by a password.

Authentication can be performed using local plain text password files (`authn_file`), local DBM password files (`authn_dbm`) or an LDAP directory (see Section 3.16.3.2.5). The only module required by the web server depends on your choice of authentication. Comment out the modules you don't need from the following:

```
LoadModule authn_file_module modules/mod_authn_file.so
LoadModule authn_dbm_module modules/mod_authn_dbm.so
```

`authn_alias` allows for authentication based on aliases. `authn_anon` allows anonymous authentication similar to that of anonymous ftp sites. `authz_owner` allows authorization based on file ownership. `authz_dbm` allows for authorization based on group membership if the web server is using DBM authentication.

If the above functionality is unnecessary, comment out the related module:

```
#LoadModule authn_alias_module modules/mod_authn_alias.so
#LoadModule authn_anon_module modules/mod_authn_anon.so
#LoadModule authz_owner_module modules/mod_authz_owner.so
#LoadModule authz_dbm_module modules/mod_authz_dbm.so
```

3.16.3.2.3 HTTP Digest Authentication

This module provides encrypted authentication sessions. However, this module is rarely used and considered experimental. Alternate methods of encrypted authentication are recommended, such as SSL (Section 3.16.4.1)

If the above functionality is unnecessary, comment out the related module:

```
#LoadModule auth_digest_module modules/mod_auth_digest.so
```

3.16.3.2.4 `mod_rewrite`

The `mod_rewrite` module is very powerful and can protect against certain classes of web attacks. However, it is also very complex and has a significant history of vulnerabilities itself.

If the above functionality is unnecessary, comment out the related module:

```
#LoadModule rewrite_module modules/mod_rewrite.so
```

3.16.3.2.5 LDAP Support

This module provides HTTP authentication via an LDAP directory.

If the above functionality is unnecessary, comment out the related modules:

```
#LoadModule ldap_module modules/mod_ldap.so
#LoadModule authnz_ldap_module modules/mod_authnz_ldap.so
```

If LDAP is to be used, SSL encryption (Section 3.16.4.1) should be used as well.

3.16.3.2.6 Server Side Includes

Server Side Includes provide a method of dynamically generating web pages through the insertion of server-side code. However, the technology is also deprecated and introduces significant security concerns.

> If the above functionality is unnecessary, comment out the related module:
>
> ```
> #LoadModule include_module modules/mod_include.so
> ```

If there is a critical need for Server Side Includes, they should be enabled with the option `IncludesNoExec` to prevent arbitrary code execution. Additionally, user supplied data should be encoded to prevent cross-site scripting vulnerabilities.

3.16.3.2.7 MIME Magic

This module provides a second layer of MIME support that in most configurations is likely extraneous.

> If the above functionality is unnecessary, comment out the related module:
>
> ```
> #LoadModule mime_magic_module modules/mod_mime_magic.so
> ```

3.16.3.2.8 WebDAV (Distributed Authoring and Versioning)

WebDAV is an extension of the HTTP protocol that provides distributed and collaborative access to web content. Due to a number of security concerns with WebDAV, its use is not recommended.

> If the above functionality is unnecessary, comment out the related modules:
>
> ```
> #LoadModule dav_module modules/mod_dav.so
> #LoadModule dav_fs_module modules/mod_dav_fs.so
> ```

If there is a critical need for WebDAV, extra care should be taken in its configuration. Since DAV access allows remote clients to manipulate server files, any location on the server that is DAV enabled should be protected by encrypted authentication.

3.16.3.2.9 Server Activity Status

This module provides real-time access to statistics on the internal operation of the web server. This is an unnecessary information leak and should be disabled.

> If the above functionality is unnecessary, comment out the related module:
>
> ```
> #LoadModule status_module modules/mod_status.so
> ```

If there is a critical need for this module, ensure that access to the status page is properly restricted to a limited set of hosts in the status handler configuration.

3.16.3.2.10 Web Server Configuration Display

This module creates a web page illustrating the configuration of the web server. This is an unnecessary security leak and should be disabled.

> If the above functionality is unnecessary, comment out the related module:
>
> ```
> #LoadModule info_module modules/mod_info.so
> ```

If there is a critical need for this module, use the `Location` directive to provide an access control list to restrict access to the information.

3.16.3.2.11 URL Correction on Misspelled Entries

This module attempts to find a document match by allowing one misspelling in an otherwise failed request.

> If the above functionality is unnecessary, comment out the related module:
>
> ```
> #LoadModule speling_module modules/mod_speling.so
> ```

This functionality weakens server security by making site enumeration easier.

3.16.3.2.12 User-specific directories

The `UserDir` directive provides user-specific directory translation, allowing URLs based on associated usernames.

> If the above functionality is unnecessary, comment out the related module:
>
> ```
> #LoadModule userdir_module modules/mod_userdir.so
> ```

If there is a critical need for this module, include the line `UserDir disabled root` (at a minimum) in the configuration file. Ideally, UserDir should be disabled, and then enabled on a case-by-case basis for specific users that require this functionality.

Note: A web server's users can be trivially enumerated using this module.

3.16.3.2.13 Proxy Support

This module provides proxying support, allowing Apache to forward requests and serve as a gateway for other servers.

> If the above functionality is unnecessary, comment out the related modules:
>
> ```
> #LoadModule proxy_module modules/mod_proxy.so
> #LoadModule proxy_balancer_module modules/mod_proxy_balancer.so
> #LoadModule proxy_ftp_module modules/mod_proxy_ftp.so
> #LoadModule proxy_http_module modules/mod_proxy_http.so
> #LoadModule proxy_connect_module modules/mod_proxy_connect.so
> ```

If proxy support is needed, load `proxy` and the appropriate proxy protocol handler module (one of `proxy_http`, `proxy_ftp`, or `proxy_connect`). Additionally, make certain that a server is secure before enabling proxying, as open proxy servers are a security risk. `proxy_balancer` enables load balancing, but requires that `mod_status` be enabled. Since `mod_status` is not recommended, `proxy_balancer` should be avoided as well.

3.16.3.2.14   Cache Support

This module allows Apache to cache data, optimizing access to frequently accessed content. However, not only is it an experimental module, but it also introduces potential security flaws into the web server such as the possibility of circumventing `Allow` and `Deny` directives.

> If the above functionality is unnecessary, comment out the related modules:
>
> ```
> #LoadModule cache_module modules/mod_cache.so
> #LoadModule disk_cache_module modules/mod_disk_cache.so
> #LoadModule file_cache_module modules/mod_file_cache.so
> #LoadModule mem_cache_module modules/mod_mem_cache.so
> ```

If caching is required, it should not be enabled for any limited-access content.

3.16.3.2.15   CGI Support (and Related Modules)

This module allows HTML to interact with the CGI web programming language.

> If the above functionality is unnecessary, comment out the related modules:
>
> ```
> #LoadModule cgi_module modules/mod_cgi.so
>
> #LoadModule env_module modules/mod_env.so
> #LoadModule actions_module modules/mod_actions.so
> #LoadModule suexec_module modules/mod_suexec.so
> ```

If the web server requires the use of CGI, enable the `cgi` module. If extended CGI functionality is required, include the appropriate modules. `env` allows for control of the environment passed to CGI scripts. `actions` allows CGI events to be triggered when files of a certain type are requested. `su_exec` allows CGI scripts to run as a specified user/group instead of as the server's user/group.

3.16.3.2.16   Various Optional Components

> The following modules perform very specific tasks, sometimes providing access to just a few additional directives. If this functionality is not required (or if you are not using these directives), comment out the associated module:
>
> - External filtering (response passed through external program prior to client delivery)
>
>   ```
>   #LoadModule ext_filter_module modules/mod_ext_filter.so
>   ```
>
> - User-specified Cache Control and Expiration
>
>   ```
>   #LoadModule expires_module modules/mod_expires.so
>   ```

- Compression Output Filter (provides content compression prior to client delivery)

  ```
  #LoadModule deflate_module modules/mod_deflate.so
  ```

- HTTP Response/Request Header Customization

  ```
  #LoadModule headers_module modules/mod_headers.so
  ```

- User activity monitoring via cookies

  ```
  #LoadModule usertrack_module modules/mod_usertrack.so
  ```

- Dynamically configured mass virtual hosting

  ```
  #LoadModule vhost_alias_module modules/mod_vhost_alias.so
  ```

3.16.3.3 Minimize Configuration Files Included

The `Include` directive directs Apache to load supplementary configuration files from a provided path. The default configuration loads all files that end in `.conf` from the `/etc/httpd/conf.d` directory.

To restrict excess configuration, the following line should be commented out and replaced with `Include` directives that only reference required configuration files:

```
#Include conf.d/*.conf
```

If the above change was made, ensure that the SSL encryption remains loaded by explicitly including the corresponding configuration file: (see Section 3.16.4.1 for further details on SSL configuration)

```
Include conf.d/ssl.conf
```

If PHP is necessary, a similar alteration must be made: (see Section 3.16.4.4.1 for further details on PHP configuration)

```
Include conf.d/php.conf
```

3.16.3.4 Directory Restrictions

The `Directory` tags in the web server configuration file allow finer grained access control for a specified directory. All web directories should be configured on a case-by-case basis, allowing access only where needed.

3.16.3.4.1 Restrict Root Directory

The Apache root directory should always have the most restrictive configuration enabled.

```
<Directory / >
    Options None
    AllowOverride None
    Order allow,deny
</Directory>
```

3.16.3.4.2   Restrict Web Directory

The default configuration for the web (`/var/www/html`) Directory allows directory indexing (`Indexes`)and the following of symbolic links (`FollowSymLinks`). Neither of these is recommended.

> The `/var/www/html` directory hierarchy should not be viewable via the web, and symlinks should only be followed if the owner of the symlink also owns the linked file.
>
> Ensure that this policy is adhered to by altering the related section of the configuration:
>
> ```
> <Directory "/var/www/html">
> # ...
> Options SymLinksIfOwnerMatch
> # ...
> </Directory>
> ```

3.16.3.4.3   Restrict Other Critical Directories

All accessible web directories should be configured with similar restrictive settings. The Options directive should be limited to necessary functionality and the `AllowOverride` directive should be used only if needed. The Order and Deny access control tags should be used to deny access by default, allowing access only where necessary.

3.16.3.5   Configure Authentication if Applicable

 *Basic authentication is handled in* plaintext *over the network. Therefore, all login attempts are vulnerable to password sniffing. For increased protection against passive monitoring, encrypted authentication over a secure channel such as SSL (Section 3.16.4.1) is recommended.*

> 1. Set up a password file.
>
>   If a password file doesn't yet exist, one must be generated with the following command:
>
>    ```
>    # htpasswd -cs passwdfile user
>    ```
>
>    *WARNING: This command will overwrite an existing file at this location.*
>
>   Once a password file has been generated, subsequent users can be added with the following command:
>
>    ```
>    # htpasswd -s passwdfile user
>    ```
>
> 2. Optionally, set up a group file (if using group authentication).
>
>   The group file is a plain text file of the following format (each group is on its own line, followed by a colon and a list of users that belong to that group, separated by spaces):
>
>    ```
>    group: user1 user2
>    group2: user3
>    ```
>
> 3. Modify file permissions so that Apache can read the group and passwd files:

```
                # chgrp apache passwdfile groupfile
                # chmod 640 passwdfile groupfile
```

4. Turn on authentication for desired directories

   Add the following options inside the appropriate `Directory` tag:

   - For single-user authentication:

     ```
     <Directory "directory">
     # ...
         AuthName "Private Data"
         AuthType Basic

         AuthUserFile passwdfile
         require user user
     # ...
     </Directory>
     ```

   - For multiple-user authentication restricted by groups:

     ```
     <Directory "directory">
     # ...
         AuthName "Private Data"
         AuthType Basic

         AuthUserFile passwdfile
         AuthGroupFile groupfile

         require group group
     # ...
     </Directory>
     ```

   - For multiple-user authentication restricted by valid user accounts:

     ```
     <Directory "directory">
     # ...
         AuthName "Private Data"
         AuthType Basic

         AuthUserFile passwdfile
         require valid-user
     # ...
     </Directory>
     ```

The `AuthName` directive specifies a label for the protected content.

The `AuthType` directive specifies the kind of authentication (if using Digest authentication, this line would instead read `AuthType Digest`)

The `AuthUserFile` and `AuthGroupFile` directives point to the password and group files (if using Digest authentication, these directives would instead be `AuthDigestFile` and `AuthDigestGroupFile`.)

The `require user` directive restricts access to a single user. The `require group` directive restricts access to multiple users in a designated group. The short-hand `require valid-user` directive restricts access to *any* user in the *passwdfile*

Note: Make sure the `AuthUserFile` and `AuthGroupFile` locations are outside the web server document tree to prevent remote clients from having access to restricted usernames and passwords. This guide recommends `/etc/httpd/conf` as a location for these files.

3.16.3.6   Limit Available Methods

Web server methods are defined in section 9 of RFC 2616 (http://www.ietf.org/rfc/rfc2616.txt). If a web server does not require the implementation of all available methods, they should be disabled.

Note: GET and POST are the most common methods. A majority of the others are limited to the WebDAV protocol.

```
<Directory /var/www/html>
#  ...
    # Only allow specific methods (this command is case-sensitive!)
    <LimitExcept GET POST>
        Order allow,deny
    </LimitExcept>
#  ...
</Directory>
```

3.16.4   Use Appropriate Modules to Improve Apache's Security

Among the modules available for Apache are several whose use may improve the security of the web server installation. This section recommends and discusses the deployment of security-relevant modules.

3.16.4.1   Deploy `mod_ssl`

Because HTTP is a plain text protocol, all traffic is susceptible to passive monitoring. If there is a need for confidentiality, SSL should be configured and enabled to encrypt content.

Note: `mod_nss` is a FIPS 140-2 certified alternative to `mod_ssl`. The modules share a considerable amount of code and should be nearly identical in functionality. If FIPS 140-2 validation is required, then `mod_nss should be used.  If it provides some feature or its greater compatibility is required, thenmod_ssl should be used.`

3.16.4.1.1   Install `mod_ssl`

```
Install mod_ssl:

    # yum install mod_ssl
```

3.16.4.1.2 Create an SSL Certificate

On your CA (if you are using your own) or on another physically secure system, generate a key pair for the web server:

```
# cd /etc/pki/tls/certs
# openssl genrsa -des3 -out httpserverkey.pem 2048
```

When prompted, enter a strong, unique passphrase to protect the web server key pair.

Next, generate a Certificate Signing Request (CSR) from the key for the CA:

```
# openssl req -new -key httpserverkey.pem -out httpserver.csr
```

Enter the passphrase for the web server key pair and then fill out the fields as completely as possible (or hit return to accept defaults); the Common Name field is especially important. It must match the fully-qualified domain name of your server exactly (e.g. www.example.com) or the certificate will not work. The /etc/pki/tls/openssl.conf file will determine which other fields (e.g. Country Name, Organization Name, etc) must match between the server request and the CA. Leave the challenge password and an optional company name blank. Next, the web server CSR must be signed to create the web server certificate. You can either send the CSR to an established CA or sign it with your CA.

To sign httpserver.csr using your CA:

```
# openssl ca -in httpserver.csr -out httpservercert.pem
```

When prompted, enter the CA passphrase to continue and then complete the process. The httpservercert.pem certificate needed to enable SSL on the web server is now in the directory.

Finally, the web server key and certificate file need to be moved to the web server. Use removable media if possible. Place the server key and certificate file in /etc/pki/tls/http/, naming them serverkey.pem and servercert.pem, respectively.

3.16.4.1.3 Install SSL Certificate

Add or modify the configuration file /etc/httpd/conf.d/ssl.conf to match the following:

```
# establish new listening port
Listen 443

# seed appropriately
SSLRandomSeed startup file:/dev/urandom 1024
SSLRandomSeed connect file:/dev/urandom 1024

<VirtualHost site-on-certificate.com:443>
    # Enable SSL
    SSLEngine On

    # Path to server certificate + private key
    SSLCertificateFile /etc/pki/tls/http/servercert.pem
    SSLCertificateKeyFile /etc/pki/tls/http/serverkey.pem

    SSLProtocol All -SSLv2
```

```
        # Weak ciphers and null authentication should be denied unless absolutely necessary
        # (and even then, such cipher weakening should occur within a Location enclosure)
        SSLCipherSuite HIGH:MEDIUM:!aNULL:+MD5


    </VirtualHost>
```

Ensure that all directories that house SSL content are restricted to SSL access only in `/etc/httpd/conf/httpd.conf`:

```
    <Directory /var/www/html/secure>
        # require SSL for access
        SSLRequireSSL
        SSLOptions +StrictRequire

        # require domain to match certificate domain
        SSLRequire %{HTTP_HOST} eq "site-on-certificate.com"

        # rather than reply with 403 error, redirect user to appropriate site
        # this is OPTIONAL - uncomment to apply
        # ErrorDocument 403 https://site-on-certificate.com
    </Directory>
```

3.16.4.2 Deploy `mod_security`

`mod_security` provides an application level firewall for Apache. Following the installation of `mod_security` with the base ruleset, specific configuration advice can be found at http://www.modsecurity.org/ to design a policy that best matches the security needs of the web applications.

3.16.4.2.1 Install `mod_security`

Install `mod_security`:

```
    # yum install mod_security
```

3.16.4.2.2 Configure `mod_security` Filtering

`mod_security` supports a significant number of options, far too many to be fully covered in this guide. However, the following list comprises a smaller subset of suggested filters to be added to `/etc/httpd/conf/httpd.conf`:

```
    # enable mod_security
    SecFilterEngine On

    # enable POST filtering
    SecFilterScanPost On
```

```
# Make sure that URL encoding is valid
SecFilterCheckURLEncoding On

# Accept almost all byte values
SecFilterForceByteRange 1 255

# Prevent directory traversal
SecFilter "\.\./"

# Filter on specific system specific paths
SecFilter /etc/passwd
SecFilter /bin/

# Prevent cross-site scripting
SecFilter "<[[:space:]]* script"

# Prevent SQL injection
SecFilter "delete[[:space:]]+from"
SecFilter "insert[[:space:]]+into"
SecFilter "select.+from"
```

3.16.4.3 Use Denial-of-Service Protection Modules

Denial-of-service attacks are difficult to detect and prevent while maintaining acceptable access to authorized users. However, there are a number of traffic-shaping modules that attempt to address the problem. Well-known DoS protection modules include:

```
mod_throttle mod_bwshare mod_limitipconn mod_dosevasive
```

It is recommended that denial-of-service prevention be implemented for the web server. However, this guide leaves specific configuration details to the discretion of the reader.

3.16.4.4 Configure Supplemental Modules Appropriately

Any required functionality added to the web server via additional modules should be configured appropriately.

3.16.4.4.1 Configure PHP Securely

PHP is a widely used and often misconfigured server-side scripting language. It should be used with caution, but configured appropriately when needed.

Make the following changes to `/etc/php.ini`:

```
# Do not expose PHP error messages to external users
display_errors = Off

# Enable safe mode
safe_mode = On
```

```
# Only allow access to executables in isolated directory
safe_mode_exec_dir = php-required-executables-path

# Limit external access to PHP environment
safe_mode_allowed_env_vars = PHP_

# Restrict PHP information leakage
expose_php = Off

# Log all errors
log_errors = On

# Do not register globals for input data
register_globals = Off

# Minimize allowable PHP post size
post_max_size = 1K

# Ensure PHP redirects appropriately
cgi.force_redirect = 0

# Disallow uploading unless necessary
file_uploads = Off

# Disallow treatment of file requests as fopen calls
allow_url_fopen = Off

# Enable SQL safe mode
sql.safe_mode = On
```

3.16.5   Configure Operating System to Protect Web Server

The following configuration steps should be taken on the machine which hosts the web server, in order to provide as safe an environment as possible for the web server.

3.16.5.1   Restrict File and Directory Access

Minimize access to critical Apache files and directories:

```
# chmod 511 /usr/sbin/httpd
# chmod 750 /var/log/httpd/

# chmod 750 /etc/httpd/conf/
# chmod 640 /etc/httpd/conf/*
# chgrp -R apache /etc/httpd/conf
```

CCE 4509-6, 4386-9, 4029-5, 3581-6, 4574-0

3.16.5.2 Configure `iptables` to Allow Access to the Web Server

> Edit `/etc/sysconfig/iptables`. Add the following lines, ensuring that they appear *before* the final `LOG` and `DROP` lines for the `RH-Firewall-1-INPUT` chain:
>
> ```
> -A RH-Firewall-1-INPUT -m state --state NEW -p tcp --dport 80 -j ACCEPT
> -A RH-Firewall-1-INPUT -m state --state NEW -p tcp --dport 443 -j ACCEPT
> ```

The default Iptables configuration does not allow inbound access to the HTTP (80) and HTTPS (443) ports used by the web server. This modification allows that access, while keeping other ports on the server in their default protected state. See Section 2.5.5 for more information about Iptables.

3.16.5.3 Run Apache in a `chroot` Jail if Possible

Putting Apache in a `chroot` jail minimizes the damage done by a potential break-in by isolating the web server to a small section of the filesystem.

In order to configure Apache to run from a `chroot` directory, edit the Apache configuration file, `/etc/httpd/conf/httpd.conf`, and add the directive:

```
SecChrootDir /chroot/apache
```

It is also necessary to place *all* files required by Apache inside the filesystem rooted at */chroot/apache*, including Apache's binaries, modules, configuration files, and served web pages. The details of this configuration are beyond the scope of this guide.

3.16.6 Additional Resources

Further resources should be consulted if your web server requires more extensive configuration guidance, especially if particular applications need to be secured.

In particular, [27] is recommended as a more comprehensive guide to securing Apache.

3.17 IMAP and POP3 Server

Dovecot provides IMAP and POP3 services. It is not installed by default. The project page at http://www.dovecot.org contains more detailed information about Dovecot configuration.

3.17.1 Disable Dovecot if Possible

> If the system does not need to operate as an IMAP or POP3 server, disable and remove Dovecot if it was installed:
>
> ```
> # chkconfig dovecot off
> # yum erase dovecot
> ```
>
> **CCE 3847-1, 4239-0**

3.17.2   Configure Dovecot if Necessary

Dovecot's main configuration file is `/etc/dovecot.conf`. The settings which appear, commented out, in the file are the defaults.

3.17.2.1   Support Only the Necessary Protocols

> Edit `/etc/dovecot.conf`. Add or correct the following lines, replacing *PROTOCOL* with only the subset of protocols (`imap`, `imaps`, `pop3`, `pop3s`) required:
>
>   protocols = PROTOCOL
>
> **CCE 4384-4, 3887-7, 4530-2, 4547-6**

Dovecot supports the IMAP and POP3 protocols, as well as SSL-protected versions of those protocols. Configure the Dovecot server to support only the protocols needed by your site.

If possible, require SSL protection for all transactions. The SSL protocol variants listen on alternate ports (995 instead of 110 for `pop3s`, and 993 instead of 143 for `imaps`), and require SSL-aware clients. An alternate approach is to listen on the standard port and require the client to use the `STARTTLS` command before authenticating.

3.17.2.2   Enable SSL Support

SSL should be used to encrypt network traffic between the Dovecot server and its clients. Users must authenticate to the Dovecot server in order to read their mail, and passwords should never be transmitted in clear text. In addition, protecting mail as it is downloaded is a privacy measure, and clients may use SSL certificates to authenticate the server, preventing another system from impersonating the server. See Section 2.5.6 for general SSL information, including the setup of a Certificate Authority (CA).

3.17.2.2.1   Create an SSL Certificate

Note: The following steps should be performed on your CA system, and not on the Dovecot server itself. If you will have a commercial CA sign certificates, then these steps should be performed on a separate, physically secure system devoted to that purpose.

> On your CA (if you are using your own) or on another physically secure system, generate a key pair for the Dovecot server:
>
> ```
> # cd /etc/pki/tls/certs
> # openssl genrsa -out imapserverkey.pem 2048
> ```
>
> Next, generate a certificate signing request (CSR) for the CA to sign, making sure to enter the server's fully-qualified domain name when prompted for the Common Name:
>
> ```
> # openssl req -new -key imapserverkey.pem -out imapserver.csr
> ```
>
> Next, the mail server CSR must be signed to create the Dovecot server certificate. You can either send the CSR to an established CA or sign it with your CA.
>
> To sign `imapserver.csr` using your CA:
>
> ```
> # openssl ca -in imapserver.csr -out imapservercert.pem
> ```

This step creates a private key, `imapserverkey.pem`, and a public certificate, `imapservercert.pem`. The Dovecot server will use these to prove its identity by demonstrating that it has a certificate which has been signed by a CA. POP3 or IMAP clients at your site should only be willing to provide users' credentials to a server they can authenticate.

3.17.2.2.2 Install the SSL Certificate

Create the PKI directory for POP and IMAP certificates if it does not already exist:

```
# mkdir /etc/pki/tls/imap
# chown root:root /etc/pki/tls/imap
# chmod 755 /etc/pki/tls/imap
```

Using removable media or some other secure transmission format, install the files generated in the previous step onto the Dovecot server:

- `/etc/pki/tls/imap/serverkey.pem`: the private key `imapserverkey.pem`

- `/etc/pki/tls/imap/servercert.pem`: the certificate file `imapservercert.pem`

Verify the permissions on these files:

```
# chown root:root /etc/pki/tls/imap/serverkey.pem
# chown root:root /etc/pki/tls/imap/servercert.pem
# chmod 600 /etc/pki/tls/imap/serverkey.pem
# chmod 600 /etc/pki/tls/imap/servercert.pem
```

Verify that the CA's public certificate file has been installed as `/etc/pki/tls/CA/cacert.pem`, and has the correct permissions:

```
# chown root:root /etc/pki/tls/CA/cacert.pem
# chmod 644 /etc/pki/tls/CA/cacert.pem
```

3.17.2.2.3 Configure Dovecot to Use the SSL Certificate

Edit `/etc/dovecot.conf` and add or correct the following lines (ensuring they reference the appropriate files):

```
ssl_cert_file = /etc/pki/tls/imap/servercert.pem
ssl_key_file = /etc/pki/tls/imap/serverkey.pem
ssl_ca_file = /etc/pki/tls/CA/cacert.pem
```

These options tell Dovecot where to find the TLS configuration, allowing clients to make encrypted connections.

3.17.2.2.4 Disable Plaintext Authentication

To prevent Dovecot from attempting plaintext authentication of clients, edit `/etc/dovecot.conf` and add or correct the following line:

```
disable_plaintext_auth = yes
```

CCE 4552-6

The `disable_plaintext_auth` command disallows login-related commands until an encrypted session has been negotiated using SSL. If client compatibility requires you to allow connections to the `pop3` or `imap` ports, rather than the alternate SSL ports, you should use this command to require `STARTTLS` before authentication.

3.17.2.3 Enable Dovecot Options to Protect Against Code Flaws

Edit `/etc/dovecot.conf` and add or correct the following line:

```
login_process_per_connection = yes
mail_drop_priv_before_exec = yes
```

CCE 4371-1, 4410-7

IMAP and POP3 are remote authenticated protocols, meaning that the server must accept remote connections from anyone, but provide substantial services only to clients who have successfully authenticated. To protect against security problems, Dovecot splits these functions into separate server processes. The `imap-login` and/or `pop3-login` processes accept connections from unauthenticated users, and only spawn `imap` or `pop3` processes on successful authentication.

However, the `imap-login` and `pop3-login` processes themselves may contain vulnerabilities. Since each of these processes operates as a daemon, handling multiple sequential client connections from different users, bugs in the code could allow unauthenticated users to steal credential data. If the `login_process_per_connection` option is enabled, then a separate `imap-login` or `pop3-login` process is created for each new connection, protecting against this class of problems. This option has an efficiency cost, but is strongly recommended.

If the `mail_drop_priv_before_exec` option is on, the `imap-login` or `pop3-login` process will drop privileges to the user's ID after authentication and before executing the `imap` or `pop3` process itself. Under some very limited circumstances, this could protect against privilege escalation by authenticated users. However, if the `mail_executable` option is used to run code before starting each user's session, it is important to drop privileges to prevent the custom code from running as `root`.

3.17.2.4 Allow IMAP Clients to Access the Server

Edit `/etc/sysconfig/iptables`. Add the following line, ensuring that it appears *before* the final `LOG` and `DROP` lines for the `RH-Firewall-1-INPUT` chain:

```
-A RH-Firewall-1-INPUT -m state --state NEW -p tcp --dport 143 -j ACCEPT
```

The default iptables configuration does not allow inbound access to any services. This modification will allow remote hosts to initiate connections to the IMAP daemon, while keeping all other ports on the server in their default protected state. See Section 2.5.5 for more information about iptables.

3.18 Samba (SMB) Microsoft Windows File Sharing Server

When properly configured, the Samba service allows Linux machines to provide file and print sharing to Microsoft Windows machines. There are two software packages that provide Samba support. The first, `samba-client`, provides a series of command line tools that enable a client machine to access Samba shares. The second, simply labeled `samba`, provides the Samba service. It is this second package that allows a Linux machine to act as an Active Directory server, a domain controller, or as a domain member. Only the `samba-client` package is installed by default.

3.18.1 Disable Samba if Possible

> If the Samba service has been enabled and will not be used, disable it:
>
> ```
> # chkconfig smb off
> ```
>
> **CCE 4551-8**

Even after the Samba server package has been installed, it will remain disabled. Do not enable this service unless it is absolutely necessary to provide Microsoft Windows file and print sharing functionality.

3.18.2 Configure Samba if Necessary

All settings for the Samba daemon can be found in `/etc/samba/smb.conf`. Settings are divided between a `[global]` configuration section and a series of user created share definition sections meant to describe file or print shares on the system. By default, Samba will operate in `user` mode and allow client machines to access local home directories and printers. It is recommended that these settings be changed or that additional limitations be set in place.

3.18.2.1 Testing the Samba Configuration File

> To test the configuration file for syntax errors, use the `testparm` command. It will also list all settings currently in place, including defaults that may not appear in the configuration file.
>
> ```
> # testparm -v
> ```

3.18.2.2 Choosing the Appropriate `security` Parameter

There are two kinds of security in Samba, share-level (`share`) and user-level. User-level security is further subdivided into four separate implementations: `user`, `domain`, `ads`, and `server`. It is recommended that the `share` and `server` security modes not be used. In `share` security, everyone is given the same password for each share, preventing individual user accountability. `server` security mode has been superseded by the `domain` and `ads` security modes. It may now be considered obsolete.

The `security` parameter is set in the `[global]` section of the Samba configuration file. It determines how the server will handle user names and passwords. Some security modes require additional parameters, such as workgroup, realm, or password server names. All security modes will require that each remote user have a matching local account. One workaround to this problem is to use the `winbindd` daemon. Please consult the official Samba documentation to learn more.

3.18.2.2.1 Use `user` Security for Servers Not in a Domain Context

> This is the default setting with a new Samba installation and the best choice when operating outside of a domain security context. The relevant parameters in `/etc/samba/smb.conf` will read as follows:
>
> ```
> security = user
> workgroup = MYGROUP
> ```
>
> Set the value of workgroup so that it matches the value of other machines on the network.

In `user` mode, authentication requests are handled locally and not passed on to a separate authentication server. This is the desired behavior for standalone servers and domain controllers.

3.18.2.2.2 Use `domain` Security for Servers in a Domain Context

When using Samba as a Primary or Backup Domain Controller, use `security = user`*, not* `security = domain`*. This tells Samba that the local machine is hosting the authentication back-end.*

> First, change the `security` parameter to `domain`. Next, set the `workgroup` and `netbios name` parameters (if necessary):
>
> ```
> security = domain
> workgroup = WORKGROUP
> netbios name = NETBIOSNAME
> ```

`domain` mode is used for any machine that will act as a domain member server. It lets Samba know that the authentication information it needs can be found on another machine. Primary and Backup Domain Controllers host copies of this information. Samba will try to automatically determine which machine it should authenticate against on a domain network. If this detection fails, it may be necessary to specify the location manually.

Unlike the Microsoft Windows implementation of the SMB standard, a Samba machine can freely change roles within a domain without requiring that the machine be reinstalled (such roles include primary and backup domain controllers, domain member servers, and ordinary domain workstations). However, there are some limitations on how each machine can fulfill each role in a mixed network.

3.18.2.2.3 Use `ads` (Active Directory Service) Security For Servers in an ADS Domain Context

> The security mode `ads` enables a Samba machine to act as an ADS domain member server. Since ADS requires Kerberos, be sure to set the `realm` parameter appropriately and configure the local copy of Kerberos. If necessary, it is also possible to manually set the `password server` parameter.
>
> ```
> security = ads
> realm = MY_REALM
> password server = your.kerberos.server
> ```

Currently, it is possible to act as an Active Directory domain member server, but not as a domain controller. Be sure to operate in mixed mode. Native mode may not work yet in current versions of Samba. Future support for ADS should be forthcoming in Samba 4. See the Samba project web site at `http://www.samba.org` for more details.

3.18.2.3 Disable Guest Access and Local Login Support

> Do not allow guest users to access local file or printer shares. In global or in each share, set the parameter `guest ok` to no:
>
> ```
> [share]
>    guest ok = no
> ```
>
> It is safe to disable local login support for remote Samba users. Consider changing the `add user account` script to set remote user shells to `/sbin/nologin`.

3.18.2.4 Disable Root Access

> Administrators should not use administrator accounts to access Samba file and printer shares. If possible, disable the root user and the wheel administrator group:
>
> ```
> [share]
>    invalid users = root @wheel
> ```
>
> If administrator accounts cannot be disabled, ensure that local machine passwords and Samba service passwords do not match.

Typically, administrator access is required when Samba must create user and machine accounts and shares. Domain member servers and standalone servers may not need administrator access at all. If that is the case, add the `invalid users` parameter to `[global]` instead.

3.18.2.5 Set the Allowed Authentication Negotiation Levels

> By default, Samba will attempt to negotiate with Microsoft Windows machines to set a common communication protocol. Whenever possible, be sure to disable LANMAN authentication, as it is far weaker than the other supported protocols.
>
> ```
> [global]
>    client lanman auth = no
> ```
>
> Newer versions of Microsoft Windows may require the use of NTLMv2. NTLMv2 is the preferred protocol for authentication, but since older machines do not support it, Samba has disabled it by default. If possible, reenable it.
>
> ```
> [global]
>    client ntlmv2 auth = yes
> ```

For the sake of backwards compatibility, most modern Windows machines will still allow other machines to communicate with them over weak protocols such as LANMAN. On Samba, by enabling NTLMv2, you are also disabling LANMAN and NTLMv1. If NTLMv1 is required, it is still possible to individually disable LANMAN.

3.18.2.6   Let Domain Controllers Create Machine Trust Accounts On-the-Fly

> Add or correct an `add machine script` entry to the `[global]` section of `/etc/samba/smb.conf` to allow
> Samba to dynamically create Machine Trust Accounts:
>
> ```
> [global]
>    add machine script = /usr/sbin/useradd -n -g machines -d /dev/null -s /sbin/nologin %u
> ```
>
> Make sure that the group `machines` exists. If not, add it with the following command:
>
> ```
> /usr/sbin/groupadd machines
> ```

When acting as a PDC, it becomes necessary to create and store Machine Trust Accounts for each machine that
joins the domain. On a Microsoft Windows PDC, this account is created with the Server Manager tool, but on a
Samba PDC, two accounts must be created. The first is the local machine account, and the second is the Samba
account. For security purposes, it is recommended to let Samba create these accounts on-the-fly. When Machine
Trust Accounts are created manually, there is a small window of opportunity in which a rogue machine could
join the domain in place of the new server.

3.18.2.7   Restrict Access to the `[IPC$]` Share

> Limit access to the `[IPC$]` share so that only machines in your network will be able to connect to it:
>
> ```
> [IPC$]
>    hosts allow = 192.168.1. 127.0.0.1
>    hosts deny = 0.0.0.0/0
> ```

The `[IPC$]` share allows users to anonymously fetch a list of shared resources from a server. It is intended to
allow users to browse the list of available shares. It also can be used as a point of attack into a system. Disabling
it completely may break some functionality, so it is recommended that you merely limit access to it instead.

3.18.2.8   Restrict File Sharing

> Only users with local user accounts will be able to log in to Samba shares by default. Shares can be limited
> to particular users or network addresses. Use the `hosts allow` and `hosts deny` directives accordingly, and
> consider setting the `valid users` directive to a limited subset of users or to a group of users. Separate each
> address, user, or user group with a space as follows:
>
> ```
> [share]
>    hosts allow = 192.168.1. 127.0.0.1
>    valid users = userone usertwo @usergroup
> ```
>
> It is also possible to limit read and write access to particular users with the `read list` and `write list`
> options, though the permissions set by the system itself will override these settings. Set the `read only`
> attribute for each share to ensure that global settings will not accidentally override the individual share
> settings. Then, as with the `valid users` directive, separate each user or group of users with a space:
>
> ```
> [share]
>    read only = yes
>    write list = userone usertwo @usergroup
> ```

The Samba service is only required for sharing files and printers with Microsoft Windows workstations, and even then, other options may exist. Do not use the Samba service to share files between Unix or Linux machines.

3.18.2.9   Require Server SMB Packet Signing

> To make the server use packet signing, add the following to the [global] section of the Samba configuration file:
>
> ```
> server signing = mandatory
> ```

The Samba server should only communicate with clients who can support SMB packet signing. Packet signing can prevent man-in-the-middle attacks which modify SMB packets in transit.

The Samba service is only required for sharing files and printers with Microsoft Windows workstations, and even then, other options may exist. Do not use the Samba service to share files between Unix or Linux machines.

3.18.2.10   Require Client SMB Packet Signing, if using `smbclient`

> To require samba clients running smbclient to use packet signing, add the following to the [global] section of the Samba configuration file:
>
> ```
> client signing = mandatory
> ```
>
> **CCE 14075-6**

A Samba client should only communicate with servers who can support SMB packet signing. Packet signing can prevent man-in-the-middle attacks which modify SMB packets in transit.

3.18.2.11   Require Client SMB Packet Signing, if using `mount.cifs`

> Require packet signing of clients who mount Samba shares using the `mount.cifs` program (e.g., those who specify shares in /etc/fstab). To do so, ensure that signing options (either `sec=krb5i` or `sec=ntlmv2i`) are used.
>
> **CCE 15029-2**

See the `mount.cifs(8)` man page for more information. A Samba client should only communicate with servers who can support SMB packet signing. Packet signing can prevent man-in-the-middle attacks which modify SMB packets in transit.

3.18.2.12   Restrict Printer Sharing

> By default, Samba utilizes the CUPS printing service to enable printer sharing with Microsoft Windows workstations. If there are no printers on the local machine, or if printer sharing with Microsoft Windows is not required, disable the printer sharing capability by commenting out the following lines, found in /etc/samba/smb.conf:

```
      [global]
      ; load printers = yes
      ; cups options = raw

      [printers]
        comment = All Printers
        path = /usr/spool/samba
        browseable = no
        guest ok = no
        writable = no
        printable = yes
```

There may be other options present, but these are the only options enabled and uncommented by default. Removing the [printers] share should be enough for most users.

If the Samba printer sharing capability is needed, consider disabling the Samba network browsing capability or restricting access to a particular set of users or network addresses. Set the valid users parameter to a small subset of users or restrict it to a particular group of users with the shorthand @. Separate each user or group of users with a space. For example, under the [printers] share:

```
      [printers]
        valid users = user @printerusers
```

The CUPS service is capable of sharing printers with other Unix and Linux machines on the local network without the Samba service. The Samba service is only required when a Microsoft Windows machine needs printer access on a Unix or Linux host.

3.18.2.13   Configure iptables to Allow Access to the Samba Server

Determine an appropriate network block, *netwk*, and network mask, *mask*, representing the machines on your network which should operate as clients of the Samba server.

Edit /etc/sysconfig/iptables. Add the following lines, ensuring that they appear *before* the final LOG and DROP lines for the RH-Firewall-1-INPUT chain:

```
    -A RH-Firewall-1-INPUT -s netwk/mask -m state --state NEW -p tcp --dport 137 -j ACCEPT
    -A RH-Firewall-1-INPUT -s netwk/mask -m state --state NEW -p tcp --dport 138 -j ACCEPT
    -A RH-Firewall-1-INPUT -s netwk/mask -m state --state NEW -p tcp --dport 139 -j ACCEPT
    -A RH-Firewall-1-INPUT -s netwk/mask -m state --state NEW -p tcp --dport 445 -j ACCEPT
```

The default Iptables configuration does not allow inbound access to the ports used by the Samba service. This modification allows that access, while keeping other ports on the server in their default protected state. Since these ports are frequent targets of network scanning attacks, restricting access to only the network segments which need to access the Samba server is strongly recommended. See Section 2.5.5 for more information about Iptables.

3.18.3   Avoid the Samba Web Administration Tool (SWAT)

SWAT is a web based configuration tool provided by the Samba team that enables both local and remote configuration management. It is not installed by default. It is recommended that SWAT not be used, as it requires the use of a Samba administrator account and sends that password in the clear over a network connection.

If SWAT is absolutely required, limit access to the local machine or tunnel SWAT connections through SSL with `stunnel`.

3.19 Proxy Server

A proxy server is a very desirable target for a potential adversary because much (or all) sensitive data for a given infrastructure may flow through it. Therefore, if one is required, the machine acting as a proxy server should be dedicated to that purpose alone and be stored in a physically secure location. The system's default proxy server software is Squid, and provided in an RPM package of the same name.

3.19.1 Disable Squid if Possible

If Squid was installed and activated, but the system does not need to act as a proxy server, then it should be disabled and removed:

```
# chkconfig squid off
# yum erase squid
```

CCE 4556-7, 4076-6

3.19.2 Configure Squid if Necessary

The Squid configuration file is `/etc/squid/squid.conf`. The following recommendations can be applied to this file.

Note: If a particular tag is **not** present in the configuration file, Squid falls back to the default setting (which is often illustrated by a comment).

3.19.2.1 Listen on Uncommon Port

The default listening port for the Squid service is 3128. As such, it is frequently scanned by adversaries looking for proxy servers.

Select an arbitrary (but uncommon) high port to use as the Squid listening port and make the corresponding change to the configuration file:

```
http_port port
```

Run the following command to add a new SELinux port mapping for the service:

```
# semanage port -a -t http_cache_port_t -p tcp port
```

3.19.2.2 Verify Default Secure Settings

Several security-enhancing settings in the Squid configuration file are enabled by default, but appear as comments in the configuration file (as mentioned in Section 3.19.2). In these instances, the explicit directive is not present, which means it is implicitly enabled. If you are operating with a default configuration file, this section can be ignored.

Ensure that the following security settings are **NOT** explicitly changed from their default values:

```
ftp_passive on
ftp_sanitycheck on
check_hostnames on
request_header_max_size 20 KB
reply_header_max_size 20 KB
cache_effective_user squid
cache_effective_group squid
ignore_unknown_nameservers on
```

CCE 4454-5, 4353-9, 4503-9, 3585-7, 4419-8, 3692-1, 4459-4, 4476-8

ftp_passive forces FTP passive connections.

ftp_sanitycheck performs additional sanity checks on FTP data connections.

check_hostnames ensures that hostnames meet RFC compliance.

request_header_max_size and reply_header_max_size place an upper limit on HTTP header length, precautions against denial-of-service and buffer overflow vulnerabilities.

cache_effective_user and cache_effective_group designate the EUID and EGID of Squid following initialization (it is essential that the EUID/EGID be set to an unprivileged sandbox account).

ignore_unknown_nameservers checks to make sure that DNS responses come from the same IP the request was sent to.

3.19.2.3 Change Default Insecure Settings

The default configuration settings for the following tags are considered to be weak security and **NOT** recommended.

Add or modify the configuration file to include the following lines:

```
allow_underscore off
httpd_suppress_version_string on
forwarded_for off
log_mime_hdrs on
```

CCE 4181-4, 4577-3, 4344-8, 4494-1

allow_underscore enforces RFC 1034 compliance on hostnames by disallowing the use of underscores.

httpd_suppress_version_string prevents Squid from revealing version information in web headers and error pages.

forwarded_for reveals proxy client IP addresses in HTTP headers and should be disabled to prevent the leakage of internal network configuration details.

log_mime_hdrs enables logging of HTTP response/request headers.

3.19.2.4 Configure Authentication if Applicable

Note: Authentication cannot be used in the case of transparent proxies due to limitations of the TCP/IP protocol.

Similar to web servers, two of the available options are Basic and Digest authentication. The other options are NTLM and Negotiate authentication. As noted in Section 3.16.3.5, Basic authentication transmits passwords in plain-text and is susceptible to passive monitoring. If network sniffing is a concern, basic authentication should not be used. Negotiate is the newest and most secure protocol. It attempts to use Kerberos authentication and falls back to NTLM if it cannot. It should be noted that Kerberos requires a third-party Key Distribution Center (KDC) to function properly, whereas the other methods of authentication are two-party schemes.

Squid also offers the ability to choose a custom external authenticator. Designating an external authenticator (also known as a "helper" module) allows Squid to offer pluggable third-party authentication schemes. LDAP is one example of a helper module that exists and is in use today.

There are comments under the `auth_param` tag inside `/etc/squid/squid.conf` that provide extensive detail on how to configure each of these methods. If authentication is necessary, choose a method of authentication and configure appropriately. The recommended minimum configurations illustrated for each method are acceptable.

To force an ACL (as discussed in Section 3.19.2.5) to require authentication, use the following directive:

```
acl name-of-ACL proxy_auth REQUIRED
```

Note: The keyword `REQUIRED` can be replaced with a user or list of users to further restrict access to a smaller subset of users.

3.19.2.5 Access Control Lists (ACL)

Be very careful with the order of access control tags. Access control is handled top-down. The first rule that matches is the only rule adhered to. The last rule on the list defines the default behavior in the case of no rule match.

The `acl` and `http_access` tags are used in combination to allow filtering based on a series of access control lists.

Squid has a list of default ACLs for localhost, SSL ports, and "safe" ports. Following the definition of these ACLs, a series of `http_access` directives establish the following default filtering policy:

- Allow cachemgr access only from localhost
- Allow access to only ports in the "safe" access control list
- Limit CONNECT method to SSL ports only
- Allow access from localhost
- Deny all other requests

The default ACL policies are reasonable from a security standpoint. However, the number of ports listed as "safe" could be significantly trimmed depending on the needs of your network. Out of the box, ports 21, 70, 80, 210, 280, 443, 488, 591, 777, and 1025 through 65535 are all considered safe. Some of these ports are associated with deprecated or rarely used protocols. As such, this list could be trimmed to further tighten filtering.

The following actions should be taken to tighten the ACL policies:

1. There is a filter line in the configuration file that is recommended but commented out. This line should be uncommented or added to prevent access to localhost from the proxy:

   ```
   http_access deny to_localhost
   ```

2. An access list should be setup for the specific network or networks that the proxy is intended to serve. Only this subset of IP addresses should be allowed access.

   Add these lines where the following comment appears:

   ```
   # INSERT YOUR OWN RULE(S) HERE TO ALLOW ACCESS FROM YOUR CLIENTS
   acl your-network-acl-name src ip-range
   http_access allow your-network-acl-name
   ```

   Note: *ip-range* is of the format xxx.xxx.xxx.xxx/xx

3. Ensure that the final `http_access` line to appear in the document is the following:

   ```
   http_access deny all
   ```

   This guarantees that all traffic not meeting an explicit filtering rule is denied.

   Further filters should be established to meet the specific needs of a network, explicitly allowing access only where necessary.

4. Consult the chart below. Corresponding `acl` entries for unused protocols should be commented out and thus denied.

CCE 4511-2, 4529-4, 3610-3, 4466-9, 4607-8, 4255-6, 4127-7, 4519-5, 4413-1, 4373-7

Port	Service	Summary	Recommendation
21	ftp	File Transfer Protocol(FTP) is a widely used file transfer protocol.	ALLOW
70	gopher	The gopher protocol is a deprecated search and retrieval protocol that is almost extinct, with as few as 100 gopher servers present worldwide. Support for gopher is disabled in most modern browsers.	DENY
80	http	A web proxy needs to allow access to HTTP traffic.	ALLOW
210	wais	The Wide Area Information Server port is similar to gopher, serving as a text searching system to scour indexes on remote machines. Today, it is deprecated and nearly non-existent on the Internet.	DENY
280	http-mgmt	No documentation of any kind could be found on the obscure service that resides on this port.	DENY
443	https	SSL traffic is likely (and recommended) for any proxy and should be allowed.	ALLOW
488	gss-http	No documentation of any kind could be found on the obscure service that resides on this port.	DENY
591	filemaker	Filemaker is a database application originally offered by Apple in the 1980s. Although development continues and it remains in use today, it should be disabled if your network does not require such traffic.	DENY
777	multiling http	No documentation of any kind could be found on the obscure service that resides on this port.	DENY

Port	Service	Summary	Recommendation
1025-65535	unregistered ports	Random high ports are used by a variety of applications and should be allowed.	ALLOW

3.19.2.6 Configure Internet Cache Protocol (ICP) if Necessary

The ICP protocol is a cache communication protocol that allows multiple Squid servers to communicate. The ICP protocol was designed with no security in mind, relying on user-defined access control lists alone to determine which ICP messages to allow.

> If a Squid server is standalone, the ICP port should be disabled by adding or correcting the following line in the configuration file:
>
> ```
> icp_port 0
> ```
>
> If the Squid server is meant to speak with peers, strict ACLs should be established to only allow ICP traffic from trusted neighbors. To accomplish this, add or correct the following lines:
>
> ```
> icp_access allow acl-defining-trusted-neighbors
> icp_access deny all
> ```

3.19.2.7 Configure `iptables` to Allow Access to the Proxy Server

> Determine an appropriate network block, *netwk*, and network mask, *mask*, representing the machines on your network which should operate as clients of the proxy server.
>
> Edit /etc/sysconfig/iptables. Add the following line, ensuring that it appears *before* the final LOG and DROP lines for the RH-Firewall-1-INPUT chain:
>
> ```
> -A RH-Firewall-1-INPUT -s netwk/mask -m state --state NEW -p tcp --dport port -j ACCEPT
> ```
>
> For *port*, use either the default 3128 or the alternate port was selected in Section 3.19.2.1.

The default Iptables configuration does not allow inbound access to the Squid proxy service. This modification allows that access, while keeping other ports on the server in their default protected state. See Section 2.5.5 for more information about Iptables.

3.19.2.8 Forward Log Messages to Syslog Daemon

The default behavior of Squid is to record its log messages in /var/log/squid.log. This behavior can be supplemented so that Squid also sends messages to syslog as well. This is useful for centralizing log data, particularly in instances where multiple Squid servers are present.

> Squid provides a command line argument to enable syslog forwarding. Modify the SQUID_OPTS line in /etc/init.d/squid to include the -s option:
>
> ```
> SQUID_OPTS="${SQUID_OPTS:-"-D"} -s"
> ```

3.19.2.9   Do Not Run as Root

Since Squid is loaded by the system's `service` utility, it starts as root and then changes its effective UID to the UID specified by the `cache_effective_user` directive. However, since it was still executed by root, the program maintains a saved UID of root even after changing its effective UID.

To prevent this undesired behavior, Squid must either be configured to run in a chroot environment or it must be executed by a non-privileged user in non-daemon mode (the `service` utility must not be used).

3.19.2.9.1   Run Squid in a `chroot` Jail

Chrooting Squid can be a very complicated task. Documentation for the process is vague and a great deal of trial and error may be required to determine all the files that need to be transitioned over to the chroot environment. Therefore, this guide recommends instead the method detailed in Section 3.19.2.9.2 to lower privileges. If chrooting Squid is still desired, it can be enabled with the following directive in the configuration file:

```
chroot chroot-path
```

Then, all the necessary files used by Squid must be copied into the *chroot-path* directory. The specifics of this step cannot be covered in this guide because they are highly dependent on the external programs used in the Squid configuration.

Note: The `strace` utility is a valuable resource for discovering the files needed for the chroot environment.

3.19.2.9.2   Modify Service Entry to Lower Privileges

The following modification to `/etc/init.d/squid` forces the `service` utility to execute Squid as the squid user instead of the root user:

```
# determine the name of the squid binary
[ -f /usr/sbin/squid ] && SQUID="sudo -u squid squid"
```

Making this change prevents Squid from writing its pid to `/var/run`. This pid file is used by `service` to check to see if the program started successfully. Therefore, a new location must be chosen for this pid file that the squid user has access to, and the corresponding references in `/etc/init.d/squid` must be altered to point to it.

Make the following modification to the Squid configuration file:

```
pid_filename /var/spool/squid/squid.pid
```

Edit the file `/etc/init.d/squid` by changing all occurrences of `/var/run/squid.pid` to `/var/spool/squid/squid.pid`

Also modify the following line in `/etc/init.d/squid`:

```
[ $RETVAL -eq 0 ] && touch /var/lock/subsys/squid
```

and add the following lines immediately after it:

```
rm -f /var/lock/subsys/squid
status squid
```

3.20 SNMP Server

The Simple Network Management Protocol allows administrators to monitor the state of network devices, including computers. Older versions of SNMP were well-known for weak security, such as plaintext transmission of the community string (used for authentication) and also usage of easily-guessable choices for community string.

3.20.1 Disable SNMP Server if Possible

The system includes an SNMP daemon that allows for its remote monitoring, though it not installed by default. If it was installed and activated, it is important that the software be disabled and removed.

> If there is not a mission-critical need for hosts at this site to be remotely monitored by a SNMP tool, then disable and remove SNMP as follows:
>
> ```
> # chkconfig snmpd off
> # yum erase net-snmpd
> ```
>
> CCE 3765-5, 14081-4

3.20.2 Configure SNMP Server if Necessary

If it is necessary to run the `snmpd` agent on the system, some best practices should be followed to minimize the security risk from the installation. The multiple security models implemented by SNMP cannot be fully covered here so only the following general configuration advice can be offered:

- use only SNMP version 3 security models and enable the use of authentication and encryption for those
- write access to the MIB (Management Information Base) should be allowed only if necessary
- all access to the MIB should be restricted following a principle of least privilege
- network access should be limited to the maximum extent possible including restricting to expected network addresses both in the configuration files and in the system firewall rules
- ensure SNMP agents send traps only to, and accept SNMP queries only from, authorized management stations
- ensure that permissions on the `snmpd.conf` configuration file (by default, in `/etc/snmp`) are 640 or more restrictive
- ensure that any MIB files' permissions are also 640 or more restrictive

3.20.2.1 Further Resources

The following resources provide more detailed information about the SNMP software:

- The CERT SNMP Vulnerabilities FAQ at `http://www.cert.org/tech_tips/snmp_faq.html`
- The Net-SNMP project web page at `http://net-snmp.sourceforge.net`
- The `snmp_config(5)` man page
- the `snmpd.conf(5)` man page

Bibliography

[1] Apache 2 with SSL/TLS: Step-by-step, Part 2. Tech. rep.

[2] *Apache 2.0 Docs.* http://httpd.apache.org/docs/2.0/.

[3] Locking down Apache. Tech. rep.

[4] Setting up a Secure Apache 2 Server. Tech. rep.

[5] Red Hat Desktop: Deployment Guide. Tech. rep., Red Hat Linux, 2005. http://www.redhat.com/docs/manuals/enterprise/RHEL-4-Manual/desktop-guide/.

[6] Red Hat Enterprise Linux 4: Reference Guide. Tech. rep., Red Hat Linux, 2005. http://www.redhat.com/docs/manuals/enterprise/RHEL-4-Manual/ref-guide/.

[7] Red Hat Enterprise Linux 4: Security Guide. Tech. rep., Red Hat Linux, 2005. http://www.redhat.com/docs/manuals/enterprise/RHEL-4-Manual/security-guide/.

[8] Red Hat Enterprise Linux 4: System Administration Guide. Tech. rep., Red Hat Linux, 2005. http://www.redhat.com/docs/manuals/enterprise/RHEL-4-Manual/sysadmin-guide/.

[9] Red Hat Enterprise Linux 5: Deployment Guide. Tech. rep., Red Hat Linux, 2006. http://www.redhat.com/docs/manuals/enterprise/RHEL-5-manual/Deployment_Guide-en-US/index.html.

[10] Common Criteria EAL4+ Evaluated Configuration Guide for Red Hat Enterprise Linux 5 on HP Hardware. Tech. rep., Hewlett Packard, May 2007. http://h20331.www2.hp.com/enterprise/downloads/RHEL5-CC-EAL4-HP-Configuration-Guide.pdf.

[11] Gentoo Security Handbook. Tech. rep., Gentoo Linux, Feb 2007. http://www.gentoo.org/doc/en/security/security-handbook.xml.

[12] *UNIX Security Checklist, V5R1.17.* DISA Field Security Operations, April 2009. http://iase.disa.mil/stigs/checklist/.

[13] BERNSTEIN, D. SYN cookies. Tech. rep. http://cr.yp.to/syncookies.html.

[14] FRANK MAYER, K. M., AND CAPLAN, D. *SELinux by Example: Using Security Enhanced Linux.*

[15] GALARNEUA, E. Security Considerations with Squid proxy server. Tech. rep., Apr 2003.

[16] GARFINKEL, S., AND SPAFFORD, G. *Practical Unix and Internet Security, 3rd Edition.* O'Reilly and Associates, 2003.

[17] HILDEBRANDT, R., AND KOETTER, P. *The Book of Postfix.* No Starch Press, 2005.

[18] HOUSEHOLDER, A., AND KING, B. Securing an Internet Name Server. Tech. rep., Aug 2002. http://www.cert.org/archive/pdf/dns.pdf.

[19] HSIAO, A. Making the Most of Pluggable Authentication Modules (PAM). Tech. rep., Mar 2001. `http://www.samspublishing.com/articles/article.asp?p=20968`.

[20] HUNT, C. *Sendmail Cookbook*. O'Reilly and Associates, 2003.

[21] LIU, C. *DNS & BIND Cookbook*. O'Reilly and Associates, Oct 2002.

[22] MIRANDA, M. Services in Fedora Core 6. Tech. rep. `http://www.mjmwired.net/resources/mjm-services-fc6.html`.

[23] MOURAN, G. Securing and Optimizing Linux: Redhat Edition - A Hands on Guide. Tech. rep., 2000. `http://www.faqs.org/docs/securing/`.

[24] PALMIERI, J. Get on D-bus. Tech. rep., Jan 2005. `http://www.redhat.com/magazine/003jan05/features/dbus/`.

[25] PETERS, M. Securing Apache. Tech. rep., Jul 2004. `http://www.linux.com/article.pl?sid=04/07/09/1935231`.

[26] PETERSON, R. Fedora 5: What's New. Tech. rep.

[27] RISTIC, I. *Apache Security*. O'Reilly and Associates, Mar 2005.

[28] SMITH, C. Linux NFS-HOWTO. Tech. rep., May 2006. `http://nfs.sourceforge.net/nfs-howto/`.

[29] TIMME, F. Secure Your Apache With `mod_security`. Tech. rep., Jul 2006. `http://www.howtoforge.com/apache_mod_security`.

[30] WAINWRIGHT, P. Building Apache the Way You Want It. Tech. rep., Apress Publishing, Aug 2005. `http://www.devshed.com/c/a/Apache/Building-Apache-the-Way-You-Want-It/`.

[31] WESSELS, D. *Squid: The Definitive Guide*. O'Reilly and Associates, Jan 2004.